Developmental Disabilities
Psychosocial Aspects

Developmental Disabilities
Psychosocial Aspects

George S. Baroff, Ph.D.
Developmental Disabilities Training Institute
Division of Continuing Education
and
Department of Psychology
University of North Carolina at Chapel Hill

8700 Shoal Creek Boulevard
Austin, Texas 78758

Printed in the United States of America

Library of Congress Cataloging-in-Publication Data

Baroff, George S.
    Developmental disabilities : psychosocial aspects / George S. Baroff
        p.   cm.
    Includes bibliographical references.
    ISBN 0-89079-412-X
    1. Developmental disabilities   2. Developmental disabilities—
Social aspects.   3. Mentally handicapped.   I. Title.
RC570.8268   1990
616.85'8806—dc20   90-43702
                                                                         CIP

8700 Shoal Creek Boulevard
Austin, Texas 78758

1 2 3 4 5 6 7 8 9 10   94 93 92 91

Contents

Preface

Developmental Disabilities: Psychosocial Aspects is about the disorders of development and learning known as *developmental disabilities*. Mental retardation, autism, cerebral palsy, and epilepsy have always been included in this "legislative" category, with epilepsy of concern chiefly because of its common association with the other conditions.

The impetus for this book lay in this author's dissatisfaction with the degree of depth with which these disabilities are typically treated in textbooks on exceptionality or psychopathology. Since these disabilities are necessarily only highlighted in books that try to cover a very wide spectrum of disorders, one is likely to gain little sense of what it *means* to be retarded or autistic or to have cerebral palsy or epilepsy. The intent of this book is to carve out a special segment of developmental disorders and to deal in depth with each, the goal being to "get inside" the disabled person in order to understand what these conditions "feel like" and how they affect one's life. The primary means of accomplishing this is through the use of autobiographical materials and interviews as supplements to the descriptive materials already widely available in the disability literature. Parenthetically, while some of the material on epilepsy refers to persons whose disorders did not arise until adulthood and so, technically, do not fall under the "developmental disability" label, often it is these individuals who have given us the most revealing descriptions of what epilepsy feels like.

The book is divided into four sections: (1) the nature of what it means to be a person, a formulation of our basic physical and psychological needs; (2) the relationship of habilitative services to the meeting of these needs; (3) the disabilities themselves; and (4) a summary of what these conditions teach us about the impact of disability on the lives of people who have one, and on all our lives.

With regard to the nature of personhood, the intent is to share with the reader a personality model and frame of reference through which the effects of disability are more readily seen. The model conceptualizes personhood in terms of two primary dimensions—human capacities and needs—and each disorder is examined with reference to its effect on these elements, with particular attention to the disorder's impact on a person's self-esteem.

The second section is concerned with the habilitative services—those that both minimize or ameliorate disability and foster optimal development. Stress is placed on viewing adaptation as a function of disability *and* services, since too much weight is sometimes given to the disability itself. I am also at pains to point out that in seeking the full array of habilitative services for disabled individuals, we are asking no more for them than we demand for ourselves. Our society expects each of us, disabled and nondisabled, to try to fulfill our potential, whatever it may be, and it seeks to accomplish this through the provision of developmentally appropriate experiences, either acquired naturally or through special intervention. Education is the most widely recognized service, but others include being reared by loving parents, having opportunities for social and recreational experiences, and, as adults, having access to a decent place in which to live and something meaningful to do. Those of us who are not disabled take these services or experiences for granted, but they are crucial to minimizing disability and to fostering a quality of life that we would wish for ourselves.

The third section of the book deals with the developmental disabilities themselves. Each chapter is organized in the same fashion: The condition is defined and its disabling aspects are described; its prevalence and causes are noted; and, most important, its effects on adaptation from infancy to adulthood are shown. It is in the description of the adaptive problems created by the disabilities that autobiographical materials have been of particular value.

The Brief Summary reviews what we have learned about the impact of these disabilities on people's lives. Particular attention is directed to the psychological and social, or psychosocial, effects residing in both the direct impact of the disability on the physical and psychological self and indirectly in the way society views the disabled individual.

Finally, I have tried to always be conscious of readability. Thinking of myself as an informed reporter, the wish is to share with the reader my interest and understanding of these disorders and, more broadly, one aspect of the human condition.

George S. Baroff

CHAPTER 1

Developmental Disabilities and Their Psychosocial Impact

OVERVIEW

This chapter (1) introduces the conditions traditionally subsumed under the category "developmental disabilities," (2) indicates their prevalence in the general population, (3) presents a new way of thinking about their psychological and social, or psychosocial, effects, and (4) identifies common adaptive problems that occur during the life of a person with one of these conditions, with special attention to the impact on self-esteem.

DEFINING DEVELOPMENTAL DISABILITIES

The term *developmentally disabled* first appeared in federal legislation of 1970—the Developmental Disabilities Assistance and Bill of Rights Act (Public Law 94-103). The act brought under a single federal legislative umbrella three major disorders: mental retardation, cerebral palsy, and epilepsy. It also included all other neurologic conditions occurring before age 18 that produce consequences similar to those of the main three. The intent of the legislation was to bring together under one law disability groups that have comparable service needs. The goal was to improve services to disabled populations with similar problems, to reduce duplication of services, and to increase coordination among the many public and private agencies that provide such services.

Following enactment of the law, however, there continued to be discussion as to both the utility of the designation and whether other disabilities also should be included under it (Kiernan, 1979; Summers, 1981). Subsequently, both autism and severe dyslexia were added, but this was soon followed by a decision to give up a *categorical* definition, one that identified the disabilities by their traditional names, and to substitute for it a *functional* definition, one that focused on their common adaptive problems. This was accomplished with the enactment of the Rehabilitation, Comprehensive Services and Developmental Disabilities Amendments of 1978 (Public Law 95-602). Disavowing any reference to specific conditions, e.g., mental retardation or cerebral palsy, the new and current definition directs our attention exclusively to the effects of these and related disabilities, especially when they are severe and chronic in nature. A *developmental disability* is now defined as a severe and chronic disorder involving mental and/or physical impairment that originates before age 22. Such a disorder is likely to persist indefinitely and will cause "substantial functional limitations" in at least three of seven areas of major life activity. These are self-care, receptive and expressive language, learning, mobility, self-direction, capacity for independent living, and economic self-sufficiency. Recent versions of this legislation retain the "functional" rather than the earlier "categorical" thrust and seek to foster increased independence, employment, and community integration (Developmental Disabilities Amendments of 1984 and 1987). Though not specific to developmental disabilities, the landmark 1990 federal Americans with Disabilities Act will support those objectives by broadening job opportunities and by increasing access to public accommodations, transportation, and community networks.

PREVALENCE

This introductory chapter provides an estimate of the *total* number of persons with developmental disabilities, and each of the individual disability chapters will provide a statement of the number of individuals with that particular disability. Combining the four major developmental disabilities (the ones treated in depth in this book)—mental retardation, autism, cerebral palsy, and epilepsy—estimates vary from 1.5 percent (Boggs and Henney, 1979) to 1.7 percent (Jacobson and Janicki, 1983) of the general population. Adding to this number individuals with head injuries that lead to permanent impairment, an estimated 50,000 to 90,000 persons nationally, we can place the prevalence[1] of developmental disabilities at between 1.5 and 2.0 percent of the general population. The reader is cautioned that these prevalence figures refer not to *all* persons with the disabilities subsumed under the traditional definition, but only to those whose impairments are sufficiently severe to cause "substantial functional limitations." One of the effects of this distinction has been to reduce by almost two-thirds the number of retarded persons considered developmentally disabled—from 2.5 to 3 percent to less than 1 percent (Baroff, 1986).

PSYCHOSOCIAL ASPECTS

Each of the developmental disabilities described in this book can be treated in great depth. Entire volumes are devoted to them and the intent here is to limit the focus to their *psychosocial* aspects. By this is meant the impact of these conditions on (1) the cognitive, social, and emotional development of the affected person, (2) on the affected person's family

---

[1]*Prevalence* refers to the frequency of a condition at either one moment in time or over time. *Incidence,* another commonly used population measure, refers to the number of *new* cases per unit of time (Maloney and Ward, 1979).

and the larger community of which the person is a part, and (3) on that person's ability to cope effectively with the challenges of daily living. The last-mentioned will include a description of the kinds of adaptive behavior difficulties encountered by developmentally disabled individuals throughout the life cycle—in the preschool years, during school age and adolescence, and into adulthood. However, to understand the psychosocial consequences of these disorders, it is necessary to consider something of what it means to be a "normal" person and then a "disabled" or "handicapped" person. With an understanding of the psychological needs of all of us, normal as well as disabled, we can better appreciate the impact of these disabilities on the lives of people so affected. Particular attention will be paid to self-esteem, a psychological need central to mental health and one that is much threatened by deviations from societal norms of whatever nature—mental, physical, or even cultural.

ON THE NATURE OF PERSONHOOD

This section presents a conception of what it means to be a person, either normal or disabled (Baroff, 1974, 1986). It offers a way of thinking about ourselves and others that is intended to sensitize us to the kinds of frustrations that are likely to accompany significant disorders of development. This conception of personhood views people in terms of three major dimensions—*resources, needs,* and *values.* Each is briefly defined here. It is these dimensions that provide the framework through which the effect of each developmental disability is explored in the later chapters.

Resources

Resources are a person's capacities or abilities. They are the basic ingredients of *all* behaviors and what a person uses as he or she tackles the problems of daily living. Our resources can be grouped into the following broad categories: (1) intelligence, (2) communication skills, (3) health, sensory, and physical skills, (4) personality (temperament, emotions, and character), and (5) aesthetic appreciation. *The essence of what it means to be disabled is to be deficient in one or more of these resources, aesthetic appreciation aside.* For example, mental retardation relates primarily to a deficiency in intelligence, whereas autism involves both communication and personality difficulties and, commonly, intellectual ones as well. Cerebral palsy and epilepsy are first problems in the health domain, but the former often includes intellectual and communication difficulties, while the latter also may be associated with intellectual and personality problems.

Intelligence (Cognitive Skills). Intelligence or cognition is equated with behaviors that reflect learning ability, especially basic academic skills; knowledge; reasoning; and the ability to cope with new situations. The developmental disability known as *mental retardation* involves principally this resource, although it commonly includes impairments in other resources as well, e.g., communication and health, sensory, and physical skills.

Communication Skills. Communication skills involve a person's ability to make himself or herself understood, typically through speech, but also through the written word as well as gestures, sign language, and the artistic modes of art, dance, and music. A communication impairment is one of the characteristics of autism.

Health, Sensory, and Physical Skills. These involve the general state of one's health; the intactness of one's senses, especially vision and hearing; the ability to use one's hands, arms, and legs; and such physical characteristics as strength, endurance, speed, and coordination. The disorders of cerebral palsy and epilepsy primarily result in problems in this resource.

Personality: Temperament, Emotions, and Character. This involves behaviors associated with personality. Though not often considered an ability, it is a major contributor to the effectiveness with which one copes.

Temperament refers to behaviors in the infant and young child that seem to be relatively independent of parental childrearing style and are presumed to be biological in origin. Behavioral differences among children are observable in infancy and give each child its individuality. Behaviors associated with developmental disabilities that relate to temperament are activity level, attention span, distractibility (Thomas, Chess, and Birch, 1968), and impulsivity (Kagan and Kogan, 1970). The hyperactive autistic child, for example, can create serious discipline problems.

Emotions are affective states that are experienced as either pleasant or unpleasant. Common pleasurable emotions are delight, pride, and joy, and common unpleasant ones are anxiety, fear, anger, and sadness.

Character refers to consistent patterns of relatedness—to people, to objects, and to events. At the "people" level, character comprises such social behaviors as cooperativeness, friendliness, and assertiveness. At the object level, character refers to such behaviors as orderliness and possessiveness. Our study of developmental disabilities will particularly note the social or interpersonal problems such disabilities create, problems that greatly affect the self-esteem of afflicted persons and those who may be associated with them, e.g., their families.

Aesthetic Appreciation. Aesthetic appreciation refers to the capacity to enjoy beauty in all its many forms—nature, art, music, dance, literature, and poetry. Aesthetic appreciation is not a resource that is involved in any primary way with disability. A person is not judged as disabled if he or she shows little or no interest in aesthetic forms of pleasure. However, special gifts in these areas are regarded as talents, and some disabled persons, even those with severe developmental disabilities, manifest genuine talent. So-called savants are retarded persons with unusual gifts, typically artistic or muscial. Dustin Hoffman as the autistic young adult in the movie *Rain Man* showed some of these unusual skills.

Needs

Needs constitute the second major component of the three-part model of personhood. Needs are the forces or *drives* that give direction to or *motivate* a person's behavior. Psychologists have commonly held that a person's most primary need or motivation is to avoid or terminate pain and to obtain pleasure. Freud referred to this as the "pleasure principle," and it is obvious that much of our behavior, at least our conscious behavior, is governed by the desire to minimize painful consequences and maximize pleasurable ones. Indeed, the effectiveness of *behavior modification*, the behavioral rather than psychodynamic approach to psychopathology, rests on this principle. Pleasurable outcomes for engaging in desired behavior are called *positive reinforcers*, whereas negative behaviors evoke unpleasant or *negative reinforcers*. In many respects, behavior modification, a widely used educational and therapeutic approach with developmentally disabled individuals, is merely the systematic application of the pleasure-pain principle.

In terms of the personhood model, states of pain or pleasure are closely tied to the degree to which needs are met—biological and psychological (e.g., Frijda, 1988). When a person's needs or desires are gratified, that person experiences a reduction in tension and increased feelings of comfort or pleasure. When a person's needs are unmet or frustrated, the individual experiences unpleasant feelings—e.g., tension, anxiety, anger, and fear. Thus feelings or emotions are seen as closely tied to the forces that motivate us. For the developmentally disabled person, chronic frustration, i.e., the inability to meet the basic human needs, is common. The effect is to produce unpleasant emotions, and the actions taken to relieve them are often what other people see as "disturbed behavior" or psychopathology (e.g., Martin, 1977).

Four major human needs are posited—survival, structure, self-esteem, and self-expression. Each is defined in the following paragraphs, and at least one example is given of the way each need affects persons with developmental disabilities.

Survival. Survival involves a person's *biological* needs. In addition to the old standbys of food, clothing, and shelter, we can add the needs for stimulation (sensation) and for sex. Satisfaction of the first three is generally not a problem for developmentally disabled persons, but the latter two can be troublesome. A culture that is uncomfortable about sexuality in general is particularly uneasy about its manifestation in disabled individuals, especially those who are intellectually impaired and dependent on others for their general maintenance. As a society, we prefer to ignore or deny the fact that our developmentally disabled peers have the same sexual needs that we have. We do not trust them to be judicious in sexual expression and just wish that the issue would "go away." Such an attitude can only lead to sexual frustration for these individuals and, in the absence of appropriate education, inappropriate sexual behaviors (Baroff, 1986).

Stimulation, too, is matter of concern. The notion that humans seek an optimum level of stimulation is an old one in psychology that finds modern expression as "arousal" theory, which ties the need for stimulation to the reticular activating system of the human brain (Berlyne, 1960; Hebb, 1955; Zuckerman, Buchsbaum, and Murphy, 1980). During the waking state, a person receives both external stimulation from the environment and internal stimulation from within the brain, e.g., daydreams, memories, and thoughts. At night, stimulation continues, but here in the form of dreams—internal stimulation. Under conditions of too little stimulation, typically of a visual or auditory nature, a person experiences boredom, restlessness, and elevated tension (Heron, 1957; Singer, 1975). Prolonged stimulus deprivation produces adverse cognitive and emotional changes, and one of the concerns related to the earlier societal pattern of institutionalizing young disabled children, such as mentally retarded ones, was the possibility of damage from exposure to settings that would fail to provide growth-enhancing stimulation (Skeels and Dye, 1939; Thompson and Grusec, 1970).

Apart from the aforementioned needs related to survival, this category refers to the life-preservation instinct itself. While life-threatening health problems do not affect most developmentally disabled persons, serious physical problems are not unusual and are especially prominent in those with the most severe degrees of mental retardation. Of course, health problems are common in the developmental disabilities that are due to clear biological abnormalities, such as cerebral palsy, epilepsy, and, to a lesser degree, autism.

Structure. Structure refers to a need for predictability, i.e., for congruence between what a person experiences and what that person expected to experience (Festinger, 1957; Osgood, Suci, and Tannenbaum, 1957). The need for structure is the need for the familiar as opposed to the strange. Structure also relates to a person's desire to understand what is expected of him or her. In childrearing, structure refers to the setting of limits and contingencies. In games, structure means the rules that govern play. To the degree that our reality has sufficient structure, things make sense to us. In the absence of such structure, we feel confusion, anxiety, and, in the extreme, bewilderment.

The need for structure is especially pronounced in autism. For autistic children, change produces anxiety. Structure is also important to retarded individuals; their intellectual difficulties cause them to feel more vulnerable when they are in an unfamiliar situation.

Self-Esteem. This is a need to which we have already referred. Self-esteem refers to self-concept, one's sense of worth or goodness. The significance of self-esteem is recognized by all personality theorists (e.g., Coopersmith, 1967; Epstein, 1973; Maslow, 1954; Rogers, 1951). Self-esteem is central to mental health (Strupp and Hadley, 1977), and much of a person's "pursuit of happiness," pleasure rather than pain, seems to be tied to behaviors designed to elevate, maintain, or defend self-esteem. Indeed, defensive behavior is generally nothing more than an attempt to ward off or deny a reality that, if accepted, would cause a person to feel less worth—in the eyes of others as well as in his or her own eyes.

Self-esteem is a complex need; some psychologists reject the notion of a single self-concept and view each person as having multiple selves (e.g., Markus and Nurius, 1986). Certainly, I have a sense of myself as having more than one self, each self being tied to a different life role—husband, father, worker, etc. For present purposes, however, let's consider self-esteem as a single entity, one that is seen as the outgrowth and reflection of three subneeds—intimacy, success, and autonomy.

Intimacy. This ingredient of self-esteem refers to the social self. The need for intimacy is a person's need to be close to other human beings. The human need for other people was attributed by Plato to the dependence of humans on each other for survival, by the psychologist McDougall to instinct, and by modern theorists to the creation of an "affectional reward system" that results from our early childhood experiences and which can only be fed by other people (Severy, Brigham, and Schlenker, 1976). The modern view echoes that of Plato. The infant or young child is absolutely dependent on its care givers, typically its parents, for its sustenance, its pleasures, and the relief of its discomforts. This extraordinary dependency means that our care givers are crucial to us, and early in life we learn that we need to please them if our own needs are to be met. Our care givers literally control our states of happiness and unhappiness. We are not likely to be consciously aware of this connection, but it operates within our psyche as a conditioned response. We learn about the necessity of pleasing those who are important to us, i.e., have power over us, a lesson that we carry throughout life.

Intimacy is the need to receive and give love. It involves the entire range of experiences that constitute positive interactions with others. At the receiving level, intimacy includes behaviors directed at us that involve attention, recognition, acceptance, approval, and love. At the giving level, intimacy refers to the expression of these behaviors toward others. Of the three ingredients that foster self-esteem, intimacy is regarded as the most important. To the extent that we have it, we feel secure, protected, and loved. To the degree that it is lacking, we feel a wide range of painful emotions—anxiety, depression, anger, and a general state of unworthiness.

The need for intimacy is often unfulfilled in developmentally disabled persons (Bogdan and Taylor, 1976; Wright, 1983; Hurley, 1965). The person's disability may evoke rejection rather than acceptance, avoidance rather than inclusion. For example, the head and body distortion and drooling often found in cerebral palsy are more likely to induce repulsion than attraction.

Intimacy needs in developmentally disabled persons are particularly likely to be frustrated during adolescence, when normal teens begin to be very sensitive about the people with whom they associate. And the adult years also may be lonely ones if there is not a peer group with whom to interact. Indeed, access to an ostensibly vocational program in a sheltered workshop may be valued by the developmentally disabled person more for its social than its vocational aspects.

Success. This second component of self-esteem refers to the sense of accomplishment that is felt when a person *successfully* tackles the significant tasks of daily life. Related terms are *achievement* (McClelland et al., 1953), *effectance*, and *competence* (White, 1959). Success evokes feelings of satisfaction, pride, and occasionally pure joy. Think of the joy shown by the winners of important athletic events. Contrariwise, failure produces feelings of disappointment, sadness, and sometimes shame and humiliation. The painfulness of shame tells us something about the importance of success in our lives.

The need for success is another significant source of difficulty for developmentally disabled persons. Cognitive deficits, such as occur in mental retardation, preclude normal school progress and can lead to a sense of inadequacy and low worth. Special education classes were created in order to give retarded children the opportunity to be successful, and they continue to serve children with at least a moderate degree of impairment. For the mildly retarded child, however, the stigma of being in a special class, especially in junior and senior high school, has led to placement of these children in regular classes (known as *mainstreaming*) while continuing to provide access to needed remediation through so-called resource programs.

Autonomy. The need for *autonomy* is the need to feel some degree of control or power over one's life. Autonomy is the sense that we are the *cause* of our own behavior, perhaps illusory (Lefcourt, 1973), but seen by at least one psychologist (deCharms, 1968) as our most fundamental motivating force. Another psychologist (Bandura, 1982) uses the term *self-efficacy* to refer to the sense of one's ability to produce and regulate events in one's own life. It is to see ourselves as at the "locus of control" (Bialer, 1961) for events that befall us. Autonomy also involves a notion of freedom, the sense that we can exercise some *choice* in our lives. With autonomy, there are feelings of pride, confidence, and even power. Without it, there can be rebellion, resignation, a sense of futility, and ultimately, apathy or surrender.

The need for autonomy is sometimes muted in persons with major developmental disabilities. Often dependence rather than independence is the adaptive mode, a not unexpected characteristic of persons whose disabilities may be of such severity as to inevitably increase their dependence on others. However, to suggest that there may *appear* to be a lesser need for autonomy in the seriously disabled population is not to say that the need does not exist. Like all people, those with developmental disabilities have preferences, tastes, and desires. Whenever they or we are not doing what we are required to do, our actions reflect those preferences. Developmentally disabled persons also want to be able to exercise some control over their lives. Indeed, we'll later read of conflicts over autonomy in complaints about excessive parental control and/or overprotection in adolescence and adulthood.

Self-Expression. Self-expression is the fourth major need in the personhood model. It refers to the need to engage in activities that are pursued simply because we enjoy them. These are the activities that make up our leisure or recreational lives, although, if we are very fortunate, they also may be pursued in our occupational life. Participation in these activities provides a wide variety of pleasurable emotions—from simple relaxation to sheer joy. When the opportunity for fun is blocked, a person experiences boredom and frustration.

Access to recreational opportunities can be much restricted by mental and physical disabilities, especially when the disabled person lives in a setting that is physically removed from community sources of recreation. The presence of physical disabilities, as in cerebral palsy, also may so interfere with a person's mobility as to make access difficult. The now common and frequently legally mandated physical modifications to public buildings, the inclusion of ramps and special lifts for wheelchair access to vans, and other accommodations, have eased the problems of providing opportunities for physically disabled people to share the same kinds of recreational pleasures that the rest of us enjoy.

Values

The concept of values has been an elusive one in psychology (Wenar, 1971), and here *values* are defined as those people, objects, activities, and ideas that we come to prize (value). We prize such people or things because they are the means through which our *needs* are met. We value health services because survival is important to us. We value a map when we are traveling because it provides us with a guide to unfamiliar territory; it gives us structure. In the self-esteem domain, parents, friends, and loved ones are prized as our chief sources of intimacy. Activities that we enjoy, in part, because we perform them well feed our need for success. Experiences reflecting a new level of independence are valued in adolescence and young adulthood as evidence of greater autonomy. I frequently cite my first solo cross-country trip at age 18 as an indication that I no longer needed the assistance of adults to manage for me.

Values are particularly evident in self-expression because we freely choose the activities to which we devote our leisure time. Since we are not *required* to engage in these activities, our involvement must indicate some interest and pleasure in them for their own sake. Our favorite forms of recreation are clearly valued.

Since values are tied to needs, like needs, they give direction and specificity to our behavior. At the recreational level, one person may enjoy a quiet game of chess, whereas another may enjoy shooting baskets or playing ball. Of course, one's recreational preferences are a mix of activities, but each is pursued for its specific pleasure or interest. When we examine the things that are important to us, those which we pursue or strongly assert, we are showing what we value.

INTEGRATING THE MAJOR
COMPONENTS OF PERSONHOOD

A model of the nature of personhood has been presented in an attempt to provide an understanding of who and what a person is and how people are affected by disability. To summarize, the personhood model consists of three major dimensions: resources, needs, and values. *Resources* are a person's capacities and abilities and are here characterized as cognitive skills (intelligence); communicative skills; health, sensory, and physical skills; personality (temperament, emotions, and character); and aesthetic appreciation. Resources are the raw materials or fundamental ingredients of all behavior. For example, in reading and understanding these lines, you are using your vision (sensory skill) to see the words and your cognition (intelligence) to understand them. Disabilities are by their very nature impairments in resources that significantly affect a person's ability to function adaptively in the world.

A person's resources are not employed randomly; rather, they are directed toward activities that are *valued* because they lead to the satisfaction of basic biological and psychological *needs*. These needs are here labeled as survival, structure, self-esteem, and self-expression. Needs are ever-present; they may be temporarily sated or gratified, as in hunger, but their demand for gratification never disappears. Needs are closely tied to emotions—feeling states that can be located on a continuum of physical and psychological pain at one end and extreme joy at the other. When needs are unmet, a person feels various states of physical or psychological discomfort (e.g., pain, anxiety, anger, sadness), and when needs are met, a person feels various states of pleasure—from simple tension relief to utter joy. These needs and the emotions they generate are seen as fundamental motivators because people are regarded as ultimately governed by the need to minimize painful states and maximize pleasurable ones.

Managing One's Emotions

In this personhood conception, the effectiveness of adaptation is seen as resulting from how one manages one's emotions and the actions they impel. Two factors are seen as determining adaptive effectiveness—awareness of the *consequences* of one's actions (reality testing) and the *intensity* of one's needs. The former is likely to be less well understood by developmentally disabled persons, especially when the disability has a significant cognitive component. The latter can create difficulties if normal opportunities for need gratification and emotional release are not available.

A Disclaimer

To be sure, not every human act can be traced to a pain-avoidance principle. Some "helping" behaviors, such as instinctively reaching out to someone who is about to fall, seem to reflect an underlying identification with others, with other living things—animals as well as people. And the war hero who throws himself on a hand grenade to protect his buddies is clearly not motivated by self-interest. Rather, these behaviors are seen as *conditioned responses* that reflect the emotional ties (identification) our social experiences engender. We become tied to other humans through our experiences of intimacy with them.

I also have not here addressed the *spiritual* aspects of human life. Most everyone recognizes this aspect of the human condition, one that seems to relate to the needs for structure and self-esteem. Religions provide structure in that their teachings offer us a way to understand our lives. And God as a source of caring and love clearly relates to our need for intimacy.

The intent of this disclaimer is to acknowledge that the model of personhood presented here is necessarily incomplete. However, it does include conceptions of personality that can help us to better understand the forces that motivate behavior in all of us, both normal and disabled.

COMMON ADAPTIVE PROBLEMS

This section presents an overview of the kinds of adaptive problems that persons with developmental disabilities are likely to encounter. Since this book deals with a wide range of disorders, from such relatively massive and severe disabilities as mental retardation to more specific and often less severe ones as epilepsy, this section will necessarily have a selective rather than total application. The purpose here is to give a sense of the typical consequences of early-arising developmental disorders. In succeeding chapters, the problems related to each of the specific disabilities will be particularly highlighted. This overview also will serve as a backdrop to further discussion of the kinds of psychosocial problems created by these developmental disorders. I have already touched on some of these problems in an effort to quickly demonstrate their relevance to the personhood model; this section examines these problems as they emerge in development—from infancy and early childhood to adulthood.

INFANCY (BIRTH TO AGE 2) AND EARLY CHILDHOOD (AGES 2 TO 6)

Depending on the nature and severity of the developmental disorder, the preschool years may find the affected child delayed in major areas of development: (1) in *motor* development—learning to sit, stand, walk, and run (gross motor skills) and hand-eye coordination (fine motor skills); (2) in *self-care*—feeding, dressing, and toileting (slow development here may be due to underlying fine motor difficulties); (3) in using and understanding *language;* (4) in acquiring *knowledge* about himself or herself and the world; and (5) in the *social* sphere—learning how to relate to others, i.e., to parents, siblings, peers, older children, and adults.

SCHOOL AGE: MIDDLE CHILDHOOD (AGES 6 TO 11), PREADOLESCENCE (AGES 11 TO 13), ADOLESCENCE (AGES 13 TO 20), AND YOUNG ADULTHOOD (AGES 20 TO 21)

Covering the sweep of four developmental periods, the school years are generally major hurdles for children and young people with developmental disabilities. Common problems are (1) difficulty in learning, i.e., in mastering the basic academic skills of reading, writing, and arithmetic; (2) difficulty in developing the level of personal responsibility and autonomy that is associated with normal adolescence and young adulthood (some diminution in independence is inevitable, however, when disabilities are severe enough to create chronic dependence on others); (3) difficulty in establishing satisfying social relationships, especially with peers, same sex and then opposite sex; (4) lack of preparation for postschool life, i.e., for the role of worker; and (5) lack of development of one's recreational or avocational life, which is also much affected by mobility and ease of access to sources of recreation.

ADULTHOOD (AGE 22 AND OVER)

The hallmark of normal adulthood in our society is the capacity to assume responsibility for one's life, to live and function independently, to no longer need the assistance or supervision of others in the management of our daily affairs. However, developmental disabilities can seriously interfere with this cultural ideal. There may be mental and physical impediments to (1) living independently, (2) working, (3) assuming the normal social roles of friend, spouse, or parent, (4) utilizing leisure time, and (5) performing common citizenship responsibilities such as voting.

AGE-RELATED ADAPTIVE PROBLEMS AND SELF-ESTEEM

Of the major needs posited in the personhood model, none is likely to be more adversely affected by developmental disabilities than self-esteem. When a person is disabled to *any* degree in body or mind, the differences that person perceives between himself or herself and the cultural norm are likely to evoke a painful response. Those who most successfully cope with their disabilities come to accept themselves for their strengths as well as their limitations, for their abilities as well as their disabilities, a perception that results from the parenting and the kinds of social and learning experiences to which they have been exposed (Zetlin and Turner, 1985; Zisfein and Rosen, 1974). This section examines how self-esteem is likely to be affected by the presence of a developmental disability, typically one recognizable in infancy or early childhood. The focus is on how the developmental experiences at each of the major developmental stages is likely to affect that important psychological need.

SELF-ESTEEM EFFECTS IN INFANCY AND EARLY CHILDHOOD

Even before there can be sufficient cognitive development for one to compare oneself with others and to be aware of a sense of being different, that is before age 3, a developmental disability may have profoundly affected the quality of *parental attachment.* The child's disorder may create obstacles to the normal expression of parental love. This will have a serious impact on the need for intimacy.

Later, as the disabled child encounters other children and more family adults, these people are added to parents (and siblings) as potential sources of intimacy. But the child who is very different from peers, and in a negative way, is more likely to experience rejection rather than intimacy. Children, for example, prefer to play with others of like developmental level; after all, it is only with others with whom there is physical, mental, and emotional compatibility that there can be cooperative play. It is because of the likely exclusion and isolation of the child who is different, in essence *immature* in mental, physical, or educational ways, that day-care programs for normal children are encouraged to include handicapped youngsters in their population mix (Guralnick, 1978). Both groups of children can benefit from contact with each other. For the disabled child, developmentally more mature youngsters can serve as models, as sources of imitation. For the nonhandicapped child, there is the opportunity for constructive interactions, those that can foster intimacy rather than rejection and shape in positive ways the attitudes the child will eventually have toward people who are different.

Experiences with nonhandicapped children may not only frustrate needs for intimacy but also can adversely affect the need for success in a developmentally disabled child. The older preschool developmentally disabled child may begin to become aware of how he or she compares with other children. As early as age 3, normally developing children start comparing themselves with others (Hurlock, 1964), thus beginning to form judgments of self-worth. If all his or her peers are functioning at higher levels of development, the less mature youngster is bound to make comparisons that are demeaning in nature. The child may perceive himself or herself as less adept in physical activities, as less able to communicate, and as requiring more assistance in self-care. All this gradually burns into the child a sense of inadequacy in relation to others. Instead of normal experiences of success in daily activities, there may be failure, frustration, and a growing sense of personal ineptitude. Admittedly, this degree of self-awareness will probably be limited only to older developmentally disabled preschoolers and those without severe intellectual deficits. The more intellectually impaired child will probably not begin to make these comparisons until school age, if at all.

The third ingredient of self-esteem and one that is also very relevant to the life experience of persons with severe handicap is autonomy. In the normally developing child, this need is expressed in growing demands for self-determination and independence. Through its gradually developing competencies, the young child begins to reduce its dependence on care givers, to assume some responsibilities for his or her own care, to establish his or her own "identity." In the preschool years, this is most evident in growing self-care skills. From a state of total dependence in infancy, there is steady growth in self-care—in learning how to feed, dress, and toilet oneself. As these skills emerge, parents can allow greater freedom, greater independence. The developmentally disabled child, however, is likely to be impaired in the mental and physical capacities that underlie self-care skills. For such a child, the period of infancy and its associated dependency is literally prolonged. The child remains dependent for a much longer period of time, and with this there is a growing expectation that others will do for him or her. This can become a problem particularly where parents persist in doing for the child what the child could learn to do for himself or herself. This occurs either because of overprotective attitudes or simply because of expediency—it's easier for parents to do it than to watch and wait for the child to learn to do it. Educators are heard to complain about families in which skills acquired in the educational setting are not expected to be performed in the home. This simply adds to the dependency that is naturally a part of severe disability and prevents the child from assuming levels of autonomy that are appropriate. In effect, the child is permanently infantilized. Admittedly, for some parents, multiple roles and family demands may make such educational cooperation unrealistic (Turnbull and Turnbull, 1982).

SELF-ESTEEM EFFECTS AT SCHOOL AGE

The school years are a crucial period for developmentally disabled children because their disability often seriously affects learning and normal school progress. This will be particularly apparent in those with mental retardation, but it also will be seen in nonretarded youngsters with cerebral palsy and autism and, to a lesser degree, in those with epilepsy. Such children can be expected to show some difficulties in acquiring basic academic skills and are also likely to manifest varying degrees of language, motor, perceptual, attentional, and personality disorder.

The consequences of these school difficulties for self-esteem appear to depend in part on the particular peer group with whom the child compares himself or herself (Baroff, 1974). Special classes were originally created for students with serious learning problems to avoid placing them in settings where failure would be inevitable (Cegelka and Tyler, 1970). Rather, they were to be in learning environments where they could progress at their own rate with a teacher who was sensitive to their learning difficulties. Such classes still are the rule for students with major intellectual impairments, and they can provide the kind of support that fosters a sense of worth. Moderately retarded students in special classes appear to compare themselves *academically* with their handicapped classmates (Schurr and Brookover, 1967; Schurr, Joiner, and Towne, 1970; Towne and Joiner, 1966), not with normal students, and in these comparisons a genuine sense of worth can be derived. At lesser degrees of intellectual impairment, special class placement can be experienced as stigmatizing. This is especially true at junior high and senior high levels (Gozali, 1972; Jones, 1972). Stigma is also reported by adults who were formerly residents of institutions for the retarded and who now reside and function independently in the community. They saw their former institutional home and the label it carried as something to be hidden. Their goal was to "pass" in normal society (Edgerton, 1967). These stigmatic concerns were the impetus for the mainstreaming of at least mildly retarded children into regular classes.

Fears of being stigmatized relate to our social sensitivities and the desire to win acceptance (intimacy) from those whom we esteem. This need is intensified in the school years, an extremely significant period in social development. In normally developing children, the school years are a time of growing demands for both autonomy and closeness with peers. With the self-consciousness of adolescence and the desire for peer approval (intimacy), there is increasing selectivity in the choice of friends. The developmentally disabled adolescent who in childhood may have had nonhandicapped friends is now likely to suffer social rejection. There is a considerable body of research that reveals the general attitudes of normal individuals toward disabled people. The reactions of normal individuals to those with physical disabilities include uneasiness in their presence, rejection of closeness, and a tendency to ridicule and derogate them (Fenderson, 1984; Wright, 1983). Our humor is replete with jokes about the infirmities of others. So-called moron stories and the use of the word *retard* as a term of ridicule make clear our attitude toward those with intellectual deficits. Perhaps we need to point out *their* deficiencies in order to bolster *our* self-esteem!

Apart from the normal preoccupation with winning peer approval in adolescence, initially with same-sex peers, later adolescence finds youngsters beginning to respond *sexually*. This domain is no less a source of anxiety to developmentally disabled young people than to nondisabled ones. For most young people today, knowledge of sexuality and its appropriate manner of expression is largely a product of "street" information gained through peers. But young people whose disabilities may restrict both their range of understanding and their degree of social contact are likely to be less informed about sex. Moreover, freedom to express sexual impulses at any level may be severely limited by lack of privacy. If, for example, one is always dependent on someone else for assistance in the bathroom, even that haven may not be available. Manifestations of sexuality in these young people, some of whom are seen as "eternal children," is often terrifying to parents (Nigro, 1975). Such parents fear exploitation of their children and the manifestation of embarrassingly inappropriate behaviors by them. The effect is to encourage a denial that their children have any sexual feelings at all or to treat the sexuality of their child as a "sleeping giant" that must not be awakened. In one book on recreational activities for retarded adolescents, for example, readers are cautioned not to encourage dancing between the sexes (Carlson and Ginglend, 1968). In my own view, it is the public expression of sexuality that creates the greatest discomfort for us. Sexuality as a topic is not easily discussed between parents and children. Parents prefer to assume that their children have some awareness of their maturing sexuality and are learning how to express it in socially appropriate ways. And privacy provides the opportunity for its nonoffensive expression. Such privacy is simply harder to come by for individuals who are dependent on others on a daily basis. Apart from the family home, disabled persons residing in facilities serving groups of individuals, e.g., group homes, often do not find privacy readily available. Moreover, the very nature of many disabled persons' handicaps often precludes parental expectations of socially appropriate outlets for sexual expression—dating and marriage.

SELF-ESTEEM EFFECTS IN ADULTHOOD

The immediate postschool period can be stressful to the young adult because access to a setting like the school within which needs for general stimulation, intimacy, and success have been met for many years may suddenly be lost. If the young adult is not ready for employment in the regular work force, then local day programs or sheltered work settings become the only avenues for continued involvement with others (intimacy) and for the performing of some kind of meaningful daily activity (success). However, the availability of such programs is limited by funding constraints that are not present during school years. At school age, there is acceptance by the community of its responsibility for the provision of programs for its handicapped youth. No such comprehensive commitment exists with regard to the postschool period. This is reflected in the denial of access to a program simply because the funds to support the person in it are not available. The current vocational thrust toward supported employment is an attempt to broaden the range of vocational opportunities open to seriously disabled adults (Wehman, 1988). For many young adults, there may be a sudden loss of purpose as the home becomes the chief place where time is spent. The family finds itself again performing full-time care as its young adult moves back into the status of "child." And often the disabled person endures this without the kind of support network that was available when he or she was young (Suelzle and Keenan, 1981). Suddenly, dependency is again increased, and activity has been narrowed to watching TV or simply vegetating. Various forms of stereotyped or self-stimulatory behaviors will increase. And with the sudden loss of friends, there may be loneliness. Trapped within the family's four walls, hard-won self-care, language, social, and vocational skills atrophy as the press for continued growth wanes.

Under such circumstances, frustration tolerance levels are likely to be reduced in care givers and in the disabled person as well. An increase in behavior problems can be expected, and these can threaten the living situation itself. Family stress is a common cause for seeking out-of-home placement for handicapped young people. This is especially true in the adult years when parents are themselves aging and are less prepared to carry on the kinds of care responsibilities that were acceptable when they were younger. There is also, of course, the mortality of parents. This will ultimately require a new living situation for the child who is unable to function independently. Many parents view planning for this as their main concern (Brotherson et al., 1984).

In addition to care-giver concerns that can threaten the disabled child's place in the family and the need for intimacy, developmentally disabled young adults are often frustrated in demands for greater self-determination (autonomy). Parental anxieties about their child's general coping skills are often intense, and such parents react by *overprotecting* and unduly curbing autonomy (Cook, 1963; Kogan and Tyler, 1973). The ironic effect of overprotection is to ensure that the child will not have the opportunity to learn those very skills that would ease parental fears.

Concerns about autonomy were prominent in a group of cerebral palsied young adults who were incensed at the restrictions imposed on them by their parents (Mowatt, 1970). They wanted greater freedom— to ride buses, visit friends, date, and to try to live independently. One member of this group, a mildly retarded as well as cerebral palsied young woman, had experienced a less restrictive upbringing. Her father insisted that she learn to cook and keep house, and he deliberately sent her on errands and bus trips to prepare her to be as independent (autonomous) as possible. Later, living in a "sheltered" apartment following the death of her parents, she expressed genuine gratitude for what her father had taught her.

This group of cerebral palsied adults felt much more confident of themselves than did their parents. Mothers in particular were seen as too protective. One wheelchair-bound member of the group noted insightfully, "It's *harder* for us to get along by ourselves, so we need *more* not *fewer* chances to learn."

In discussing the school years, reference was made to sexuality. This, of course, can continue to present stresses to the disabled person and the family. The concerns of parents have been indicated; it is only necessary to repeat that where evidence of sexual desire is ignored or denied and where there is no recognition of culturally normative needs for privacy, sexuality may produce problems. However, parents are not necessarily of one mind regarding sexuality in their developmentally disabled children. While parental denial of sexuality in the developmentally disabled young adult may simply be consistent with a perception of the young adult as a "child" who is unable to enter into normal heterosexual roles, e.g., that of spouse or parent, others who accept their child's sexuality may see marriage as a desirable outcome. They may, however, see a parent role for their child as inappropriate. This is, at least, true for those with significant intellectual impairment (e.g., Goodman, Budner, and Lesh, 1971).

In older developmentally disabled adults, apart from self-esteem concerns, health needs are going to be more prominent. There may be earlier signs of physical and mental decline, as in Down syndrome (Miniszek, 1983), or chronic associated physical disabilities may produce a generally weakening state of health. Concerns about the needs of the elderly segment of the developmentally disabled population are increasingly heard (Janicki and Wisniewski, 1985).

From the standpoint of meeting basic psychological needs in adulthood, a developmentally disabled person requires a residential setting in which there is acceptance; access to stimulation, recreation, and meaningful daily activity—preferably some form of work; and the opportunity for social relationships, commonly but not exclusively with other handicapped individuals (college students have established friendships with mildly retarded young adults). To the degree that these needs are met, the developmentally disabled person, no less than the rest of us, can be regarded as leading a happy and fulfilling life. *However, accomplishment of these goals depends on the services that communities provide.* These are described in Chapter 2.

REFERENCES

Bandura, A. (1982). Self-efficacy mechanism in human agency. *American Psychologist, 37,* 122–147.

Baroff, G. S. (1974). *Mental retardation: Nature, cause, and management.* New York: Hemisphere.

Baroff, G. S. (1986). *Mental retardation: Nature, cause, and management,* 2d Ed. New York: Hemisphere.

Berlyne, D. E. (1960). *Conflict, arousal and curiosity.* New York: McGraw-Hill.

Bialer, I. (1961). Conceptualization of success and failure in mentally retarded and normal children. *Journal of Personality, 29,* 303–320.

Bogdan, R., and Taylor, S. (1976). The judged, not the judges. *American Psychologist, 31,* 47–52.

Boggs, E. M., and Henney, R. L. (1979). *A numerical and functional description of the developmentally disabled population in the United States by major life activities as defined in the Developmental Disabilities Assistance and Bill of Rights Act as amended in PL 95-602.* Philadelphia: EMC Institute.

Brotherson, M. J., Backus, L. H., Summers, J. A., and Turnbull, A. (1986). Transition to adulthood. In J. A. Summers (Ed.), *The Right to Grow Up.* Baltimore: Paul H. Brookes.

Carlson, B. W., and Ginglend, D. R. (1968). *Recreation for retarded teenagers and young adults*. Nashville, TN.: Abingdon Press.

Cegelka, W. J., and Tyler, J. L. (1970). The efficacy of special class placement for the mentally retarded in proper perspective. *Training School Bulletin, 67*, 33–68.

Cook, J. J. (1963). Dimensional analysis of child-rearing attitudes of parents of handicapped children. *American Journal of Mental Deficiency, 68*, 354–361.

Coopersmith, S. (1967). *The antecedents of self-esteem*. San Francisco: Freeman.

deCharms, R. (1968). *Personal causation: The internal affective determinants of behavior*. New York: Academic Press.

Edgerton, R. B. (1967). *The cloak of competence: Stigma in the lives of the mentally retarded*. Berkeley: University of California Press.

Epstein, S. (1973). The self-concept revisited: On a theory of a theory. *American Psychologist, 28*, 484–416.

Fenderson, D. A. (1984). Opportunities for psychologists in disability research. *American Psychologist, 39*, 524–528.

Festinger, L. (1957). *A theory of cognitive dissonance*. New York: Harper & Row.

Frijda, N. H. (1988). The laws of emotion. *American Psychologist, 43*, 349–358.

Goodman, L., Budner, S., and Lesh, B. (1971). The parents' role in sex education for the retarded. *Mental Retardation, 9*, 43–45.

Gozali, J. (1972). Perception of the EMR special class by former students. *Mental Retardation, 10*, 34–35.

Guralnick, M. J. (1978). *Early intervention and the integration of handicapped and nonhandicapped children*. Baltimore: University Park Press.

Hebb, D. O. (1955). Drives and the CNS (central nervous system). *Psychological Review, 62*, 243–254.

Heron, W. (1957). The pathology of boredom. *Scientific American, 196*, 52–56.

Hurley, J. R. (1965). Parental acceptance-rejection and children's intelligence. *Merrill-Palmer Quarterly, 11*, 19–31.

Hurlock, E. G. (1964). *Child development*, 4th Ed. New York: McGraw-Hill.

Jacobson, J. W., and Janicki, M. P. (1983). Observed prevalence of multiple developmental disabilities. *Mental Retardation, 21*, 87–94.

Janicki, M. P., and Wisniewski, H. M. (Eds.). (1985). *Aging and developmental disabilities: Issues and approaches*. Baltimore: Paul H. Brookes.

Jones, R. L. (1972). Labels and stigma in special education. *Exceptional Children, 38*, 553–564.

Kagan, J., and Kogan, N. (1970). Individual variation in cognitive processes. In P. H. Mussen (Ed.), *Carmichael's manual of child psychology*, Vol 1, 3d Ed. New York: Wiley.

Kiernan, W. (1979). Rehabilitation planning. In P. R. Magrab and J. O. Elder (Eds.), *Planning services to handicapped persons: Community, education, health*. Baltimore: Paul H. Brookes.

Kogan, K. L., and Tyler, N. (1973). Mother-child interaction in young physically handicapped children. *American Journal of Mental Deficiency, 77*, 492–497.

Lefcourt, H. M. (1973). The function of the illusions of control and freedom. *American Psychologist, 28*, 417–425.

Maloney, M. P., and Ward, M. P. (1979). *Mental retardation and modern society*. New York: Oxford University Press.

Markus, H., and Nurius, P. (1986). Possible selves. *American Psychologist, 41*, 954–969.

Martin, B. (1977). *Abnormal psychology: Clinical and scientific perspectives.* New York: Holt, Rinehart and Winston.

Maslow, A. H. (1954). *Motivation and personality.* New York: Harper & Row.

McClelland, D. C., Atkinson, J. W., Clark, R. A., and Lowell, E. L. (1953). *The achievement motive.* New York: Appleton-Century-Crofts.

Miniszek, N. A. (1983). Development of Alzheimer disease in Down syndrome individuals. *American Journal of Mental Deficiency, 87,* 377–385.

Mowatt, M. H. (1970). Group therapy approach to emotional conflicts of the mentally retarded and their parents. In F. J. Menolascino (Ed.), *Psychiatric approaches to mental retardation.* New York: Basic Books.

Nigro, G. (1975). Sexuality in the handicapped: Some observations on human needs. *Rehabilitation Literature, 36,* 202–205.

Osgood, C. E., Suci, G. J., and Tannenbaum, P. H. (1957). *The measurement of meaning.* Urbana, IL: University of Illinois Press.

Rogers, C. R. (1951). *Client-centered therapy.* Boston: Houghton-Mifflin.

Schurr, K. T., and Brookover, W. (1967). *The effect of special class placement in the self-concept ability of the educable mentally retarded child* (U.S. Office of Education). East Lansing, MI.: Michigan State University Press.

Schurr, K. T., Joiner, L., and Towne, R. C. (1970). Self-concept research on the mentally retarded: A review of empirical studies. *Mental Retardation, 8,* 39–43.

Severy, L. J., Brigham, J. C., and Schlenker, B. R. (1976). *A contemporary introduction to social psychology.* New York: McGraw-Hill.

Singer, J. L. (1975). Navigating the stream of consciousness: Research in day dreaming and related inner experience. *American Psychologist, 30,* 727–738.

Skeels, H. M., and Dye, H. B. (1939). A study of the effects of differential stimulation on mentally retarded children. *Proceedings and Addresses of the Sixty-Third Annual Session of the American Association on Mental Deficiency, 44,* 114–130.

Strupp, H. H., and Hadley, S. W. (1977). A tripartite model of mental health and therapeutic outcomes: With special reference to negative effects in psychotherapy. *American Psychologist, 32,* 187–196.

Suelzle, M., and Keenan, V. (1981). Changes in family support networks over the life cycle of mentally retarded persons. *American Journal of Mental Deficiency, 86,* 267–274.

Summers, J. A. (1981). The definition of developmental disabilities: A concept in transition. *Mental Retardation, 19,* 259–265.

Thomas, A., Chess, S., and Birch, H. G. (1968). *Temperament and behavior disorders in children.* New York: New York University Press.

Thompson, W. R., and Grusec, J. E. (1970). Studies of early experience. In P. H. Mussen (Ed.), *Carmichael's manual of child psychology.* New York: Wiley.

Towne, R. C., and Joiner, L. M. (1966). *The effects of special class placement on the self-concept of ability of the educable mentally retarded child.* East Lansing, MI.: Office of Educational Publications.

Turnbull, A. P., and Turnbull, H. R., III. (1982). Parent involvement in the education of handicapped children: A critique. *Mental Retardation, 20,* 115–122.

Wehman, P. (1988). Supported employment: Toward equal opportunity employment for persons with severe disabilities. *Mental Retardation, 26,* 357–361.

Wenar, C. (1971). *Personality development from infancy to adulthood.* Boston: Houghton-Mifflin.

White, R. W. (1959). Motivation reconsidered: The concept of competence. *Psychological Review, 66,* 297–333.

Wright, B. A. (1983). *Physical disability: A psychological approach,* 2d Ed. New York: Harper & Row.

Zetlin, A. G., and Turner, J. L. (1988). Salient domains in the self-conception of adults with mental retardation. *American Journal of Mental Deficiency, 89,* 570–579.

Zisfein, L., and Rosen, M. (1974). Self-concept and mental retardation: Theory measurement, and clinical utility. *Mental Retardation, 1,* 15–19.

Zuckerman, M., Buchsbaum, M. S., and Murphy, D. L. (1980). Sensation seeking and its biological correlates. *Psychological Bulletin, 88,* 187–214.

CHAPTER 2

Services: The Key to Meeting Biological and Psychological Needs

OVERVIEW

This chapter focuses on the means by which persons with developmental disabilities are provided the experiences that both strengthen their resources or abilities and help them meet their biological and psychological needs. The topics covered are (1) the importance of services, (2) an introduction to the full array of services, and (3) an elaboration of major services in infancy and early childhood, school age, and adulthood.

SERVICES: THE KEY TO DEVELOPMENT AND THE MEETING OF NEEDS

A WAY OF THINKING ABOUT SERVICES

We tend to think of our capacities or skills as something that is *within us*. The achievement of our goals is viewed with pride, the product of *our* capacities and *our* motivation. But what is often overlooked is that that which is within us is largely the result of what has *happened to us*— our experiences. Your potential and mine are determined not only by our inherent, or biological, capacities, but also by the opportunities we have had to develop them. These opportunities can be regarded as *services*, the particular experiences that our society encourages us to participate in or provides for us because it values what they can do for us.

Education is a service with which we are all familiar. Societies provide education because it is a means of transmitting to its young the skills and values the society wishes to inculcate. The reader of these words may be a student who is planning for a career that involves working with people in need, including those who are disabled. Such a career goal requires access to the kind of education that transmits the relevant knowledge and skills. This means an educational program typically provided by an educational institution. In its absence, such career hopes cannot be realized. Most people take for granted the institutions that make it possible for us to fulfill our career aspirations, but if such institutions were suddenly unavailable or if we were living where only a small elite could be admitted to them, *availability* would have a very different meaning. We would be frustrated in our goals and angry at a society that is unfair and ignores *our* developmental needs.

This serves to emphasize that many of the problems encountered by disabled persons and their families are not inherent in the disability, but rather are a normal emotional response to the failure of our society to assist them in the attainment of their basic needs through services. Disabled citizens are no less entitled to these services than are normal individuals. All that can be expected of anyone, normal or disabled, is the maximal development of his or her potential, *whatever that potential may be* (Baroff, 1986). Nor are disabled persons entitled to less because they have less potential. We are all limited in one fashion or another. We can all look around and see others who are brighter, physically more attractive, better coordinated, more talented, and so on. Differences among us are the norm, not the exception. It is only when the differences are great enough to create problems in our daily lives that attention is called to them. Under such comparisons, the smaller differences among normal individuals are muted, and we mistakenly think in terms of only two levels of difference—we and they—rather than in terms of a continuum of differences of which we are all a part.

NORMALIZATION: A PHILOSOPHY OF TREATMENT

Beginning in the 1960s, there was a tremendous growth in services to persons with developmental disabilities, especially at the community level. Stirred (1) by the interest of John F. Kennedy and the Kennedy family (the late president had a sister with mental retardation), (2) by evidence of gross abuse in some institutional settings, and (3) by the *normalization* movement in Scandinavia (Bank-Mikkelson, 1969), a movement developed in the United States to provide developmentally disabled persons with conditions of life that, as closely as possible, parallel those afforded to nondisabled persons. As elaborated in the United States and Canada, the focus of this movement is on the *means* by which training objectives are attained by developmentally disabled individuals (Perske, 1972; Wolfensberger, 1972; Wolfensberger and Glenn, 1973, 1975). Particularly concerned with the negative image that our society has of handicapped persons, especially those with serious cognitive impairments, the intent of the originators of this movement was to reduce both the *degree* of disability of developmentally disabled individuals and our *perception* of them as "deviant" by offering services in settings that maximize opportunities for daily contact with nonhandicapped persons. More specifically, this has meant serving developmentally disabled individuals *within* the community rather than in the traditionally isolated and segregated setting of the large state institution. Integration of the disabled population rather than separation and exclusion is seen as offering nonhandicapped role models to disabled persons and lessening the likelihood of exposure to physical and psychological abuse. Recently, I encountered a group of retarded young adults, some of whom I had known earlier in an institutional setting, dining at a local restaurant. The encounter reminded me of the value of integration. In that "normal" setting, the disabled diners were not distinguishable from the other diners, except, perhaps, by appearance. They were dignified by being seen in an environment associated with normality. Indeed, the setting itself teaches behaviors through modeling or imitation that might be less strongly communicated in a setting in which only disabled persons interact.

Although the strongest arguments for normalization were based on institutional exposés (Blatt, 1970; Blatt and Kaplan, 1966), there is a growing body of research that documents the developmental advantages of living in community settings (Eastwood and Fisher, 1988; Eyman et al., 1977; Eyman, Demaine, and Lei, 1979; MacEachron, 1983). Increased levels of competence are found (1) with movement from large institutions to the community (Conroy, Efthimiou, and Lemanowicz, 1982; Kleinberg and Galligan, 1983; Thompson and Carey, 1980) and to such smaller residential settings as group homes (most often serving up to six residents), (2) with continued residence in the community (Aanes and Moen, 1976), and (3) even with movement from larger to smaller units within the same institution (Hemming, Lavender, and Pill, 1981; MacEachron, 1983; Witt, 1981).

In a comprehensive study of matched populations of institutionalized and community-residing older adults, not only did the community group show significantly greater gain in virtually every domain studied, but benefits also were found in those with more severe levels of cognitive impairment. The greatest impediment to utilization of the growth potentials of small-group community residences was physical disability (Eastwood and Fisher, 1988). Physical disability affects ease of access to the potentially growth-enhancing experiences available in community resources.

Amidst this picture of enhanced functioning, several skill areas in particular seem to be responsive to community residential settings—language, household skills, and socialization (Kleinberg and Galligan, 1983). In commenting on the gain in domestic skills, Kleinberg and Galligan note that there is much greater opportunity to practice such activities in the smaller community settings. Like members of a family, residents are expected to contribute in whatever way they can, and in so doing, they practice domestic and community skills, such as cooking and shopping, that could enable them to function at even higher levels of independence (e.g., in a sheltered apartment). Residents of small group homes can learn a variety of cooking skills, for example, because their residence is feeding 6 people, not 600 people. Cooking is done in a regular family kitchen using the kinds of equipment found in all our homes. There is time to teach, to learn, to practice, and to make mistakes. Care givers are not operating under the kinds of pressures that require cooks in large settings to prepare meals for hundreds or even thousands of persons. And shopping can be done at neighborhood stores. Residents can accompany care givers and learn about the selection and purchase of food. Residential programs serving large numbers of individuals do not buy their groceries at local supermarkets; groceries are trucked in.

Two other very important benefits of normalization are commonly overlooked. First, by serving disabled people in settings that most nearly parallel those of nondisabled people, the so-called least restrictive settings, the programs do not overprotect. Such settings provide an opportunity for exposure to the most complex (most normal) environment to which the disabled person can adapt. It is in such a milieu that maximal competency can develop (Baroff, 1986). Second, the provision of services within communities rather than in more isolated settings ensures *our* more frequent exposure to people who are different. For example, shopping malls are a popular hangout for disabled as well as nondisabled people, and we commonly encounter disabled people there. However, since disabled individuals are the very people we tend to stigmatize, it is only by frequent exposure to them in settings where they can demonstrate their abilities (as well as their disabilities) that we can learn to reduce our avoidance tendencies toward them. Given time and appropriate kinds of contacts, we can gradually come to recognize that underneath the obvious intellectual or physical differences there is a person, one who shares the same biological and psychological needs as ourselves. Let's see how one college student describes her personal growth experience as a result of tutoring a mentally retarded and cerebral palsied child:

> Working with Toni this semester has been quite an experience for me. . . . I had never worked with or been around . . . anyone who was retarded. I must admit my first feeling toward her was shock. I was really surprised that I, an inexperienced college junior, was being presented with a severely retarded child to tutor, . . . as the sessions with Toni continued . . . I gained a great deal of confidence in myself. I completely lost my feeling of shock and uneasiness and developed an assured, satisfied, confident feeling . . . around her. I came to realize that she was a person, just as I, but that her physical and mental nature, being as limited as it was, made her stand out in needs [survival, structure, self-esteem, self-expression]. . . . She was a young girl who was in great need of love, attention, and patience. But above all else, she needed a means of developing self-esteem.
>
> . . . This is probably the most unique relationship . . . I have ever had— and one of the most rewarding. By rewarding I do not mean gratifying in terms of academic success [the tutoring experience is a part of a college course], but rather, I mean the pleasure of knowing that I have reached this girl. (Baroff, 1986, p. 334)

Table 2-1. Array of services

Services	Service agents	Service disciplines
	PRENATAL	
Prevention: Genetic counseling, prenatal care, amniocentesis, therapeutic abortion	Health agents: Primary physician, local health department, hospital clinic, fetology service	Physician, public-health nurse, genetic counselor
	INFANCY AND PRESCHOOL	
Prevention (medical): Metabolic screening (e.g., PKU), adequate diet, immunization, avoid toxic substances, follow-up of high-risk neonates, routine medical care	Health agents: Primary physician, well-baby clinic at local health department, hospital	Physician, public-health nurse, nutritionist
Prevention (psychological): Stimulation	Child care agents: Home, foster care (social service), infant stimulation, developmental day care	Parents or parent surrogate, teacher, aide, social worker, volunteer
Identification: Screening, diagnosis, parent counseling, medical treatment, early intervention: sensory stimulation, physical therapy, encouraging motor, language, and cognitive development	Health agents: Well-baby clinic (health department, hospital), physician (general practitioner or specialist, e.g., pediatrician or neurologist), special diagnostic clinic	Public-health nurse, pediatrician, psychologist, social worker, audiologist, physical therapist, occupational therapist, speech therapist, educator, dentist
Training and education: Self-help (feeding, dressing, toileting), gross motor and fine motor, language, cognitive, social-emotional skills	Early childhood workers: Infant stimulation in the home, child development center (generic and specialized)	Teacher, teacher aide, physical therapist, occupational therapist, speech therapist, social worker, psychologist
Residential	Care givers: Home, adoptive home, foster home, small group home, respite care, "medical support" home	Parent, foster parent, group home parent
Parental: Training in child development, emotional support, respite care, parent organizations, social services	Early childhood workers, social service agencies, parent associations (local and regional)	Parent trainers, social workers

30

Coordination and advocacy: Coordination of multiagency services (as needed), helping parents become "advocates" for their child	Case managers and advocates: Case management agency; advocacy agency	Case managers (social workers, etc.), volunteers, lawyers, paralegals

SCHOOL AGE

Training and education: As in preschool plus academic, prevocational and vocational preparation; sex and family life education; stress on acquisition of skills in activities of daily living	Education, vocational rehabilitation, health, and special therapies: Public school, special school, homebound program, institution; vocational rehabilitation agency and health department; physical, occupational, and speech therapy	Teacher, aide, school psychologist, guidance counselor, rehabilitation counselor, sex educator, physical therapist, occupational therapist, speech therapist
Residential: As in preschool but adding programs for special populations	As in preschool years plus special facilities for youthful offenders and behaviorally disabled	As in preschool years plus behavior management specialists
Recreational	Community parks and recreational programs: Generic and special recreational resources; day programs, camping—day and overnight, summer, year-round; scouting, Special Olympics	Recreator, group worker, volunteer (e.g., student)
Coordination and advocacy: As in preschool years but with special emphasis on assuring that schools fulfill their responsibilities under Education for Handicapped Children Act (PL 94-142)	As in preschool years	As in preschool years but with paralegal advocates assisting in school hearings

ADULTHOOD

Vocational: Prevocational, vocational (as appropriate), and on-the-job training; competitive employment, sheltered employment	Semiskilled and unskilled jobs in industry, services, and government; sheltered workshop, vocational rehabilitation agency	Employer, job coach, rehabilitation counselor, staff of sheltered workshop (administrator, work evaluator, work supervisor, personal adjustment counselor, instructor)

31

Table 2-1 (*continued*)

	ADULTHOOD	
Day "activity" program: Primarily for severely and profoundly retarded adults and providing continued training in basic self-care skills and activities of daily living, recreation, and prevocational activities	Day "activity" center	Teacher, aide
Educational: Courses on money management, human relations, music appreciation, health, sexuality, cooking, camping, etc.	Community colleges, e.g.,: Metropolitan State, Denver; College of Staten Island, N.Y.; Northern Virginia Community College, Annandale, Va.; Mesa Community College, Mesa, Ariz.	Educators
Residential: From semi-independent living to specialized residential facilities for profoundly retarded and medically involved	Care givers and counselors: Supervised/supported boarding placements, apartment clusters, and coresidential living; subsidized family living placement; minimum-supervision group home, intensive-training group home, health care facility, specialized facility for persons with chronic medical problems (ICF/MB)	As in earlier years plus health workers
"Support" services home	Respite resources, homemaker, personal care, and chore services	"Respite" care givers, homemakers, personal care attendants
Health	Medical and dental	Health professionals
Transportation	Community agencies	
Social and recreational	Organizations and community recreation resources	As in earlier years
Advocacy	Advocacy agency	As in earlier years
Coordination	Case management agency	As in earlier years

HABILITATIVE SERVICES: A CONTINUUM OF CARE

The concept of normalization offers guidance as to how and where services should be delivered, but now let's look at the services themselves. An appropriate array of services would meet our most basic needs as human beings—food and clothing, a decent place to live, something meaningful to do, and satisfying social relationships. The idea of a *continuum* of care refers to the multiplicity of services that may be required at any one moment in time or over time. A child with a developmental disability may be simultaneously in need of health services and educational services. A preschool-aged cerebral palsied child, for example, commonly would need physical and occupational therapy for motor problems and, possibly, medical treatment for epilepsy. There may be a need for a day educational program (developmental day care) and respite services for the family for temporary relief from care giving. However, the kinds of services required also can change with age. For the older child, the school would be expected to replace day care. Social, vocational, and recreational services also are important at school age, and while the school might be their main provider, other community agencies also are commonly involved—notably recreation and vocational rehabilitation. In the postschool years, an array of services is necessary to meet social, vocational, and recreational needs, and in the case of a disabled adult who is not able to achieve independence, residential ones are needed as well.

Table 2-1 presents the array of available services organized by developmental period—from prenatal status to adulthood (Baroff, 1986). At each stage there are identified (1) the required services, (2) the agencies that deliver them, and (3) the professional disciplines that offer them. The table makes clear the extraordinary number of agencies and disciplines that serve developmentally disabled individuals and their families. It is also this diversity that creates problems of coordination, a concern expressed by mental retardation workers in the early sixties and still so timely as to cause one set of authors to have viewed it as one of the major challenges of the 1980s (Magrab and Elder, 1979). It is my impression that the same challenges still exist in the 1990s, and it is likely that the problem will still not have been solved by the turn of the next century.

PREVENTION OF DEVELOPMENTAL DISABILITIES

Preventive services are those which support the conception and birth of a healthy infant. Such services include, as appropriate, the planning of a pregnancy, provision of knowledge regarding possible abnormalities based on maternal age (as in Down syndrome) and/or genetic history (an inherited disorder such as phenylketonuria), encouragement and provision of prenatal care, access to prenatal diagnosis as needed (e.g., regarding Down syndrome), and the prospective mother's avoiding the use of substances that can harm the unborn baby, such as alcohol, hard drugs (e.g., heroin), and even drugs used for therapeutic purposes (e.g., anticonvulsants). Prevention in the neonatal period involves the identification of high-risk babies, routine laboratory screening for genetic disorders (e.g., phenylketonuria or galactosemia), and utilization of medical care. In infancy and early childhood, prevention entails such standard health measures as immunization, avoidance of exposure to toxic substances (e.g., lead), and periodic medical examinations. Unfortunately, what is standard and routine care in our society is related to socioeconomic status, and the quality of care, prenatal as well as postnatal, available to or utilized by economically disadvantaged families often leaves much to be desired. This is starkly reflected in social class and racial differences in the use of prenatal care and in the frequency of low-birth-weight babies and the high infant mortality rates among the poor.

A survey conducted by the U.S. General Accounting Office in 1987 found that almost two-thirds of poor women (63 percent) had inadequate prenatal care as opposed to only 19 percent of more affluent women. Inadequate care means a failure to begin prenatal care during the first trimester of pregnancy or having less than nine medical contacts over the course of the pregnancy. This difference was associated with a nearly doubled frequency of low-birth-weight babies, babies weighing less than 5½ pounds at birth (12.4 versus 6.8 percent). A similar finding was obtained with regard to infant mortality, that is, death before the first birthday. With a national rate of infant mortality in 1984 of 11 per 1000, the rate for black children was 18.4, while the rate for white children was 9.4.

DIAGNOSIS OF DEVELOPMENTAL DISABILITIES

The diagnosis of a developmental disability usually occurs in infancy and certainly by age 2 years if the disorder is more than mild in degree. Where there are pronounced physical abnormalities, as in Down syndrome, the condition is recognizable at birth. In cerebral palsy, abnormalities in motor development are seen during the first year. Where there are no gross physical abnormalities, only delays in development may signal an underlying disorder. Autism in some children, for example, is not recognized until the second year. By then it will be evident that these children have failed to develop normal speech, and they will be showing patterns of social withdrawal and repetitive behaviors.

The diagnostic process itself, especially in the young child, is a complex procedure that should include evaluation of the family as well as the child. With reference to the child, there will be an assessment of resources—cognitive; communicative; health, sensory, and motor; and personality. This assessment is best performed in a multidisciplinary setting and one in which evaluation is tied to intervention. The clinical and behavioral picture presented by the child will dictate the range of assessments needed, those most often employed being in pediatrics, psychology, social work, education, speech and hearing, physical and occupational therapy, public health nursing, and child psychiatry. Serious physical problems such as cerebral palsy or epilepsy will, of course, require medical specialists in neurology, surgery, and orthopedics. Increasingly, there also should be early dental evaluation.

Of these disciplines, all except social work have the child as their focus. The social worker will be involved primarily with the family, helping members to understand the nature of the child's disorder, determining their needs, marshalling their resources to meet the child's needs, and helping them to reach out to other services in the community that the child may require. The family has taken on a new significance in the diagnostic process. It is now recognized that the goals sought for the child and their method of accomplishment are affected by family attitudes and resources (Bailey, 1987). Indeed, recent legislation refers to the diagnostic and treatment formulation as an "individual family service plan."

A comprehensive treatment of multidisciplinary diagnosis in mental retardation is described elsewhere (Johnston and Magrab, 1976; Koch and Dobson, 1971). For the psychologist and educator, the often multiply handicapped developmentally disabled child can present special assessment difficulties (Simeonnson, 1986). Of particular interest in this regard are detailed treatments of the psychological assessment of children with autism (Marcus and Baker, 1986) as well as those with severe motor impairments (e.g., cerebral palsy) (Wilhelm, Johnson, and Eisert, 1986).

Two other diagnostic concerns are nutrition and dental status. Nutritional problems accompany metabolic disorders or are associated with motor difficulties in chewing and swallowing. With regard to dental health, tooth abnormalities are increased in children with developmental disorders, and prophylactic measures should begin with the eruption of teeth in the first year and certainly by age 2½.

POSTDIAGNOSTIC SERVICES

Infant and Preschool-Age

Home-Based Services. Programs for high-risk infants or those with clear developmental disorders are commonly offered in the home beginning in the first year of life and continuing until age 3. Their focus is on the stimulation and total development of the child and the provision of guidance to the family.

Developmental Day Care. At about age 3, if not earlier, children with developmental disabilities may begin to attend day-care centers. These centers offer social and educational experiences to the child and also may provide assistance to families. Although commonly housed in special centers for disabled children, handicapped preschoolers also can be served in day-care programs for nondisabled children (Guralnick, 1978). The potential benefits of mutual exposure of normal and disabled children to each other were mentioned earlier.

In 1986, federal legislation was enacted (Public Law 99-457) that extends to 3- to 5-year-old handicapped children by 1991 all the rights and protections of the landmark educational legislation of 1975 (Education for All Handicapped Children Act, Public Law 94-142). This legislation also encourages the development of services for infants and toddlers (ages 1 to 2).

Respite Care. This is an important service to families (see, for example, Apolloni and Triest, 1983; Marc and MacDonald, 1988). Respite workers provide temporary care in the family home or in their own homes. Overnight care or care for up to 30 days also may be offered in respite homes. The goal of these programs is to provide relief to parents from the continuous care responsibilities entailed in the rearing of seriously disabled children. Other forms of respite care include after-school services, e.g., from 3 o'clock to 5 o'clock, and drop-in centers, for example, two Saturdays a month from 9 A.M. to 2 P.M.

Health Services. The population of concern varies from those who are apparently free of any health problems to those with chronic and life-threatening conditions.

Epilepsy. The frequency of seizure disorders or epilepsy is much increased in developmental disabilities. Occurring in only about 1 percent of the general population, much higher frequencies of epilepsy are found in children with mental retardation (Richardson et al., 1981), autism (Lotter, 1978), and cerebral palsy (Shapiro et al., 1983). Perhaps as many as 25 percent of retarded youngsters are so affected, especially those with more severe degrees of cognitive impairment. By adolescence, a similar proportion of autistic children will have had seizures, while a third of the cerebral palsied population will be so affected.

Seizures can be fairly well controlled through anticonvulsant medications in about 80 percent of cases. For the remainder, seizures are a continual medical-management problem, and their persistence may itself adversely affect adaptation. (Seizures are dealt with in depth in Chapter 6.)

Motor or Physical Disability. Motor impairment and physical disability are prominent in cerebral palsy (see Chapter 5) and in spinal cord deformity (i.e., spina bifida). The latter disorder is not otherwise treated in this book, but it sometimes includes a degree of cognitive deficit in addition to motor impairment. The spinal deformity causes varying degrees of paralysis in limb and body functions below the level of the spinal cord lesion and also may be associated with hydrocephalus, an excessive buildup of cerebrospinal fluid in the brain. It is the latter that can adversely affect cognitive functioning.

Sensory Loss. Hearing and visual impairments also occur in developmental disabilities and at a higher rate than in the general population. In mental retardation, hearing loss is found in children with congenital rubella, a prenatal viral infection that can produce multiple defects. Rubella is now largely preventable through a vaccine. Hearing loss associated with middle ear infections (otitis media) has recently been found in Down syndrome children and may contribute to their language problems (Balkany et al., 1979; Whiteman, Simpson, and Compton, 1986).

Visual disorders also can result from the kinds of neurologic conditions that cause developmental disability and are particularly prominent in cerebral palsy. These can range from impairment in spatial and depth perception to blindness (Mitchell, 1983).

Residential Services. There has been a strong trend toward rearing developmentally disabled children within their family home and avoiding out-of-home placements, especially those of an institutional nature. But not all children, normal or disabled, are assured of a family home. For these, social service agencies ordinarily choose between foster care and adoption. While disabilities can affect adoptability, the adoptive potential of even severely disabled children has been much underestimated by social agencies (Franklin, 1969; Wolfensberger, 1972). More commonly, however, out-of-home care means temporary placement with a foster family. Foster homes can offer the kind of individual care that is so important in infancy and are generally to be preferred to any form of group care for very young children.

School Age

Education. It is during the school years, if not earlier, that the developmentally disabled child is exposed to the wider community and, hopefully, given the opportunity to acquire the skills necessary to optimize adjustment. The landmark federal educational legislation, the Education for All Handicapped Children Act (Public Law 94-142), has had a dramatic effect on the provision of public education to these children. There has been an increase in access to education in the public schools and in regular class as well as in special class settings. Under the impetus of mainstreaming, students with mild levels of retardation (educably mentally handicapped) typically split their day between regular classes and a "resource" room. The latter provides the special academic assistance their learning difficulties require. Children with more severe degrees of intellectual impairment are still found in self-contained special classes, but these are now much more likely to be physically located in settings that also serve normal children.

Educational goals for developmentally disabled children vary with the nature and severity of impairment. For children with mild retardation, the focus is on the acquisition of some functional reading and number skills and on vocational preparation. At more severe levels of intellectual impairment, irrespective of the particular type of disability, stress is on the development of self-care, language, social, recreational, and prevocational skills (Kirk and Gallagher, 1979). Prevocational training primarily involves strengthening the interpersonal behaviors essential to employment in any setting. Whereas schools have traditionally prepared students with moderate to profound levels of retardation for transition to adult day care or noncompetitive employment in sheltered workshops, the current emphasis on "supported" employment is intended to open up the possibility of regular or competitive employment for at least some of these individuals.

Residential Services. During the school years, the family home usually will continue to be the chief residential resource. If the family home is not available, either foster care or group homes are community-based alternatives. The latter may be preferred for some developmentally disabled adolescents because it is likely to offer greater opportunities for peer relationships.

Mental Health Services. The school years, especially adolescence, may see the emergence of significant emotional and behavior problems. The developmentally disabled child is maturing physically, and the combination of larger size and greater emotionality can lead to behaviors that are difficult to manage. Studies of retarded youths and adults indicate that about one third will have significant mental health problems (Jacobson, 1982; Reiss, 1990), though only about ten percent will have a formal psychiatric diagnosis (Borthwick-Duffy and Eyman, 1990; Reiss, 1990). Among the autistic population, one that tends to manifest its greatest emotional and behavioral disturbances in the preschool years, adolescence may be associated with diminished emotionality and its replacement by a general state of apathy (DeMyer, 1978).

Given the stresses imposed on the developmentally disabled child, as well as on his or her family, it is not surprising that emotional upsets and behavior disorders are common outcomes. However, the mental health community—psychiatrists, psychologists, social workers, and counselors—has traditionally been reluctant to serve children with major cognitive and learning problems. Only the autistic segment of the population covered in this book has been regarded as psychiatric, and within the scope of disorders dealt with in child psychiatry, these children have been among the most difficult to treat.

Several misconceptions appear to influence the attitude of mental health professionals toward developmentally disabled children and young people, especially toward those with mental retardation (Phillips, 1966). First, behavior problems are viewed as a direct expression of the cognitive impairment rather than as a consequence of the interaction of a stress-vulnerable individual with his or her environment. In fact, adaptive behavior is clearly related both to biological capacities (or incapacities) and to the degree to which the child's environment maximizes developmental potential. A second misconception is the perception of emotional disorders in developmentally disabled individuals as different from those in nondisabled individuals. While among those with mental retardation, for example, there *are* differences in the range of disorders seen (e.g., fewer paranoid reactions and less complex ideation in psychoses), such individuals still exhibit the same broad group of psychiatric conditions found in nonretarded persons—personality disorders, neuroses, and psychoses. Third, symptoms may be regarded as merely expressions of organic brain damage. However, the population of individuals with organic brain damage is extraordinarily diverse—all the way from children of normal parents with lower-than-expected IQs and no clearcut neurologic abnormalities to those with gross brain pathology (e.g., anencephaly or the absence of a cortex) and only vegetative behaviors. It is true that some behaviors seen in developmentally disabled children appear to be direct expressions of their specific disability (organicity), for example, hyperactivity and distractibility, but even these can be worsened or eased through manipulation of the child's psychological environment (Ross and Ross, 1976). In effect, the label *organicity* tells us little about the *why* of specific behavior problems in a given child.

While many mental health professionals offer their own lack of training in developmental disorders as a reason for not serving this population, it is likely that a more relevant reason is a preference for clients who have good verbal skills and for whom *insight* is a reasonable goal. Moreover, with mental health services generally in short supply, the demands of the less disabled population can be used as a justification for serving them in lieu of serving more severely disabled individuals. Finally, there may simply be a wish to avoid being identified with a population that tends to be much devalued in our society, especially those with mental retardation.

After reviewing the literature on the use of psychotherapy with retarded individuals, those least likely to have access to this form of treatment, Szymanski (1980) concluded that the indications for psychotherapy for retarded persons are the same as for nonretarded persons. The indicators for treatment include (1) the presence of a behavior disorder in which psychological factors are either causative or aggravating, (2) the potential for establishing a relationship with the therapist by an individual in whom there is some ability to communicate, verbally or nonverbally, and (3) the expectation that symptom removal will permit fuller use of *whatever* potential the individual possesses. The goal is not to cure or eliminate the basic developmental disorder, currently not a realistic option, but rather to free the already burdened individual from additional burdens. Interestingly, Szymanski maintains that the degree of intellectual impairment does not determine suitability for psychotherapy, but rather fixes the choice of therapeutic techniques and goals. In other words, symptom relief is a justifiable treatment objective at whatever degree of impairment. Psychological treatment will vary as a function of the degree of cognitive deficit—from psychotherapy, counseling, behavioral therapies, and social skills training for those with mild cognitive impairment to a concentration on behavioral treatments in those with more severe deficits. Psychologists working with individuals with both retardation and psychiatric disorders (the dually diagnosed) see these procedures as beneficial at all but the most severe levels of impairment (Jacobson and Ackerman, 1989).

Psychotropic drugs have been heavily used as an alternative to psychological methods in the developmentally disabled population (Aman, 1987; Buck and Sprague, 1989; Chadsey-Rusch and Sprague, 1989) and their medical misuse is widely acknowledged (e.g., Bates, Smeltzer, and Arnoczky, 1986; Rivinus, 1980). While psychotropics have a legitimate role as a supplement to psychological procedures, all too often they have been used as "chemical strait jackets," as substitutes for trained staff and appropriate programming and services. Recognition of a possible neurologic disorder as a consequence of long-term psycho-tropic drug use, "tardive dyskinesia" (Gualtieri, 1985), appears to have resulted in diminished use (e.g., Briggs, 1989; Poindexter, 1989).

Special Mental Health Programs. Given the problems of accessing general mental health services, one alternative is the development of mental health programs specifically for the developmentally disabled popula-tion. Such programs can consist of mental health centers, necessarily in metropolitan areas, where the population size would merit such a set-ting, or intinerant teams, a service appropriate to more rural areas or for clients with major mobility limitations. A model of such a special mental health center is found at the University of Illinois at Chicago (Reiss and Trenn, 1984). Its special focus is on clients with intellectual impairments at all levels. It largely serves an adolescent and young-adult population, ages 15 to 29, two-thirds of whom are male. Clients are commonly referred by local agencies already serving these individuals, and the chief referral problems are inappropriate aggression, depressive and psychotic-like symptoms, and personality disorders. Treatment services are broad and include individual and group psychotherapy, cognitive-behavior therapy, family therapy, behavior modification, drug therapy, and art therapy. The cognitive-behavior therapy consists of structured programs designed to teach social skills, management of anger, and re-laxation. Therapy is generally offered on a weekly basis.

A variant of the special mental health center model is one that utilizes institutional facilities for time-limited treatment (Fidura, Lindsey, and Walker, 1987). In Virginia, young people 16 years of age and older are admitted to a special behavior residential center for periods of either 30 or 90 days. The most common referral problems are aggression and non-compliance. An important feature is the provision of training to the fam-ily or to the staff of the community agency to which the person will return. Reporting a success rate of 40 to 50 percent, based on subsequent retention of the client in the community, the program is said to be more effective with individuals who reside in group homes than with those who are returned to the family.

An alternative to the special-centers model is one that serves clients in the settings in which they live and work, a mobile or traveling mental health professional or professionals (itinerant treatment team). Provid-ers of residential and day services particularly value visits by profession-als to their settings because typically they have to transplant the client to the professional's "turf."

A related issue pertains to the treatment of persons with major cog-nitive impairments in psychiatric hospitals. Sovner and DesNoyers

(1986) have called attention to problems of unfamiliarity with mentally retarded persons by psychiatric staff and the need for consultation with mental retardation professionals in treatment planning.

Adulthood

Vocational Services. Central to adult self-esteem, whether a disabled or nondisabled adult, is the opportunity to be productively employed—to work. Even as our culture seems to be offering the opportunity for increased leisure activities, the work ethic continues to have a powerful hold on our cultural consciousness. Indeed, with the dramatic increase in the number of women in the work force, the proportion of individuals who find their identity and self-esteem in their occupation may be increasing. For those of us reared in homes where both parents worked, the expectation for ourselves is that we will follow in their footsteps and that in achieving a "successful" occupational adjustment, there will be important material and psychological rewards. The latter is epitomized in the aphorism "You are what you do."

While the power of the work ethic is likely to be muted in persons whose disabilities are of such a nature and severity as to seriously narrow their occupational potential, for many disabled people, including those with developmental disabilities, the desire to work is very powerful. To be productively employed is to be perceived as normal. I was very impressed many years ago when I visited a sheltered workshop in Los Angeles where a large number of clearly seriously disabled individuals were sitting around a long table packaging decks of playing cards. In that setting there was pride in doing something valuable. After all, people paid for the product these people were producing, and at the end of the week, their efforts were rewarded with a paycheck, prima facie evidence of their worth. These individuals could feel productive, competent, and part of the mainstream of a society in which work is accepted as a normal adult role. The psychological importance of work to persons with developmental disabilities is dramatically revealed in the following description of its impact on a mildly retarded young man.

Johnny Robertson was 22 years old, unemployed, and considered unemployable except in a sheltered workshop or a day activity program. He had attended a private school until he was 16 and then returned home, where for 6 years he led a life characterized as one of "intolerable emptiness." He was shunned and teased by peers, lost what confidence he had developed at school, and came to spend his time locked in his room with a television set. He had been recommended for placement in a sheltered workshop, but his parents viewed that employment setting as recreational rather than as one in which there was real work. Admittedly, this can be a problem in settings where there may be much "down" time or where nonwork activities such as educational or recreational ones predominate. John had worked at a riding academy cleaning stalls. He loved horses, but the academy had closed. Then John's parents learned about the opening of a pet shop that was specifically to employ cognitively impaired youth. It was a project conceived by a young couple who had worked with retarded youth in a sheltered workshop but who felt that, with proper supervision, their charges could function in the regular work world (Graham and Poling, 1963). They came to see the pet shop as a setting that offered handicapped youth exposure to the rhythm of daily life. There was the constant challenge of new problems, new customers, and different jobs to stretch the minds of the handicapped workers. Instead of being limited to simple, repetitive assembly-type operations, they could grow vocationally. "Our kids are constantly stimulated—and they grow, amazingly."

This is how his parents describe the effect on Johnny of working in the pet store:

> We still find it hard to believe. . . . Our Johnny who had no life, now has a full and happy one—a job and a place to go every day, a place where he is actually needed [self-worth] a place where he has puppies and people to love and be loved by [intimacy]. The change is unbelievable. Now he goes to the movies alone, eats by himself in restaurants, buys his own clothes [all newfound autonomy], does everything he was afraid to do before. And he laughs! . . . Believe me, it's a welcome sound in a house that heard none for years. (Graham and Poling, 1963, p. 28)

Johnny and his coworkers continued to develop vocationally, and some moved to regular jobs of comparable complexity in a department store. Others would remain in the more sheltered setting of the pet shop. Irrespective of the level of employment, however, work had been the means for dramatic changes in the self-images of these individuals. They moved into life's mainstream; they came to feel a sense of value and worth as human beings. These events of an earlier decade laid the groundwork for the current thrust toward "supported employment," the placing of developmentally disabled persons in supervised environments within regular work settings (Wehman et al., 1982).

Within the populations described in this book are found all levels of employability—from regular competitive employment, to various forms of sheltered employment, to day programs that mix education and work. While we tend to think that only normal people are employable, people like ourselves, exposure to the reality of work potential in even very disabled individuals is a humbling and broadening experience. For those with serious cognitive and academic limitations, work will necessarily be unskilled in nature, but many such jobs still exist, primarily in service industries. For those with intact cognitive skills, it will be their physical impairment that will constitute the greatest vocational impediment. And increasingly our society is removing the physical barriers to employment for these individuals.

As we have seen, even mentally retarded individuals are employable. Apart from special placements in regular employment, sheltered workshops and day activity centers can be expected to continue to be impor- tant job settings, especially for those with at least a moderate degree of intellectual impairment. Mildly retarded individuals, on the other hand, have long been known to be capable of unskilled regular employment (Brickey, Campbell, and Browning, 1985; Deno, 1966). And even profoundly retarded persons can, over time, learn to perform simple assembly tasks at a level comparable to that of normal workers (Bellamy, Inman, and Yeates, 1978). For disabled individuals, job potential is not what you *can* do, but what you can *learn* to do!

Residential Services. It is during the adult years, if not earlier, that residential alternatives to the family home become an important consideration. In some families, movement of the disabled individual into a nonfamily residential situation is perceived as a step toward greater independence. While the child may not be expected to achieve full self-sufficiency, in the potentially less protective context of a nonfamily residence, pressures for greater personal responsibility may be increased. In such settings there is the opportunity to learn how to deal with nonfamily adults and peers, to begin to separate oneself psychologically from family ties, and to move toward greater autonomy and independence.

Still another condition that may encourage such placement is the parents' recognition of their own mortality. If the parents cannot always be there to provide a home for their child, someone else will have to. While siblings may assume this responsibility, it is now common to find other alternatives to permanent care by family members.

Prior to the 1970s, the most common nonfamily settings were institutional ones, principally those serving persons with mental retardation and mental illness. These were centers that housed populations of from hundreds to even thousands. They were self-contained environments that sought within their walls to meet all the needs of their residents. In the field of mental retardation, apart from special educational services in the schools, institutions were the most prominent symbol of services to this developmentally disabled population. In the 1960s, however, media exposés of horrendous conditions in some of these institutions and such pictorial essays as *Christmas in Purgatory* (Blatt and Kaplan, 1966) led to dramatic changes. A picture emerged of generally inadequate care coupled with numerous instances of outright physical abuse. It was

these revelations that fueled the normalization and deinstitutionalization movements. In the field of developmental disabilities, formerly institutionalized persons were subsequently moved to a wide array of
community-based residences. (Parenthetically, the nightmare of former
adult *psychiatric* patients currently sleeping on our streets, so-called
street people, does not include this population.) Society has provided a
seemingly wider range of residential alternatives to developmentally
disabled persons than to those with chronic mental illness. Former psychiatric patients are less likely to be perceived as always in the need of
some degree of residential care, although the problems of those with
chronic mental illness suggest that alternatives to the street will be necessary.

For persons with developmental disabilities, three types of community-based nonfamily residential options are available: domiciliary, intermediate care, and skilled nursing care. In addition to these, one can
also find rural village-like programs that serve particular populations,
such as those with autism or mental retardation.

Domiciliary settings are those which limit themselves to the provision
of residential care; other services are provided elsewhere in the community. The current array of domiciliary settings includes family care
(foster) homes, most group homes, rest homes, and sheltered apartments.

Intermediate care facilities (ICFs) and *skilled nursing care facilities* (SNFs)
are residential options for persons needing more than just living accommodations. The former serves individuals with either some medical or
behavioral problems, while the latter is reserved for those with major
medical needs.

As well as the community residential alternatives to the family home,
the traditional state institution (public residence facility, PRF) continues
to be available. Although the numbers of individuals found in such settings had been reduced by about 40 percent between 1967 and 1982,
from 194,650 to 117,160 (Rotegard, Bruininks, and Krantz, 1984), in
1982, institutions were still serving at least half of all the retarded individuals who were in nonfamily residential care (Hauber et al., 1984).
With the growth in residential options, however, the institutions have
come largely to house persons with the most severe intellectual and/or
physical impairments or behavior problems (Lakin et al., 1983; Scheerenberger, 1982). Indeed, behavior problems are the single largest cause
for institutional admission—principally behaviors that are injurious to
others, very unusual, or disruptive to care givers being the main ones
(Lakin et al., 1983). This again calls attention to the need for strengthening mental health services to the developmentally disabled population in order to avoid unnecessary institutionalization.

Interestingly, despite deinstitutionalization and a 40 percent reduction in the institutionalized population, the number of public residential facilities has actually increased; it is only that their average size has diminished, from a median of 506 residents in the mid-1960s to 393 in 1981 (Epple, Jacobson, and Janicki, 1985).

Educational Services. Formal schooling for those with developmental disabilities generally ends with high school, although the 1975 Education for All Handicapped Children Act encourages its provision to age 21. It is clear, however, that where learning problems are prominent, there is need for a longer learning period than that fixed by age 18 or 21. Even before enactment of the Education for All Handicapped Children Act in 1975, federal legislation in 1974 (Education Amendments of 1974; Public Law 93-380) had encouraged the states to provide educational services to adults who were then institutionalized. So-called adult basic education is, in fact, a major component of adult day activity programs and is also offered to developmentally disabled individuals on the campuses of community colleges.

Depending on the individual's level of cognitive impairment, learning experiences may be directed toward continued growth in self-help and academic skills as well as in arts and crafts (Kiernan, 1979). The goal is to maximize self-sufficiency, and where functional academic skills have not yet been acquired, the focus will be on teaching those skills essential to daily living. These include time telling, use of the telephone, an understanding of money, reading single-word signs, and using public transportation. While all these learning activities would have been part of the formal school experience, for those with more than mild degrees of intellectual impairment, their continued study and practice are necessary on into the young-adult years.

Recreational Services. Of the services needed by developmentally disabled persons, the recreational domain has been the most neglected, often regarded only as a frill (Kiernan, 1979). Paradoxically, it is through recreation that activities are found that provide the teachable kinds of experiences for the population of concern. Where severe learning difficulties exist, the standard classroom group-learning situation may be the least functional setting. The concept of *therapeutic recreation* is relevant here. When an activity is enjoyed for its own sake, interest and motivation are naturally enhanced and the activity's teaching potential is magnified.

Bingo and bowling are examples of fun activities that have built-in properties for strengthening all kinds of skills. Bingo is a popular classroom method for helping students learn to recognize numbers and letters. Recognition leads to progress in the game and the possibility of winning. The pleasure interest in the game translates into high motivation to succeed. Bowling also provides a mix of fun and learning opportunities (Fitzimmons, 1970). Apart from the pleasure of knocking down pins and the exercise itself, bowling affords a golden opportunity through score keeping to teach basic number skills. Bowling with others also can teach social relationships, while the milieu of the bowling alley can provide socially appropriate peer models and experiences in purchasing and money management.

Arts, crafts, and various table games (Wehman, 1979) also lend themselves to the combining of fun and learning. But recreation, of course, is also to be enjoyed for its own sake. Whether solitary or social, active or sedentary, recreation provides a chance for relaxation, for a nonstressful change of pace. Recreational activities have long been a standard part of adult day activity programs and are increasingly available to developmentally disabled young people and adults through our local parks and recreation departments.

The Aged Adult. With increasing proportions of developmentally disabled adults being served in community rather than in institutional programs, there is dawning awareness that these individuals have life spans not very different from our own and that they are in need of services on into old age (Janicki and Wisniewski, 1985; Seltzer, 1988). In a survey of the New York State developmentally disabled population, 16 percent were age 53 and older, eight percent were 53 to 62, and eight percent were 63 and older. We are just beginning to study the question of how programs serving older nondevelopmentally disabled individuals can be of assistance to their developmentally disabled aged counterparts. One statewide survey has revealed that to an unexpected degree, elderly retarded persons were utilizing the standard aging services in their communities (Seltzer, 1988).

COORDINATION OF SERVICES: CASE MANAGEMENT

A persistent concern in developmental disabilities, especially in mental retardation, but also in other disorders (Bilenker, 1983), has been the coordination and monitoring of services provided to affected individuals. The developmentally disabled person, often multihandicapped, commonly needs a range of services, for example, residential, vocational, social, health, mental health, and educational, each of which may be provided by a different agency. The long-felt recognition of the need to coordinate services offered by different care givers has led to the creation of *case managers* and *case management* as an essential service itself. The case manager, or *case coordinator*, should be capable of interpreting the disabled individual's needs to the family, assist in securing appropriate services, monitor their effectiveness, and participate with the family (and disabled individual) in ongoing planning. Now required in the federal legislation pertaining to developmentally disabled preschoolers, case management should be the one constant in a service array that will necessarily vary from early childhood to old age.

REFERENCES

Aanes, D., and Moen, M. (1976). Adaptive behavior changes of group home residents. *Mental Retardation, 14*, 36–40.

Aman, M. (1987). Overview of pharmacotherapy: Current status and future direction. *Mental Deficiency Research, 31*, 121–130.

Apolloni, A. A., and Triest, G. (1983). Respite services in California: Status and recommendation for improvement. *Mental Retardation, 21*, 240–243.

Bailey, D. (1987). Collaborative goal setting with families: Resolving differences in values and priorities for services. *Topics in Early Childhood Special Education, 7*, 59–71.

Balkany, T. J., Downs, M. P., Jafek, B. W., and Krajicek, M. J. (1979). Hearing loss in Down's syndrome: A treatable handicap more common than generally recognized. *Clinical Pediatrics, 18*, 116–118.

Bank-Mikkelson, N. E. (1969). A metropolitan area in Denmark: Copenhagen. In R. Kugel and W. Wolfensberger (Eds.), *Changing patterns in residential services for the mentally retarded.* Washington: President's Committee on Mental Retardation.

Baroff, G. S. (1986). *Mental retardation: Nature, cause, and management,* 2d Ed. New York: Hemisphere.

Bates, W. J., Smeltzer, D. J., and Arnoczky, S. M. (1986). Appropriate and inappropriate use of psychotherapeutic medications for institutionalized mentally retarded persons. *American Journal of Mental Deficiency, 90*, 363–370.

Bellamy, G. T., Inman, D. P., and Yeates, J. (1978). Workshop supervision: Evaluation of a procedure for production management with the severely retarded. *Mental Retardation, 16*, 317–319.

Bilenker, R. M. (1983). Coordination of services. In G. H. Thompson, I. L. Rubin, and R. M. Bilenker (Eds.), *Comprehensive management of cerebral palsy.* New York: Grune & Stratton.

Blatt, B. (1970). *Exodus from pandemonium: Human abuse and a reformation of public policy.* Boston: Allyn & Bacon.

Blatt, B., and Kaplan, F. (1966). *Christmas in purgatory: A photographic essay on mental retardation.* Boston: Allyn & Bacon.

Borthwick-Duffy, S. A., and Eyman, R. K. (1990). Who are the dually diagnosed? *American Journal of Mental Retardation, 94*, 586–595.

Brickey, M. P., Campbell, K. M., and Browning, L. J. (1985). A five-year follow-up of sheltered workshop employees placed in competitive jobs. *Mental Retardation, 23*, 67–73.

Briggs, R. (1989). Monitoring and evaluating psychotropic drug use for persons with mental retardation: A follow-up report. *American Journal of Mental Retardation, 93*, 633–639.

Buck, J. A., and Sprague, R. L. (1989). Psychotropic medication of mentally retarded residents in community long-term care facilities. *American Journal of Mental Retardation, 93,* 618–623.

Chadsey-Rusch, J., and Sprague, R. L. (1989). Maladaptive behaviors associated with neuroleptic drug maintenance. *American Journal of Mental Retardation, 93,* 607–617.

Conroy, J., Efthimiou, J., and Lemanowicz, J. (1982). A matched comparison of the developmental growth of institutionalized and deinstitutionalized mentally retarded clients. *American Journal of Mental Deficiency, 86,* 581–587.

DeMyer, M. K. (1979). *Parents and children in autism.* New York: Wiley.

Deno, E. (1966). Vocational preparation of the retarded during school years. In S. G. DiMichael (Ed.), *New vocational pathways for the mentally retarded.* Washington: American Personnel and Guidance Association.

Eastwood, E. A., and Fisher, G. A. (1988). Skills acquisition among matched samples of institutionalized and community-based persons with mental retardation. *American Journal on Mental Retardation, 93,* 75–83.

Epple, W. A., Jacobson, J. W., and Janicki, M. P. (1985). Staffing ratios in public institutions for persons with mental retardation in the United States. *Mental Retardation, 23,* 115–124.

Eyman, R. K., Demaine, G. C., and Lei, T. (1979). Relationship between community environments and resident changes in adaptive behavior: A path model. *American Journal of Mental Deficiency, 79,* 573–582.

Eyman, R. K., Silverstein, A. B., McLain, R. E., and Miller, C. R. (1977). Effects of residential settings on development. In P. Mittler and J. DeJong (Eds.), *Research to practice in mental retardation: Care and intervention,* Vol. 1. Baltimore: University Park Press.

Fidura, J. G., Lindsey, E. R., and Walker, G. R. (1987). A special behavior unit for treatment of behavior problems of persons who are mentally retarded. *Mental Retardation, 25,* 107–111.

Fitzimmons, M. (1970). Bowling. In L. L. Neal (Ed.), *Recreation's role in the rehabilitation of the mentally retarded* (Monograph No. 4). Eugene, OR: University of Oregon Rehabilitation Research and Training Center in Mental Retardation.

Franklin, D. S. (1969). The adoption of children with medical conditions: Pt. 1. Process and outcome. *Child Welfare, 48,* 459–467.

Graham, J., and Poling, J. (1963). Help is a warm puppy. *Ladies Home Journal, 80,* 28.

Gualtieri, T. (1985). The problem of tardive dyskinesia litigation. *Psychiatric Aspects of Mental Retardation Reviews, 4* (4), 13–16.

Guralnick, M. J. (1978). *Early intervention and the integration of handicapped and nonhandicapped children.* Baltimore: University Park Press.

Hauber, F. A., Bruininks, R. H., Hill, B. K., Lakin, K. C., Scheerenberger, R. C., and White, C. C. (1984). National census of residential facilities: A 1982 profile of facilities and residents. *American Journal of Mental Deficiency, 89,* 236–245.

Hemming, H., Lavender, T., and Pill, R. (1981). Quality of life of mentally retarded adults transferred from large institutions to new small units. *American Journal of Mental Deficiency, 86,* 157–169.

Jacobson, J. W. (1982). Problem behavior and psychiatric impairment in a developmentally disabled population I: Behavior frequency. *Applied Research in Mental Retardation, 3,* 127–129.

Jacobson, J. W., and Ackerman, L. J. (1989). Psychological services for persons with mental retardation and psychiatric impairments. *Mental Retardation, 27,* 33–36.

Janicki, M. P., and MacEachron, A. E. (1984). Residential, health, and social service needs of elderly developmentally disabled persons. *The Gerontologist, 24,* 128–137.

Janicki, M. P., and Wisniewski, H. M. (Eds.). (1985). *Aging and developmental disabilities: Issues and approaches.* Baltimore: Paul H. Brookes.

Johnston, R. B., and Magrab, P. R. (Eds.). (1976). *Developmental disorders: Assessment, treatment, education.* Baltimore: University Park Press.

Kiernan, W. (1979). Rehabilitation planning. In P. R. Magrab and J. O. Elder (Eds.), *Planning for services to handicapped persons. Community, education, health.* Baltimore: Paul H. Brookes.

Kirk, S. A., and Gallagher, J. J. (1979). *Educating exceptional children,* 3d Ed. Boston: Houghton-Mifflin.

Kleinberg, J., and Galligan, B. (1983). Effects of deinstitutionalization on adaptive behavior of mentally retarded adults. *American Journal of Mental Deficiency, 88,* 21–27.

Koch, R., and Dobson, J. C. (Eds.). (1971). *The mentally retarded child and his family: A multidisciplinary handbook.* New York: Brunner/Mazel.

Lakin, K. C., Hill, B. K., Hauber, F. A., Bruininks, R. H., and Heal, L. W. (1983). New admissions and readmissions to a national sample of public residential facilities. *American Journal of Mental Deficiency, 88,* 13–20.

Lotter, V. (1978). Follow-up studies. In M. Rutter and E. Schopler (Eds.), *Autism: A reappraisal of concepts and treatment.* New York: Plenum.

MacEachron, A. E. (1983). Institutional reform and adaptive functioning of mentally retarded persons: A field experiment. *American Journal of Mental Deficiency, 88,* 2–12.

Magrab, P. R., and Elder, J. O. (1979). *Planning for services to handicapped persons: Community, education, health.* Baltimore: Paul H. Brookes.

Marc, D., and Macdonald, L. (1988). Respite care—Who uses it? *Mental Retardation, 26,* 93–96.

Marcus, L., and Baker, A. (1986). Assessment of autistic children. In R. J. Simeonnson (Ed.), *Psychological and developmental assessment of special children.* Boston: Allyn & Bacon.

Mitchell, P. R. (1983). Ophthalmologic problems. In G. H. Thomson, I. L. Rubin, and R. M. Bilenker (Eds.), *Comprehensive Management of Cerebral Palsy.* New York: Grune & Stratton.

Perske, R. (1972). The dignity of risk and the mentally retarded. *Mental Retardation, 11,* 18–19.

Phillips, I. (1966). Children, mental retardation, and emotional disorder. In I. Phillips (Ed.), *Prevention and treatment of mental retardation.* New York: Basic Books.

Poindexter, A. R. (1989). Psychotropic drug patterns in a large ICF/MR facility: A ten-year experience. *American Journal of Mental Retardation, 93,* 624–626.

Reiss, S. (1990). Prevalence of dual diagnosis in community-based day programs in the Chicago metropolitan area. *American Journal of Mental Retardation, 94,* 578–585.

Reiss, S., and Trenn, E. (1984). Consumer demand for outpatient mental health services for people with mental retardation. *Mental Retardation, 22,* 112–116.

Richardson, S. A., Koller, H., Katz, M., and McLaren, J. (1981). A functional classification of seizures and its distribution in a mentally retarded population. *American Journal of Mental Deficiency, 85,* 457–466.

Rivinus, T. M. (1980). Psychopharmacology and the mentally retarded patient. In L. S. Szymanski and P. E. Tanguay (Eds.), *Emotional disorders of mentally retarded persons.* Baltimore: University Park Press.

Ross, D. M., and Ross, S. A. (1976). *Hyperactivity: Research, theory, and action.* New York: Wiley.

Rotegard, L. L., Bruininks, R. H., and Krantz, G. C. (1984). State-operated residential facilities for people with mental retardation, July 1, 1978–June 30, 1982. *Mental Retardation, 22,* 69–74.

Scheerenberger, R. C. (1982). Public residential services (1981): Status and trends. *Mental Retardation, 20,* 210–215.

Seltzer, M. M. (1988). Structure and patterns of services utilization by elderly persons with mental retardation. *Mental Retardation, 26,* 181–185.

Shapiro, B. K., Palmer, F. B., Wachtel, R. C., and Capute, A. J. (1983). Associated dysfunctions. In G. H. Thompson, I. L. Rubin, and R. M. Bilenker (Eds.), *Comprehensive management of cerebral palsy.* New York: Grune & Stratton.

Simeonnson, R. (1986). *Psychological and developmental assessment of special children.* Boston: Allyn & Bacon.

Sovner, R., and DesNoyes, A. (1986). Guidelines for the treatment of mentally retarded persons on psychiatric inpatient units. *Psychiatric Aspects of Mental Retardation Reviews, 6,* 7–14.

Szymanski, L. S. (1980). Individual psychotherapy with retarded persons. In L. S. Szymanski and P. E. Tanguay (Eds.), *Emotional disorders of mentally retarded persons.* Baltimore: University Park Press.

Thompson, T., and Carey, A. (1980). Structured normalization: Intellectual and adaptive changes in a residential setting. *Mental Retardation, 18,* 193–197.

Wehman, P. (1979). *Curriculum Design for the Severely and Profoundly Handicapped.* New York: Human Sciences Press.

Wehman, P., Hill, M., Goodall, P., Cleveland, P., Brooke, V. and Pentecost, J. H., Jr. (1982). Job placement and follow-up of moderately and severely handicapped individuals after three years. *Journal of the Association for the Severely Handicapped, 7,* 5–16.

Whiteman, B. C., Simpson, G. B., and Compton, W. C. (1986). Relationship of otitis media and language impairment in adolescents with Down syndrome. *Mental Retardation, 24,* 353–356.

Wilhelm, C., Johnson, M., and Eisert, D. (1986). Assessment of motor-impaired children. In R. J. Simeonnson (Ed.), *Psychological and developmental assessment of special children.* Boston: Allyn & Bacon.

Witt, S. (1981). Increase in adaptive behavior level after residence in an intermediate care facility for mentally retarded persons. *Mental Retardation, 19,* 75–79.

Wolfensberger, W. (1972). *The principle of normalization in human services.* Toronto: National Institute on Mental Retardation.

Wolfensberger, W., and Glenn, L. (1973). *PASS (Program Analysis of Service Systems).* Toronto: National Institute on Mental Retardation.

Wolfensberger, W., and Glenn, L. (1975). *PASS 3: A method for the quantitative evaluation of human services.* Toronto: National Institute on Mental Retardation.

CHAPTER 3

Mental Retardation

OVERVIEW

As defined by the American Association on Mental Retardation, a definition also adopted by the American Psychiatric Association, *"mental retardation* refers to significantly subaverage general intellectual functioning existing concurrently with deficits in adaptive behavior, and manifested during the developmental period" (Grossman, 1973, 1977, and 1983; American Psychiatric Association, 1980). This chapter explores (1) important aspects of intelligence itself, (2) the nature of the intellectual deficit in mental retardation, (3) its prevalence, (4) its causation, (5) its associated or secondary disabilities, (6) its effect on adaptation, and (7) its special-service needs.

NATURE OF INTELLIGENCE

ESSENTIAL CHARACTERISTICS

Intelligence is generally equated with the abilities to learn and profit from experience, to reason, and to adapt to changing conditions (Sternberg, 1981). Each of these can be regarded as mental or cognitive in nature. To a lesser degree, intelligence also has been associated with a motivational dimension, the will to succeed (Sternberg, 1981).

The ability to learn seems to be particularly relevant because difficulty in basic school learning is the most characteristic adaptive impairment in mental retardation. In the academic realm, retarded individuals learn more slowly and to a lesser degree. But *learning ability* is only an end product or outward manifestation of intelligence. Underlying it are more fundamental elements, defined as *abilities* or *processes*.

Ability Models

Popular ability models have tended to equate intelligence with the capacity to infer relationships—that is, to reason (Resnick and Glaser, 1976; Spearman, 1923). Inferred understanding is the way our receptive vocabularies develop (Sternberg and Powell, 1983). Our knowledge of the meanings of words is typically acquired neither through a dictionary nor by having them explained. Rather, it occurs through repeated exposure to words in a particular context, and through that context their meaning gradually becomes apparent (is inferred).

Other ability models broaden the conception of intelligence to include other abilities beside reasoning—the abilities to remember (memory), to understand numerical and spatial relationships, to know facts, and to evaluate or judge in terms of some standard (Guilford, 1967; Thurstone,

1938). More recent research has indicated a hierarchical structure for intelligence under which these abilities are subsumed (Fredericksen, 1986). Two of these higher-order abilities are fluid and crystallized intelligence (Cattell, 1963; Cattell and Horn, 1978). *Fluid intelligence* is primarily tied to inferential reasoning and is perhaps reflective of our basic biological cognitive capacities, while *crystallized intelligence* refers to abilities more heavily influenced by experience and education. The current edition of the Stanford-Binet Intelligence scale (Thorndike, Hagen, and Sattler, 1986) purports to measure these two higher-order mental abilities, along with short term memory. Tests of verbal and quantitative reasoning are examples of crystallized intelligence while tests of abstract and visual reasoning ability are examples of fluid intelligence. The verbal and quantitative measures are regarded as more school related.

Information-Processing Models

Information-processing theories categorize problem-solving behavior in terms of cognitive activities called *components*. These consist of planning *(metacomponent)*, executing plans *(performance component)*, learning *(acquisition component)*, memory *(retention component)*, and generalization of learning from one situation to another *(transfer component)* (Sternberg, 1980). Adherents of this approach in mental retardation have been particularly active in the realm of memory, where they have sought to improve this component or ability by teaching strategies to strengthen retention (Belmont and Butterfield, 1971; Borkowski and Cavanaugh, 1979; Campione and Brown, 1977). Strategy training has produced improved memory performance, but the strategies tend not to be used outside the training setting (Landesman and Ramey, 1989). In my view, there seemed to be no emphasis on teaching the idea or concept of a strategy itself. More recently, strategy training has taken as one of its goals the hope that the child will come to recognize its general utility (Borkowski and Turner, 1988).

Another process activity that relates to retardation is speed of response. Retarded persons are slower to make even simple decisions, for example, whether two visual stimuli, such as two letters, are the same or different (Lally and Nettelbeck, 1977). Retarded persons are also slower to retrieve learned material from memory (Merrill, 1985).

MEASUREMENT OF INTELLIGENCE

Intelligence Tests

The instruments that measure intelligence (intelligence tests) consist of questions and tasks that involve the aforementioned basic mental abilities and processes. Such tests require their takers to reason, remember, calculate, compare, judge, and explain. Although these tests are a source of much controversy because of intergroup differences favoring economically more advantaged segments of our population (e.g., Mercer, 1973), they are best understood as predictors of school achievement, that is, as measures of scholastic aptitude (Anastasi, 1988). A good score on an intelligence test does not ensure good school achievement because other factors such as motivation are also important, but a poor score essentially precludes it.

Intelligence Quotient (IQ)

The score on an intelligence test is expressed in an *intelligence quotient (IQ)*. The tests are constructed such that the average score is 100, and about half the population has an IQ that falls between 90 and 110. This is the so-called average intelligence range. IQs above 110 represent above-average intelligence, with an upper limit of about 170, depending on the test used (Terman and Merrill, 1973; Wechsler, 1967; 1974, 1981). Some extraordinarily gifted individuals have had an IQ as high as 200; they are considered to be geniuses. IQs of less than 90 represent below-average intelligence, and the range that has traditionally been associated with mental retardation is 70 and below (see Fig. 3-1). This represents approximately 2 percent of the general population (Wechsler, 1974; 1981), although the segment of it considered developmentally disabled is about 1 percent (Baroff, 1982). In the below-70 IQ range, four levels of retardation are distinguished—mild, IQ 55–69; moderate, IQ 40–54; severe, IQ 25–39; and profound, IQ 0–24.[1] In school terminology, the mildly retarded range includes all children classified as educable and the moderately and severely retarded ranges include those classified as trainable.

NATURE OF INTELLECTUAL DEFICIT IN MENTAL RETARDATION

THEORIES OF MENTAL RETARDATION

Two kinds of theories have been dominant in mental retardation. The so-called deficit or difference theory attributes retardation to deficits or impairments in one or more cognitive abilities or processes (e.g., mem-

---

[1]These IQ ranges relate specifically to the Wechsler Intelligence Scales. The corresponding Stanford-Binet ranges are 52–67, 36–51, 20–35, and 19 and below (Grossman, 1977). Test-specific IQ ranges are not presented in the most recent classification revision (Grossman, 1983).

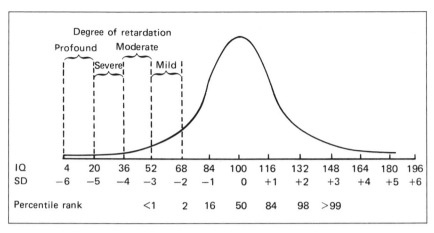

FIGURE 3-1. Distribution of measured intelligence in the normal and retarded range (based on Stanford-Binet IQs).

ory) (Ellis, 1969; Ellis and Cavalier, 1982). The developmental theory views retardation as the result of a slower *rate* of cognitive development that causes the retarded person to function at a lower level of mental development (mental age) than the normally developing individual at any given chronological age (Zigler, 1969; Zigler and Balla, 1982). This theory also appears to assume that persons of the same mental age (to be explained shortly), whether retarded or normal, are comparable in their mental functioning, an assumption that can be questioned and one that will be addressed later in a description of the quality of thought in retarded individuals. Both theories are regarded by Detterman (1987) as referring to different aspects of a more general theory that views retardation as the effect of deficits in one or more basic abilities that have a particularly powerful influence on overall functioning. Of the primary mental abilities, reasoning probably would have such a role, whereas among the information processes, the metacomponent would have a similar influence. The material that follows illustrates how the developmental model can help us to understand retardation, although attention also will be paid to areas of relative deficit and strength.

IQ AND MENTAL AGE

To further understand the nature of the intellectual impairment in mental retardation, it is necessary to go beyond IQ and to describe another important feature derived from intelligence tests, namely, mental age (M.A.). Although not incorporated in the now more widely used Wechsler Intelligence Scales [Wechsler Preschool and Primary Scale of Intelligence (WPPSI), Wechsler Intelligence Scale for Children, Revised

(WISC-R), and Wechsler Adult Intelligence Scale, Revised (WAIS-R)], nor in the latest version of Stanford-Binet, *mental age*[2] is extremely useful in understanding the mental abilities of persons who are retarded, especially as these relate to academic potential. Furthermore, the Wechsler scales are least accurate at the extremes of the intelligence range. A 5-year-old, for example, would obtain an IQ of 45 on the WPPSI even with zero scores on all items. This precludes the possibility of distinguishing between levels of retardation in young children or of determining the mental level at which the child does function. The more venerable Stanford-Binet test permits this distinction because it can sample mental abilities as low as age 2. It is mental age through which IQ is determined, and the meaning of both will now be illustrated.

A 6-year-old boy is performing well below his first-grade classmates. He seems to want to succeed, has no visual or hearing problems, and the language of the class is his native tongue. In addition to difficulties in learning first-grade reading, writing, and number skills, the child seems generally less mature than his classmates. More assistance is needed from the teacher in dressing, and he has less dexterity than classmates. His speech is simpler in structure, his utterances are shorter, and the words spoken are less clearly articulated. And social interactions with peers and the teacher, as well as his play, seem more like those of a younger child. In trying to understand why this youngster is having so much difficulty in mastering first-grade content, the teacher would eventually request an educational evaluation, which would typically include an intelligence test. Intelligence testing of a 6-year-old, depending on the child's precise age, can be done with one of several scales, the WPPSI, the WISC-R, or the Stanford-Binet. For this discussion, the pre-1986 version of the Binet will be used because it provides a direct measure of mental age. For the purpose of explaining the nature of mental retardation, mental age is extremely useful.

The Binet test consists of a series of tasks that are grouped by chronological age. At each age, or, in the case of very young children, at 6-month intervals, six test items are presented, each of which is accomplished by a majority of children of that age. At the 6-year level, for example, the test items consist of defining words, giving differences between common objects, finding a missing part in a familiar object, understanding number concepts up to 10, and solving a simple maze. Most of the test items count for 2 months each, and the total of the items passed gives the total number of months of mental age. Mental age

---

[2]The WPPSI and WISC-R provide a *test age,* a score roughly equivalent of mental age. The 1986 revision of the Stanford-Binet test offers age score equivalents of raw scores, but not an *overall* age or mental age score.

(M.A.) is recorded in years and months, e.g., 4 years 6 months, or an M.A. of 4–6.

A 6-year-old of average intelligence would have a mental age roughly equivalent to his or her chronological age, that is, a mental age of approximately 6 years. But the child described earlier might only attain a mental age of 4 years, a level that is two years below expectancy and more appropriate to a child of 4 rather than one of 6. Together with other evaluations, the teacher would recognize that the immaturity of this child in all aspects of development, including academics, is at least partly attributable to a current level of mental development that is well below that expected for his age. The child's learning difficulties are now understandable. He is having to deal with school content at a first-grade or 6-year mental-age level when his actual degree of mental development is more like that of a 4-year-old. One would not expect the average 4-year-old to succeed at first-grade tasks, but this is the learning situation that confronts this child.

Computing the IQ

Intelligence testing gives us both a mental age and an IQ. The IQ tells us how the child's (or youth's or adult's) present level of mental development compares with that of others of the same chronological age. The IQ is computed by dividing mental age by chronological age and then multiplying by 100 to eliminate any decimals:[3]

$$\frac{\text{Mental age (M.A.)}}{\text{Chronological age (C.A.)}} \times 100 = \text{IQ}$$

The IQ of the first grader we have been discussing, if he were just 6 years old, that is, 6 years and no months, would be 67, that is,

$$\frac{\text{M.A.}}{\text{C.A.}} = \frac{4}{6} = \frac{2}{3} = 0.67 \times 100 = 67$$

Given the overall picture of developmental lag, and assuming that the test score is an accurate reflection of this child's current ability level, this youngster would fall within the range of mild mental retardation. Already this child is 2 years behind classmates of average intelligence and at least 3 years behind any who are of above-average ability. The latter would have mental ages of at least 7 years. Moreover, the disparity between the retarded child's mental age and that of his classmates will not diminish. If his mental development continues at the rate suggested

---

[3]This is the original *ratio* IQ. It has been supplanted by statistically more sophisticated measures, but its use here for explanatory purposes is deemed appropriate.

by his present IQ, the difference between his mental age and that of his normal classmates will grow even greater with time.

IQ as a Measure of the Rate of Mental Growth

In addition to serving as a comparative measure with regard to others of the same chronological age, IQ also can be considered an indicator of the rate of mental development. An IQ of 67 suggests a mental-age growth rate that is two-thirds (67 percent) of expectancy. The child with an IQ of 100 gains 12 months of mental age over the course of 1 year, while the youngster with an IQ of 67 gains only two-thirds as much—8 months of mental age. If this child's rate of mental growth is relatively constant, and this is more characteristic in the retarded IQ range (Walker and Gross, 1970), then there will be an ever-widening mental-age gap between the retarded and the normally developing child. The gap will increase by 4 months each year for much of the period during which mental growth occurs, mental growth being equated with increase in mental age (see Fig. 3-2). At age 6, there is a 2-year mental age difference, and it will increase to 4 years at age 12 and 5 years at age 18.

The Mental-Age Growth Period

Now let's consider another very important aspect of intelligence, one that is obscured by the usual meaning of the word *retarded*. In its usual sense, *retarded* refers to "delay" rather than to "arrest." It might be thought that mental retardation is simply a condition of slower than average mental growth, and therefore, given enough time, the difference in growth (mental age) would eventually disappear. However, this could only occur if the mental-age growth period for retarded persons was longer than that for nonretarded ones, which is *not* the case.

Let us consider what the mental-age growth period means. Mental growth is like physical growth in that it occurs only during a specific time period. We know that we grow in height from birth on into adolescence and that by late adolescence, if not earlier, our maximum height is reached. The same principle applies to mental growth. Our mental powers, as reflected in mental age, increase from infancy on into young adulthood, at which time growth in mental age virtually ceases. On the Stanford-Binet test, for example, mental-age scores essentially do not increase after age 18 (see Fig. 3-3). It is clear, however, that the 18-year limit relates to the specific content of the Stanford-Binet test itself, since on the WAIS-R, scores increase up to age 26 (Bayley, 1970). In any case, scores on these tests do not increase beyond the young-adult period, and this same age limit applies to retarded persons. Whatever differences exist between retarded and nonretarded individuals at the end of

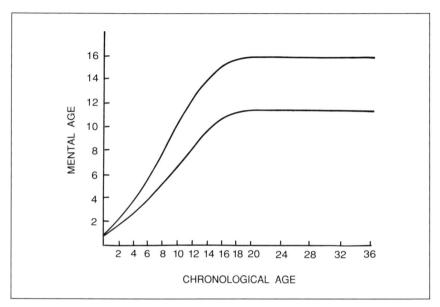

FIGURE 3-2. Mental age growth curves corresponding to IQs of 100 and 67 [adapted from Bayley (1970) and based on 1960 Binet IQs (Terman & Merrill, 1960)].

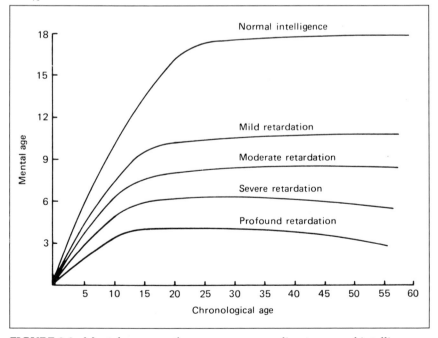

FIGURE 3-3. Mental age growth curves corresponding to normal intelligence and to the four levels of retardation. Adapted from Fisher & Zeaman (1970).

the mental-age growth period will persist thereafter. Happily for all of us, scores on these tests remain fairly constant into old age, and even then there is very little decline except as health begins to fail.

The Mental-Age Growth Period and Learning

Although the comparable mental-age growth period for retarded and nonretarded persons precludes any "catching up," it is important to distinguish between the period during which our mental powers grow and that during which we can learn. Although out mental powers are essentially complete by young adulthood, this does not affect learning ability. People can and do learn throughout their lives whether they are retarded or not. The reader of this material may have reached the end of his or her mental-age growth period, but learning is taking place at this very moment as the material is read and digested. Learning, for all of us, goes on throughout our lives; it is necessary only that the material that we seek to learn does not exceed in complexity that which is beyond our mental-age grasp.

Mental Age and Mental Retardation

Mental age provides a general measure of mental powers and, in the case of retarded mental development, permits us to identify both the mental-age level at which the retarded person currently functions and the degree of mental-age disparity from normal expectancy. However, knowledge of mental age per se (e.g., M.A. 4 in the 6-year-old discussed earlier) tells us only that in some fashion, the 6-year-old is mentally more like a 4-year-old than a 6-year-old. Nevertheless, while there are similarities between the retarded 6-year-old and his (or her) 4-year-old mental-age counterpart, there are also differences. The retarded 6-year-old is likely to be more advanced physically than the 4-year-old and to have better self-help skills. The retarded 6-year-old's interests and play activities may be more mature than those of his or her mental-age counterpart. On the other hand, the retarded 6-year-old's speech and knowledge of letter and number concepts may be less developed than those of the normal 4-year-old. The 6-year-old also may appear to be less curious, less stimulated by new experiences, less spontaneous, and less creative than the average 4-year-old (Baroff, 1986).

STRENGTHS AND WEAKNESSES ON INTELLIGENCE TESTS

On intelligence tests, one tends to find that retarded individuals perform relatively better on nonspeech tasks—those which involve motor or manual responses and do not require verbal responses. Retarded individuals are more likely to succeed on such tasks as copying geometric designs, solving jigsaw-like puzzles, creating block designs from a visual pattern, and identifying missing parts in pictures. Not only do these tasks not require a verbal response, but the problem is always before the person in visual form. On the other hand, tasks that are primarily verbal and require reasoning, judgment, and memory tend to be more difficult for them. This includes defining words, solving arithmetic problems, finding similarities among things that are different (categorizing), and demonstrating general knowledge.

Retarded persons tend to do better on practical and concrete tasks than on those that primarily involve language. This pattern is particularly true of mildly retarded individuals and those without evidence of organic brain damage. Individuals with an organic brain abnormality have more difficulty in the reproduction of visual patterns (Achenbach, 1970; Baroff, 1959; Sattler, 1974; Silverstein, 1968).

THE QUALITY OF THINKING IN RETARDED PERSONS

Given this pattern of strengths and weaknesses, what is the quality of thinking in retarded persons as it is expressed in our encounters with them?

Suggestibility

Retarded persons are more suggestible than normal individuals; they are more easily influenced by external factors (Zigler, 1966). This vulnerability has at least two bases. First, retarded individuals have particular difficulty in considering more than one factor at a time in complex situations. The tendency is to fix or center attention on only one aspect in such situations. This quality was referred to by the Swiss psychologist Piaget as "egocentric thought," and it also happens to be particularly characteristic of the normal preschool-age child (Flavell, 1963; Piaget, 1952). This type of egocentric thought also is seen in retarded persons with mental ages of less than 7 years (Ferretti and Butterfield, 1989). A second source of greater suggestibility is thought to relate to the usual life experience of the average retarded person. The chronic frustration in coping that retarded people usually experience is bound to diminish self-confidence and to cause a greater reliance on others. This is particularly true in unfamiliar situations where there is reduced confidence in one's own abilities (Balla, Styfco, and Zigler, 1971; Turnure, 1970a, 1970b).

Specific Problem-Solving Deficiencies

Probably related to excessive suggestibility in retarded individuals is a kind of passivity of thought (Baroff, 1986). This is evident in the way in which retarded individuals approach a problem whose solution would be abetted by the initiation of one or more strategies. This is a metacomponent (information-processing) deficit in retarded individuals. When a normal person is confronted with a problem, he or she "sizes it up" and decides what will help to solve it. Such a person may, for example, seek more information, call on others for assistance, or even try to modify the problem to make it less complex. Retarded persons, however, seem to lack awareness that they might create ways in which to help themselves. This has been shown in studies of memory in which there is an apparent lack of understanding of how material that is to be remembered might be organized to facilitate retention. Although retarded individuals know that they will be asked to recall something on a test, for example, they seem to be unaware that rehearsal or repetition of the material will aid retention.

Apart from the obvious benefit of rehearsal, memory is also enhanced by reorganization of the material to be remembered. In such reorganizations, links are created that bind individual items. Items may be combined in an image (Segal, 1971), in a sentence, in an acronym, or in a category (concept). The use of concepts, for example, can reduce the total number of initially separate items to one (e.g., the concept "breakfast" is a good link for orange juice, cereal, bread, and coffee—one item standing in the place of four). Recall of a series of numbers is facilitated by "chunking" (Dember, 1974), that is, by combining them into groups. The last four digits of a telephone number, for example, 1-9-2-4, can be reduced to two by grouping the numbers to produce a new number, 19-24.

Whether employing reorganization (MacMillan, 1972; Rohwer, 1968) or rehearsal (Anders, 1971; Ellis, 1969), the normal learner _actively_ engages the task and carries out activities that will strengthen retention. Retarded individuals, however, do not _spontaneously_ employ such strategies. Interestingly, this failure to strategize may not be inherent in mental retardation, but rather may be a mental-age–related phenomenon. Normal children with mental ages of less than 8 years also do not spontaneously use such strategies (Corsale, 1977). One of the important developments in the field of mental retardation has been the attempt to teach retarded youth to use strategies. This was referred to earlier (Belmont and Butterfield, 1971; Borkowski and Cavanaugh, 1977). There is evidence that retarded youth can benefit from such training, at least with regard to memory (Belmont and Butterfield, 1971; Brown et al., 1973), and increasingly, researchers are focusing on attempts to strengthen general strategy use (e.g., Borkowski and Cavanaugh, 1979).

Lack of Critical Judgment

Retarded persons seem to be less critical in their thinking. They may appear careless and indifferent to inconsistencies (Baroff, 1986). Perhaps this quality, too, is a reflection of a history of difficulty with thinking kinds of activities. Any solution, irrespective of quality, becomes a way of terminating an anxiety-arousing situation.

Concreteness of Thought

Concreteness of thought is a prominent characteristic of retarded individuals. Thinking tends to be bound to the particular and to be situation-specific. Retarded persons have difficulty in generalizing or applying what has been learned in one setting to a different but comparable one. This is the *transfer* information-processing component. The problem is an inability to ignore surface differences and to recognize underlying similarities. Thus a mildly retarded adolescent when asked how a ship and an automobile are alike insists that they are not alike because "a ship rides on the water and an automobile rides on the land." Even though the reply indicates a recognition that both "ride," it is the difference in where they ride rather than their underlying similarity of action that dominates his thinking. What is probably occurring here is the continued influence of egocentric thought in a youth who is functioning at a mental-age level of about 8 years.

Another aspect of concreteness is seen in the way that retarded individuals interpret proverbs. Retarded people do not recognize that the language of a proverb is not to be taken literally but rather is to be understood at a symbolic level. Thus "a stitch in time . . ." is likely to be understood as relating to the maintenance of clothing rather than as a general warning about the value of prevention.

Concreteness, Planfulness, and Foresight. Concreteness also involves a focus on what is directly knowable as opposed to what might be. We can *know* directly through our senses—we can see a glass and touch a glass—but what might be, that is, the future, has no current reality—it is only hypothetical, to be imagined, not directly apprehended. Planning and foresight, however, deal with the future, and as such, they are concerned with possibilities rather than realities. They are also affected by one's ability to consider multiple possibilities, and the limitation of retarded people in considering more than one aspect of a situation at a time has already been noted. All this has the effect of limiting the retarded person's capacity to think ahead, the metacomponent. Nevertheless, there is some indication that planning ability can be strengthened in retarded persons through teaching them how to generate and consider possible alternative courses of action (Tymchuk, Andron, and Rahbar, 1988).

Concreteness, Imagination, and Creativity. Another consequence of concreteness of thought is to limit imagination, the faculty that enables normal individuals to go beyond that which is directly given to the senses and to create something new. Although some retarded people show true creative talents in music and art, the so-called idiot savant (Hill, 1974), as a rule these abilities are also diminished.

Slowness of Thought

Retarded persons tend to be slower in their responses. This is true even on tasks involving well-practiced skills such as simple letter discrimination for the retarded child who can read (Hunt, 1976), or in speed of reading itself in mildly retarded adult readers (Ellin et al., 1989).

Adaptive Behavior

The definition of mental retardation includes a reference to adaptive behavior as well as subaverage intelligence. *Adaptive behavior* refers to the degree to which one's behavior reflects the standards of personal and social responsibility expected for one's age and cultural group (Grossman, 1983). Measures of adaptive behavior give particular weight to age-related expectations in personal independence and self-sufficiency (Bruininks, McGrew, and Maruyama, 1988), traditional hallmarks distinguishing retarded from nonretarded persons. The inclusion of adaptive behavior as a criterion for classification as mentally retarded also implies that not all persons with subaverage intelligence will show a major impairment in adaptive behavior. This is a distinction that particularly applies to socioeconomically disadvantaged individuals who test in the mildly retarded intelligence range but who are free of any organic basis for their intellectual impairment. Their primary adaptive behavior deficit will be in the academic realm; in other areas of general functioning they will perform much like their peers, although such people are more likely to be followers than leaders and to be perceived as "slow." Once an individual drops into the below-50 IQ range, the distinction between intelligence and adaptive behavior is likely to be academic, since almost all such individuals will show significant impairment in virtually all developmental domains and will need at least some degree of assistance and supervision throughout their lives.

SECONDARY OR ASSOCIATED DISABILITIES

In terms of the personhood model presented in Chapter 1, retardation represents an impairment in the resource known as intelligence. However, other resources or abilities are also much affected.

COMMUNICATION SKILLS

Speech and language difficulties are pervasive in mental retardation (McLean, Yoder, and Schiefelbusch, 1972; Schiefelbusch and Lloyd, 1974; Spradlin, 1963). In a Canadian study of retarded 7- to 10-year-olds, almost two-thirds (66 percent) had a speech disorder, more than twice the frequency of the next most common problem, behavior disorders (McQueen et al., 1987). The typical developmental course includes slow speech acquisition, especially in children with some organic impairment (Kirk, 1964; Spradlin, 1963). In a study of mildly retarded children aged 5 to 12, about half (45 percent) had speech impairment (Chess and Hassibi, 1970).

Most prominent are problems in articulation (pronunciation) and speech clarity (Yoder and Miller, 1972), also one of the characteristic abnormalities in Down syndrome (Dodd, 1975). As the degree of retardation increases, speech clarity tends to decline, and in persons with severe and/or profound retardation, speech may be limited to only brief utterances or be absent altogether. In fact, at severe and profound levels of retardation especially, one finds that the ability to understand language much exceeds the ability to produce it.

Apart from articulation problems, spontaneous utterances tend to be briefer in length (Mecham, 1955; Siegel, 1962) and more concrete in word usage (Papania, 1954). Studies have tied the quality of the retarded child's speech to mental age (e.g., Schlanger, 1953; Siegel, 1962), with their speech seen as simply less complex than that of their mental-age counterparts (Lenneberg, Nichols, and Rosenberger, 1964). Other workers see the retarded child's speech as deficient relative to that of nonretarded younger children of comparable mental age (e.g., Jordan, 1967). This would definitely appear to be the case in Down syndrome (Thompson, 1963). All this suggests a deficit not wholly explicable in terms of mental age.

Where speech problems are due to neuromuscular disorders, as in cerebral palsy, nonverbal or augmentative forms of communication are widely employed. These are illustrated in Chapter 5.

HEALTH, SENSORY, AND PHYSICAL SKILLS

Health

Numerous health problems are found in mental retardation (McLaren and Bryson, 1987), including such neurologic ones as cerebral palsy and epilepsy (Alvarez, 1989; Richardson et al., 1981); infectious and parasitic diseases, especially in group-care settings (Yoeli and Scheinesson, 1976); and metabolic disorders (Milunsky, 1975). The metabolic disorders, typically genetic in origin, often require dietary management (e.g., phenylketonuria and galactosemia). Apart from the metabolic conditions, Down syndrome, which is a chromosomal disorder, includes a variety of health problems of which congenital heart defects and respiratory infection in particular threaten survival in early childhood (Gorlin, 1977). Upper respiratory, chest, and ear infections are also common (Kavanagh, Kahane, and Kordan, 1986).

Persons with cerebral palsy are frequently retarded, and this neuromuscular disorder includes a host of health problems (see Chapter 5), as well as nutritional difficulties (Springer, 1987). Only mentioned here are feeding and respiratory problems tied to poor motor control of swallowing and sucking. These difficulties are also found in extremely physically impaired individuals without cerebral palsy.

Occasionally associated with retardation (National Institutes of Health, 1986), the congenital spinal cord abnormality spina bifida involves chronic medical problems involving the cerebrospinal fluid and the bladder and bowel. Only in recent years are children with spina bifida surviving into adulthood.

Deafness and blindness occur with increased frequency, especially in the moderate to profound ranges of retardation (Payne, 1971). Individuals with retardation and cerebral palsy, along with these sensory losses, are frequently found to have diminished tactile sensitivity as well.

Apart from health and sensory problems, dental ones are also common in retardation. In addition, there is a particularly high susceptibility to periodontal disease in Down syndrome (Barnett et al., 1986; Barnett et al., 1988).

Physical Skills

Abnormalities in motor development are found in retardation, especially in the organic segment of the population, such as those with Down syndrome (Henderson, Morris, and Ray, 1981). For the person who is slow in motor development, there is delay in acquisition of all physical skills and greater awkwardness and incoordination. Again, as in the sensory area, organically impaired retarded people are particularly affected.

Physical skills will be most impaired in persons with neurologic disorders that affect the brain, as in cerebral palsy (Johnston, 1976), or in persons with the most severe degrees of retardation, as in the nonambulatory profoundly retarded individual (with or without cerebral palsy).

PERSONALITY: TEMPERAMENT, EMOTIONS, AND CHARACTER

Within the personality resource domain there are numerous problems, some of which were discussed in Chapter 1 (see Mental Health Services). In the young retarded child, one often encounters hyperactivity, easy distractibility, low frustration tolerance, and general impulsivity (Chess and Hassibi, 1970; Webster, 1970). Play is generally solitary, often repetitive in nature, and may involve odd-appearing motor activities that seem to be enjoyed for the sensory experiences they are presumed to evoke—tactile, kinesthetic, visual, and auditory. Emotions tend to be easily aroused and occasionally are explosive in quality. Emotional behavior characteristic of a younger child is a hallmark of retardation and gives the retarded individual the quality of being immature.

In older retarded children, hyperactivity tends to diminish, but a variety of potentially maladaptive behaviors can be seen—undue fearfulness in new situations, fears of rejection (the intimacy need), fears of failure (the success need), shyness or withdrawal tendencies, negativism, and compulsiveness (Baroff, 1986).

Psychoses also are found in retardation; hallucinations, delusions, and major mood disorders have been described in retarded adults (Reid, 1972a, 1972b), whereas acute psychoses have been described in young children (Menolascino, 1965). For example, a 4-year-old child with Down syndrome began to withdraw and to show catatonic posturing and bizarre speech after the hospitalization of his father, with whom he had a very close relationship. The symptoms disappeared after a brief period of inpatient hospital care.

As indicated in the Mental Health Services section in the previous chapter, psychiatric disorders are widely seen in retarded youth and young adults. Major problems consist of (1) schizophrenic-like behaviors—social withdrawal, flattened affect, paranoid tendencies (blaming others), and anxiety (Reiss, 1982); (2) antisocial behavior—aggression, lying, stealing, and oppositional behavior, primarily found in younger and less-retarded males (Koller et al., 1983; Myers, 1987); (3) excessive dependency; and (4) depression (Pawlarcyzk and Beckwith, 1987; Reiss and Benson, 1985; Reynolds and Baker, 1988).

Chapter 2 stressed that the presence of serious personality difficulties cannot be divorced from the availability of appropriate services. Where individuals do not have access to activities that can meet basic psychological needs for intimacy, success, and autonomy, frustration and disordered behavior are inevitable. Thus lack of friendships and deficits in social skills combine to cause depression in retarded adults (Reiss and Benson, 1985; Benson et al., 1985; Matson, DiLorenzo, and Andrasik, 1983).

AESTHETIC APPRECIATION

Among retarded individuals are some with unusual gifts—artistic or cognitive. Referred to in Chapter 2, so-called savants function in retarded fashion in all areas except for their gift. The most common talents are calendar calculating, memory, music, and art (Hill, 1974; Hoffman, 1971; Miller, 1987).

Calendar calculators can tell the day of the week on which a particular date will fall for past and future. They are unable to explain how they do it, although it appears that they memorize a series of base dates from which the number of days in each month are used to count forward or backward to the desired date. These calculations are done in the head, yet despite this remarkable ability, when not calendar calculating, these individuals are frequently unable to carry out even very simple arithmetic operations. I once evaluated a pair of retarded (and autistic) identical twins who, though able to calendar calculate, could not solve addition or subtraction problems of sums of less than 10.

In the musical domain, a mildly retarded adult (IQ 67) was an outstanding pianist. In addition, he had a remarkable memory and was capable of repeating, word for word, two pages of print after reading them once silently (Anastasi and Levee, 1960).

In painting, several gifted retarded persons have been described. For example, Gottfried Mind was famed in Europe for his paintings of children and animals (Hill, 1974). His retardation was due to congenital hypothyroidism (cretinism), a condition now treatable if detected early in infancy. Unusual painting talent has been observed in two Japanese youths, one of whom is autistic as well as retarded (Morishima and Brown, 1976, 1977). The nonautistic youth has had his work exhibited in Japan and the United States, and except for his gift, his language, thinking, and general behavior are consistent with retardation.

The savant is a constant challenge to our understanding of how the brain functions and clearly suggests the possibility of areas of autonomous development.

PREVALENCE OF MENTAL RETARDATION

In Chapter 1, the prevalence of mental retardation was given as 0.9 percent. Although about 2.5 percent of the general population have an IQ below 70, only about a third of them (0.9 percent) are currently considered developmentally disabled. Figure 3-1 shows the IQ distribution in the general population and the subgroups that comprise the mentally retarded population. Within the below-70 range, the great majority have only mild retardation, the respective proportions being mild 89 percent, moderate 7 percent, severe 3 percent, and profound 1 percent (President's Committee on Mental Retardation, 1967). A review of the recent literature (McLaren and Bryson, 1987) suggests prevalence rates in the moderate to profound ranges of 3 to 4 per 1000: moderate, 1 to 2 per 1000; severe, 1 per 1000; and profound, 0.4 per 1000.

CAUSES OF MENTAL RETARDATION

Mental retardation may arise from either biological or psychosocial causes. *Biological* causes involve damage to the brain and may be due to heredity, chromosomal abnormalities, or events occurring during pregnancy, at birth, or in early childhood.[4] *Psychosocial* causes refer to retardation in nonorganically impaired children, generally from impoverished families in which retardation is also found in parents and siblings (Grossman, 1983). In this situation, while emphasis is placed on an adverse learning environment, a role for heredity cannot be ruled out. For an in-depth treatment of causation, the reader is referred to any of the major textbooks in mental retardation (e.g., Baroff, 1986; Payne and Patton, 1981; Robinson and Robinson, 1976).

The term *psychosocial* has been used in a variety of ways, one of which pertains to the causes of mental retardation. The term is used differently in the title of this book, where it is intended to convey both the psychological and social consequences of disability.

---

[4]Damage to the brain after early childhood tends to produce specific rather than general impairment, such as paralysis and speech disorders following a stroke. If the brain damage is massive, however, there is often a widespread loss of previous mental functioning and the creation of states either characterized as mental retardation or equivalent to it.

BIOLOGICAL CAUSES

Prenatal Factors

Genes and Chromosomes. At conception itself, events can occur that will adversely affect brain development. Some forms of retardation are hereditary, transmitted from parents to children through the genes in the reproductive cells, the sperm and the egg. Most often the mode of transmission is recessive, which means that "carrier" parents are not affected and the children have a 1 in 4 risk of inheriting the disorder. Recessive disorders have been clearly tied to gene-caused biochemical abnormalities, and phenylketonuria (PKU) is one of the best-known forms. Interest in PKU stems both from its preventability if detected at birth and the risk of retardation in the babies of normal phenylketonuric women. Less often in mental retardation the genetic mode of transmission is dominant, wherein, typically, the parents and the child are affected, although the symptoms in the parent or parents may be very mild. Tuberous sclerosis is an example of a dominantly inherited condition in which only the child is likely to show retardation. In a dominantly inherited disorder, the risk of inheriting the condition from a parent is one in two.

Apart from gene-determined disorders, abnormalities of the chromosomes, the structures on which genes are found, may themselves cause retardation. The abnormalities consist of extra chromosomes, missing chromosomes, and loss of small parts of a chromosome. The best known chromosomal disorder is Down syndrome (mongolism), a condition caused by the presence of an extra chromosome number 21. Loss of a small part of the X chromosome (fragile X syndrome) can cause retardation, typically more so in males than in females, while females with two or more extra X chromosomes also can have intellectual impairment.

Nongenetic Prenatal Causes. During pregnancy, the fetus may be exposed to a variety of biological insults that can impair brain development. These can consist of maternal infections transmitted to the fetus through the placenta (e.g., rubella, toxoplasmosis, cytomegalovirus, syphilis, and now the AIDS virus), blood incompatibility between mother and fetus (e.g., Rh disease), fetal exposure to potentially toxic agents (alcohol, drugs, tobacco, or radiation), and maternal hypertension or diabetes. With regard to fetal drug exposure, moderate to heavy regular maternal consumption of alcohol very early in pregnancy has been most clearly implicated in increased fetal risk of retardation, notably in the *fetal alcohol syndrome* (Jones et al., 1973; Landesman-Dwyer, Ragozin, and Little, 1981).

Perinatal Factors

In health terms, the first 28 days of life is the most important period in childhood (Phibbs, 1977). This is the time of greatest infant mortality, as well as a period when sublethal damage can occur. Injury to the brain during labor or delivery or in the early neonatal period is a major cause of cerebral palsy (see Chapter 5), deafness, and mental retardation. In particular, it is the premature newborn (small for age) who is at risk, especially those with birthweights of less than 3 lbs (1500 gm). Potentially injurious conditions to which the premature baby is vulnerable include severe oxygen deprivation (anoxia), head trauma, and herpes infection contracted from the mother during delivery (Chamberlin, 1975). Herpes is a sexually transmitted viral infection which when present in a pregnant woman is particularly dangerous to the newborn. It can cause retardation, blindness, or death (Nahmias and Tomeh, 1977), and women at risk are delivered by cesarean section.

Postnatal Factors

Although biological causes of retardation are usually of prenatal origin, illnesses and head trauma during infancy and early childhood also can create problems. These postnatal potential causes of retardation consist chiefly of (1) infectious diseases of the brain—encephalitis (Hodes, 1977) and meningitis (Sells and Bennett, 1977); (2) head injury—often as a result of motor vehicle accidents, but also, sadly, from child abuse; and (3) exposure to lead. Lead exposure has been a special public health concern. Eating flaking old lead-based paints from walls can cause brain inflammation (lead encephalitis) and retardation. At lower levels of exposure or in children dwelling near lead battery dumps or lead smelters, there is some suggestion of impairment in attention span (Needleman et al., 1979) and an approximate 10-point reduction in IQ (Milar and Schroeder, 1983). One of the responses to the lead paint problem has been to reduce the lead level of paints currently available.

Another threat to normal development is inadequate nutrition. In developed countries, whatever dietary deficiencies exist generally are not severe enough to affect brain growth and mental development. In countries where moderate to severe undernourishment (inadequate calorie intake) is the norm, however, some effects are seen. In particular, severe malnutrition in infancy, such as kwashiorkor (protein deficiency) or marasmus (calorie deficit), conditions that affect about 5 percent of the world's children, results in retardation of both growth and mental development. The infant is especially vulnerable to these conditions during the first six months of life (Birch et al., 1971).

PSYCHOSOCIAL CAUSES

Although there is no doubt that biological damage to the brain can cause mental retardation, one could ask whether a child's psychological environment also can produce a similar effect. While the research that relates to this question is less explicit than its biological counterpart, the evidence from a number of lines of study indicates that it can. Let's examine what I regard as the most persuasive evidence for a major psychological influence on cognitive development.

Effects of Dramatic Change in Environment on Development

Case studies of children reared under conditions of extraordinary deprivation (e.g., confinement to a single room) reveal not only severe stunting of mental development but also a remarkable capacity to recover mental functions if intervention occurs in childhood (Davis, 1947; Koluchova, 1972; Mason, 1942). It would appear, as Hunt (1979) has suggested, that "a major share of early losses can be made up if the develop-fostering . . . experience improves." And contrary to the traditional view of the time period during which this can occur, such change is reported in children first assisted as late as ages 6 and 7.

Less dramatic but equally persuasive are the striking gains in mental growth found in children originally reared in an unstimulating hospital setting and moved in the second year of life to a setting in which there was a tremendous amount of both stimulation and loving attention. Children originally seen as retarded but without any biological abnormality came to function normally (Skeels and Dye, 1939). I conclude (Baroff, 1986) along with other workers (e.g., Ramey and Landesman, in press; Scarr-Salapatek, 1975; Zigler and Seitz, 1982) that, in biologically intact children, the environment can produce effects of from 20 to 30 IQ points, a magnitude sufficient to make the difference between mental retardation and normalcy.

Environments that depress mental development are deficient in general stimulation—personal, object, and experiential—and by their deprivation interfere with opportunities for learning. I have characterized such settings as sparse in experiences of *contingent stimulation* (the child's response to a stimulus produces an effect on its environment) and lacking an adult who can provide individual, responsive care and who can serve as a *verbal mediator* (teacher) to the child (Baroff, 1986).

Early Foster or Adoptive Placement of Children at Risk for Mental Retardation

As early as the 1940s, studies have shown that children of mothers with subaverage intelligence (borderline or retarded) will show essentially normal (average) intelligence when reared in foster or adoptive homes of normal parents (Schiff et al., 1978; Skeels and Harms, 1948; Skodak and Skeels, 1949; Willerman, 1979). Moreover, the earlier the placement, the better the child is likely to do (Speer, 1940). Indeed, the early studies revolutionized child care and led to the current preference for family rather than institutional placement of young children. The findings of these early studies were unexpected:

> Perusal of the child's social history . . . and comparison [of it] with the field agent's preplacement evaluation of the adoptive home was disheartening. It did not seem possible that children with such meager possibilities as projected from the intellectual, academic, and occupational attainments of their parents could measure up to the demands of cultured, educated parents. Yet careful examination of one child after another showed none of the retardation anticipated. (Skodak and Skeels, 1949, p. 89) [Although the quality of parenting is clearly crucial to development, we are too quick to presume that the child's cognitive level will mirror that of the parents.]

In the study from which the preceding quotation came, the average IQ of the biological mothers was 86 and that of their children, reared since infancy in adoptive homes, was 107. Perhaps most startling was the finding in a subgroup of children whose mothers were retarded (mean IQ 63). The mean IQ of these children at age 13 was 96. Despite being born to retarded mothers, these children were functioning in the average intelligence range.

An analogous phenomenon is seen in a cross-racial study of black children adopted in infancy by advantaged white families in Minnesota (Scarr and Weinberg, 1976). The average IQ of these black children was 106 (N = 130), which exceeded by 16 points the average IQ of black children in that region. Again, the earlier the adoption, the greater were the effects. Even for late adoptees, i.e., those adopted after age 1 year, the gain was at least 10 points, and this doubled to 20 points for early-placed children.

The Skodak and Skeels study discloses more than just an environmental effect on intelligence, however. The children themselves differed from each other, those of the brighter biological mothers functioning at a higher level than those of the low-scoring biological mothers. Although early adoption elevated IQ scores for all the children, there remained differences between them that correlated with the IQs of their biological mothers. This correlation is regarded as a genetic effect, heredity being seen as influencing the child's capacity to respond to the adoptive home. This study and that of Willerman (1979) are viewed as revealing the simultaneous working of both heredity and environment.

Twin Studies and the Heredity-Environment Interaction

The strongest evidence for the effect of environment on intelligence is found in studies of twins, especially identical twins separated in childhood and reared in different homes. The rationale of twin research is that differences between identical (monozygotic) twins, products of a single fertilized egg, must be nongenetic or environmental in origin because the twins are genetically identical. On the other hand, differences between fraternal (dizygotic) twins, products of two different fertilized eggs, may be genetic or environmental. Fraternal twins are no more alike genetically than ordinary single-born siblings; they just happened to have been conceived at the same time. Studies of IQ differences among identical twins reared apart reveal that they are greater than among identical twins reared together, evidence of an environmental effect (Erlenmeyer-Kimling and Jarvik, 1963; Jensen, 1971). However, if only the environment influenced intelligence, then fraternal twins reared in the same home would be more similar than identical twins reared apart. This is not the case. Identical twins reared apart are actually more similar in IQ than fraternal twins reared together, evidence for a genetic effect. As in the studies cited earlier, both heredity and environment influence mental development. With regard to heredity, genetic factors appear to particularly influence verbal and spatial abilities (Plomin, 1988).

It is clear that a child's environment can either enhance or depress intelligence, and to a degree, that makes the difference between essentially normal ability and mental retardation. A child is not infinitely malleable, however. Even within a shared environment, be it home or institution, variations between children in IQ rather than sameness are the rule. These variations are attributed to genetically determined differences in the capacities of the children to respond to a common environment. This interdependence is the essence of the conception of heredity as the capacity to use an environment in a particular way (Fuller, 1954).

AGE-RELATED ADAPTIVE BEHAVIOR PROBLEMS AND PSYCHOSOCIAL EFFECTS

Impairment in the capacity for prudent self-management and personal responsibility leads to difficulties in activities of daily living and, in mental retardation in particular, causes the individual to appear to be immature. Such a person's behavior seems more like that of a younger person. This quality of immaturity, especially pronounced in those with more than mild retardation, results in the perception of them as "eternal children," a perception that tends to deny the more developed, mature, or adult aspects of the person and one that may itself diminish opportunities for further development. This is especially problematic in the case of the retarded person who is no longer, chronologically, a child. Whether the person is an older child, an adolescent, or an adult, the perception of him or her as an "eternal child" leads to behavioral expectations and programmatic activities that strengthen the image of immaturity and preclude further growth. This has led in recent times to an emphasis on providing activities and experiences for such people that reflect their chronological as well as their mental age.

Impairment in judicious self-management is also found in mental illness, but in retardation it is tied to cognitive rather than emotional factors. Retardation is itself no protection against mental illness, however, and where both are present, in the so-called dual-diagnosis individual, adjustment is further weakened. Apart from the potentially adverse effects of the personality disorder, the nature of the retarded person's general adaptation will largely reflect his or her level of cognitive impairment. Where retardation is not more than mild in degree, and especially where there is no indication of an organic causation, impairment may be largely associated with the consequences of extremely limited reading and math skills. For example, money-management problems are a commonly cited difficulty for this subgroup (LaCampagne and Cipani, 1987; McDevitt et al., 1978). On the other hand, the general expectation is that mildly retarded people will achieve independent functioning in adulthood (e.g., Kushlick and Blunden, 1974; Cobb, 1972), although there will be a greater vulnerability to stress of whatever kind. However, where retardation is more than mild in degree, from moderate to profound, the attainment of a fully independent adult adjustment is increasingly improbable. Within these ranges of retardation, academic problems will be compounded by difficulties in the areas of basic self-care, language, socialization, and work.

However, coping difficulty is not only tied to intellectual or emotional problems, it is also much affected by the availability of needed services. The relationship between adaptation and services was stressed in Chapter 2. A moderately retarded young adult, for example, who has had no vocational training nor the opportunity to be employed is likely to be perceived as lacking the *capacity* for work. However, if this individual were given access to vocational training and to sheltered or supported employment, we might suddenly discover a hitherto invisible work potential. It is again stressed that the adaptive potential of retarded or otherwise disabled individuals is as much related to the *opportunities* they have had to develop their resources as it is to the disabilities themselves.

Characterization of retardation only in terms of its disabling aspects, however, is to grossly distort how we come to know, befriend, love, teach, employ, and socialize with these individuals. Retarded individuals are _people_ first, and in our contact with them, over time, the differences or disabilities are muted—they are just another aspect of the person. Indeed, the lack of sophistication in persons who are retarded can be reflected in personal characteristics that we prize but tend to lose with age, such as directness, trust, spontaneity, and gentleness (Wolfensberger, 1988). I remember quite well how impressed I was at the friendliness of the residents of a church-operated farm-residence for retarded adults. And when I think of the retarded adults with whom I bowled in a league, I think only of George and Cliff, my friends. In the context of bowling, it was their bowling skill and general sociability, not their retardation, that was relevant. Indeed, disabilities can become a source of great joy when they are overcome. Success and achievement count for much more when they do not come easily. Marcia, the mother of 4-year-old Emily, a child with tuberous sclerosis, had this to say:

> Emily's first doctor painted a very bleak picture. That was devastating. We thought she was going to be a vegetable, a blob that would never sit up. You're told they aren't going to do anything, so when she learned to walk on time we were beside ourselves. When she was about a year old the whole family was here and she took a step toward my nephew. You could have heard everybody scream all over Durham. The roof could have come off this house. (Kosterman, 1987, p. 11)

The "peopleness" of a retarded child with Down syndrome and his mother's love for him are seen in the following letter sent to a newspaper. In part, it illustrates the quality of spontaneity noted above.

> If this turns out to be a Pollyanna-like story, I hope no one reads it, or else reads it and writes a nasty letter. Being a Pollyanna can be tolerated in some instances I suppose, but never in regard to retardation. And that's what this is about, mental retardation, or more precisely, certain feelings I have toward my eight-year-old son who is mentally retarded.
>   Now believe me, I have had my moments of weeping and despair. When I first learned that our baby, that rosy, dimpled infant was retarded, I almost died of agony. The doctors were wrong [grief and denial are common initial reactions to catastrophic events]. . . . Our Ben couldn't be what they said, a child with Down's syndrome . . . a mongoloid. But he was, and he is, and that's a primary fact of his life and ours [ultimate acceptance of reality]. Today Ben is a sturdy eight-year-old. And I sometimes find tears in my eyes at the sight of him trying to keep up with his neighborhood peers who are so brightly normal, but I more often find myself smiling, sometimes even belly-laughing at the sheer exuberance with which this child faces life. The very idea for writing this at all is that not an hour ago I witnessed the most ecstatic, uninhibited reaction to a fried chicken TV commercial that any sponsor could hope for in his wildest dreams. Who else can raise his arms in gustatory

triumph over a dancing chicken and shout, "Wow!" in such a way as Ben? What an ability to translate the mundane into something terrific! It gives his life an added flavor at every turn.

He is lucky, this little boy of mine. He will not conquer the worlds of the academic, the scientific, or the great doers. But he has a unique appreciation for those ordinary rites of life that seem only dull and jaded to the rest of us. And it goes way beyond fried chicken. The neighbor's dog comes loping by covered with mud from a nearby creek and all we see is one big messy mutt. But Ben sees a friend, and they sit on the walk together, Ben's arms around the dog's neck, dog licking Ben's face; sheer joy in one another. We go to the ocean and contemplate its vast magnificence. The ocean fills a hole Ben has dug in the sand. "Beat it, ocean," says Ben. Around 3:20 every afternoon the front door bangs open and various articles are dropped on the floor. "I'm back, Mommie," shouts Ben and comes to give me my home-again hug. . . .

One recent Saturday morning the whole family had slept late, and as my husband and I were struggling awake, Ben came into our room to say good morning. He looked at his stubble-chinned, disheveled father and in the tone of a true believer announced, "Daddy is Prince Charming." At that moment I could see more of a resemblance to Godzilla but Ben saw Prince Charming. And then he turned to me—a half-unconscious Phyllis Diller—and said, "Mommie is the Sleeping Beauty." How wonderful to wake to laughter. And how wonderful to live with someone who can look at a couple of creaky parents and see a prince and a princess.

Pollyanna, go fly a kite.

But, Ben . . ., oh how I love you! (*Mental Retardation News*, 1976)

INFANCY AND EARLY CHILDHOOD (BIRTH TO 6 YEARS)

In infancy and early childhood, retardation results in a slower rate of development—in the self-care skills of feeding, dressing, and toileting; in language; in understanding; and in social and motor skills. It is the slower rate of development that causes the child to appear immature, since his or her developmental level is more like that of a child who is younger. This is the phenomenon earlier described in terms of the 6-year-old first grader who is functioning more like a 4-year-old.

The early years are also important in personality development, in how the child comes to feel about himself or herself and relates to others. In large measure this will be the result of the degree to which parents/care givers provide experiences that foster self-esteem—intimacy, success, and autonomy.

Chapter 1 noted that a child's disability may interfere with normal parental bonding or attachment and thus threaten the child's need for intimacy (see Self-Esteem: Intimacy). Parents frequently see their children as psychological extensions of themselves (Ryckman and Henderson, 1965). Thus young children with characteristics in which parents take pride, e.g., beauty, learning ability (intelligence), and speech, elevate parental self-esteem, and the converse is true when the child's characteristics are culturally undesirable. Coming to terms with a painful reality can take time. Witness, for example, Ben's mother's initial agony, grief, and attempt at denial in the preceding quotation. Where the parents have reasonable mental health, reality is ultimately accepted, although there may be a residual of sorrow (Olshansky, 1962) and an unquenchable hope that something can make the child normal. Parents who have the greatest difficulty in accepting the reality of their child's retardation are vulnerable to so-called purveyors of cure or diagnosticians who tell them what they want to hear. However, the likelihood of a relatively conflict-free parental attachment is least where extraordinary value is placed on the very abilities that the child lacks. Thus extremely achievement-oriented parents, more often the father, may have great difficulty in accepting their retarded child. The effect is to make the child more dependent on the mother or other care givers for intimacy and to render the child generally more sensitive to criticism and rejection.

Admittedly, the rearing of a seriously retarded child does create stresses that are unknown to parents of normal children (e.g., Gabel, McDowell, and Cerreto, 1983). Apart from the psychological stresses already noted, there are a prolongation of the usual period of childhood dependency, possible health problems and their attendant financial as well as mental demands, uncertainty about the future, possible dearth of needed services, a sense of isolation from others, and a more or less continuous pressure on one's coping abilities. In general, these stresses are greatest in families of children with severe or profound retardation, major health and motor disorders, and persistent behavior problems (Blacher, Nihira, and Meyers, 1987; Dunst, Trivette, and Cross, 1986; Minnes, 1988).

Let's look at the experience of Clara and Jim, parents of a child with medical problems and delayed development. Both illustrate common psychological stresses in their families, especially where the nature of the disorder is not immediately evident. More often it is not until about age 2 that a diagnosis of mental retardation is reasonably firmly established. Prior to this, there is likely to be prolonged uncertainty (lack of structure), a questioning of often "reassuring" professionals, and a more or less continuous state of anxiety and tension.

> When Bobby was born I [Clara] beamed as the pediatrician wrote 100 percent normal infant [pride in having produced a presumably normal child and elevation in self-esteem]. I was not prepared for what the future would bring.
>
> Bobby's first 3 years were like a roller-coaster ride. We experienced our share of grief and uncertainty [depression and anxiety]. Bobby was diagnosed as having tuberous sclerosis at 7 months of age [a dominantly inherited condition referred to earlier in the section on biological causes]. We were in disbelief as the neurologist gave us the diagnosis. Jim and I went through an immediate grieving process for Bobby [mourning for the child that was not]

and for his uncertain future [What will become of him? Why did this happen to him and to us? Who can help us?]. The security of our normal daily routines was gone [a clear example of the loss of structure in their lives; stability is replaced by turmoil].

Bobby had seizures during his first year and underwent medical treatment for it. He began to walk at 16 months [a little delayed], but in the latter half of his second year significant delays in development were evident.

We lived in a large city but knew no other family with the same disorder, and we felt very isolated [the sense of being alone with one's tragedy is very common]. I didn't want to be with friends who had young children [by avoiding them she is adding to her sense of isolation].

When Bobby was 2 we found a preschool program for him and other families with retarded children. They had very positive attitudes toward their children's prospects and represented an extremely important "support" group for us. Although the causes of our children's disabilities were different, we shared the common bond of not being alone and we could learn from their experience in dealing with our own. [In North Carolina, the tuberous sclerosis chapter has established a statewide information and support network for parents.]

At age 5, Bobby attends a special school in the morning and receives language and occupational therapies at home in the afternoon. He has a tutor and enjoys a therapeutic riding program. Outwardly he doesn't seem to perceive himself as different from other children. [Most of the people around him are "normal," and they become the mirror in which he sees himself. This is also strikingly apparent in the self-images of children with serious physical abnormalities, which is illustrated in Chapter 5.] He loves to ride bikes, play in the sandbox, swings on tires, look at books, play with cars and trucks, and paint at the easel.

I feel that we've adjusted fairly well [as do most parents]. The milestones any child achieves are a source of pride in any family [the child as a source of pride and self-esteem for the parents], and those of Bobby are an even greater source of pride [for him and his parents] because they require such an effort. While the stress of a "special needs" child is emotionally and financially exhausting, the sharing of decisions about Bobby has made Jim and me work very hard to try to make the right decisions. This has been a very positive experience [we learn about our own capacities when they are stressed]. We've drawn from each other's strengths. [Those families who have specifically chosen to adopt a retarded child are positive about the adoption and tend to view themselves as better persons for doing so.] (Glidden, Valliere, and Herbert, 1988)

SCHOOL AGE

Academic Concerns

The school years are a particularly important period in the life of a retarded child because it is then, if not before, that the extent of the cognitive disability become clearest. The retarded child will not make normal school progress. It is the academic area that is always affected by retardation, and it was the associated school learning difficulties that led to the development of modified educational programs, so-called special education. Among retarded children, it is usually only the mildly retarded (educable) youngster who will achieve some basic reading and arithmetic skills, although the average level of attainment is only third grade (Gunzburg, 1968). Third-grade skills are hardly functional for activities of daily living. Reading a newspaper requires about a sixth-grade achievement level, while at least fourth-grade arithmetic competency is required for even the simplest daily money-management activities. Money-management problems were mentioned earlier as one of the most common difficulties for mildly retarded adults. Moderately retarded young people usually do not achieve beyond a first-grade level, although some do acquire functional reading skills. The education of the "trainable" pupil is nonacademic in emphasis and stresses the continued development of self-help, language, social, and motor skills. These same nonacademic areas will be the focus of educational programs for severely and profoundly retarded children, a population only recently served in the public schools.

Social Issues

The school years are a very important period in a child's social development. In the nondisabled youngster, school provides a time for loosening ties with parents and intensifying those with peers—first with same-sex peers and then opposite-sex peers. The same pattern is seen in retarded children, although at a slower rate. During adolescence in particular, efforts by retarded children to achieve greater autonomy, to define themselves, and to express sexuality can be particularly troublesome and create conflicts with parents (Zetlin and Turner, 1985).

Opposite-sex interest is common in mildly and moderately retarded youth, although in the latter it is likely to have a particularly immature quality. Where the retardation is severe or profound, there may be relatively little interest in peers and sexuality, when expressed, tends to be limited to masturbation.

Conflicts over autonomy and the resultant adolescent rebellion are undoubtedly more common and more intense in nondisabled youth than in those with retardation, but they are still present. Mildly retarded adolescents frequently demand greater freedom than their parents are willing to give. As with normal children, the effect is one of frustration and an increase in behavior problems. For the parent of a child with a cognitive disability that interferes with the capacity for age-appropriate decision making, however, loosening of the reins is bound to be unnerving. There is uncertainty regarding the child's future adult role, and this interferes with the normal parental function of helping the teenage child make the transition to adulthood. Parents in this situation are more likely to encourage dependency, obedience, and childlike behavior rather than independence, self-direction, and personal responsibility (Paulson and Stone, 1973; Zetlin and Turner, 1985).

A central feature of adolescence is the clarification of who one is, the defining of self (Erikson, 1968). In a study of 25 mildly retarded adults, all of whom came from normal family backgrounds, the great majority (84 percent) reported that it was during adolescence that they became aware of their "differentness" and the effect of their social identity (as "retarded") on their lives (Zetlin and Turner, 1985).

Adolescence represented the beginning of their coming to terms with their school learning difficulties. For the first time they began to identify themselves in terms of their disability—as "slow learners" (a less demeaning label than "retarded"). This realization was, nevertheless, damaging to their self-esteem; they felt as though they were failures. As a part of this coming to terms, these adolescents and their parents began to recognize that their long-held expectations or hopes for normalcy might not be realized. These adolescents wanted to do the same things as their siblings and nonretarded peers, aspirations that produced frustration when, for example, a younger sibling was accomplishing things they themselves had not yet achieved. There is no more important goal to the person who is different than to be perceived as normal, as just like everyone else. It is this hope that is most likely to be dashed with the growing self-awareness of adolescence.

Another aspect of the painfulness of the situation for these retarded adolescents relates to intimacy, the need for acceptance. Of this group of young adults, about two-thirds (68 percent) reported rejection by family members or peers. Some saw themselves as a disappointment to their parents or as being held in lower regard than their siblings. They felt that they were less loved than their brothers and sisters.

Rejection by peers was even more common (Luftig, 1988). Most reported experiences of being teased and taunted by schoolmates and neighborhood children. Some also were beaten up. Examples of the price one pays in our society for disability are found throughout this book—notably in this chapter and in the chapter on cerebral palsy (Chapter 5). Experiences of rejection, however, are not necessarily tied only to childhood. About a quarter (23 percent) of these retarded adolescents were unhappy that, unlike their normal peers, they had no boyfriend or girlfriend. Their feelings were summed up in one young man's appraisal: "You were looked down upon as a person with not too much intelligence or smarts, *(diminished self-worth)* and what people were trying to tell you was 'too bad you couldn't live in our world and too bad you couldn't be and act like us.' I felt very much left out of it."

Vocational Concerns

During the later part of the school years, vocational considerations loom. The serious academic limitations of the retarded student will reduce the possibilities for any postsecondary education as well as for formal vocational training. Many trades require reading and arithmetic skills as well as manual abilities. Those mildly retarded young people who are physically normal, however, can develop some craft-related skills and have been employable as helpers in some trades (DiMichael, 1964).

Nevertheless, despite minimal academic skills, most mildly and moderately retarded young people are employable, the former in regular though unskilled jobs and the latter in sheltered employment (Kiernan, McGaughey, and Schalock, 1988). The supported competitive employment thrust of the 1980s has demonstrated that with support, moderately and even some severely retarded individuals are capable of working in regular jobs, typically in food and janitorial/custodial services[5] (Kregel, Hill, and Banks, 1988; Wehman and Kregel, 1989).

Wherever mentally retarded young people are employed, vocational success depends in part on the presence of good work-related social behaviors—punctuality, reliability, cooperativeness, the ability to follow directions, and the ability to accept supervision (Menchetti and Rusch, 1988; Rusch et al., 1982). The fostering of these behaviors is an important school objective, as is instruction in the nonvocational skills necessary for community living—health, safety, shopping, use of public transportation, money management, telephone use, household skills, and recreation.

The employability of even profoundly retarded individuals has been demonstrated on an experimental basis (Bellamy, Peterson, and Close, 1975; Gold, 1973). This involves breaking down assembly tasks into their most elementary components, "chaining" them, and teaching persistence and speed, primarily through the use of rewards contingent on production.

Parental/Care Giver Stresses

In the school years, adolescence is the time that is likely to exert the most stress on parents. The demands of retarded adolescents for greater independence, including access to girlfriends and boyfriends, have been mentioned. The emergence of sexuality is particularly anxiety evoking. Parents fear exploitation of their children and/or pregnancy, and frequently either deny that their children have sexual feelings or

---

[5]Personal communication: The jobs held by these individuals were described to the author in a letter from Kregel.

excessively restrict and limit their exposure to situations that might encourage such feelings.

These various tensions of adolescence press very hard on parents who are now perhaps less hopeful of any dramatic future changes in their children's status. The parents, too, must come to terms with the child's disability, and at a developmental stage when there tends to be less support from community agencies than was available when their child was much younger. The generally diminished support to families of older retarded (and otherwise disabled) persons will be discussed again later in relation to postschool adjustment.

Roger Meyers is a mildly retarded young man whose life was described by his brother in a newspaper series on mental retardation. The focus here will be limited to Roger's schooldays.

Roger first attended private school; this was followed by public school and some private tutoring. The parents thought that Roger had more ability than his tests indicated and they sought to stimulate his development by giving him as many "real life" experiences as possible.

His father, an advertising executive, took Roger to the rodeo, the circus, and to his office on Saturdays. His mother spent hours with him on his school work and socialization—making sure he knew the importance of personal appearance and teaching him to brush his teeth and comb his hair.

In school he was teased and he'd say, "Well Mom, I hate to tell you this, but they're making fun of me again." He was laughed at because he couldn't keep up with peers or because of his speech impediment. A gang made him sing and dance to their jeers. Cornered by kids at a park, they made him take off his clothes. [Some people are often cruel to those who are "different," and use this difference to bolster their self-esteem. Is it any wonder that a retarded person wants to be considered "normal"?]

His mother sought support from a school guidance counselor, but all he could suggest was that Roger be sent to a state institution for the retarded ["resolving" the teasing and harassment problems]. The mother was furious at the recommendation. "All the work I'd done with him, every book I taught him to read, all of his manners—to throw everything away in some place where he'd be taunted and sexually abused and placed in a corner (an earlier image of institutional life)—never, I never for one minute considered it. I wouldn't have been able to live with myself. I could barely live with myself as it was" [there was continuous stress on the parents, especially the mother].

Roger was becoming a young man, handsome, and willing to tell everyone he met that he was retarded. He liked movies and sports on TV, especially golf, "perhaps because it is a game of understandable moves." He spent most of his time at home.

He'd become interested in girls and wrote a Valentine's Day poem to a girl who at the same time received an obscene letter. Although the most explicit line in Roger's poem was, "A Valentine is sweet, because its sharing warm, affectionate love," a subsequent police investigation labeled him as the prime suspect. It was thought by one of the policemen that because he was retarded he was supposed to be "different." (*The Washington Post*, Aug. 22, 1977. Reprinted with permission.)

ADULTHOOD

Adjustment in adulthood in our culture is measured by the degree to which we can live independently, work, use leisure time, fulfill roles as spouse and parent, and conform to community mores. As in the pre-adult years, the quality of this adjustment is much affected by the degree of retardation, as well as by the availability of support services.

Mildly Retarded Adults

Mildly retarded individuals have the capacity to meet most normal standards for an adequate adult adjustment. They are capable of living independently, working, marrying, using leisure time, and presenting no special behavior problems (Edgerton and Bercovici, 1976; Richardson, 1978; Zetlin and Turner, 1985). Major adaptive obstacles pertain to managing money, job vulnerability during periods of economic hardship, and social isolation. Social isolation relates to the likelihood of fewer friends and a lower rate of marriage—a more socially isolated existence. This was mentioned earlier in a mental health context—the common complaint of loneliness in persons with depression.

In some sense, the population of "mildly retarded adults" is a residual one. A substantial proportion of individuals so classified at school age disappear from the mentally retarded rolls as adults because of the adequacy of their adjustment. These people will commonly be the non-organic segment of the retarded population, persons coming from families with similarly affected individuals and generally functioning at lower socioeconomic levels. The residual mildly retarded group is made up of individuals with some evident or presumed organic impairment, and these individuals are found in families at all levels of the socioeconomic spectrum. It is chiefly this population that will continue to receive services from community agencies serving the developmentally disabled; these individuals represent only about 20 percent of the population with IQs in the 55 to 69 range.

The adjustment of this group has been studied by Zetlin and Turner (1985). In their late twenties or thirties, such individuals were all living independently. Over half had been or were married at the time, and about two-thirds were employed, primarily in regular job settings. Some were maintaining a fully adult-like adjustment. They were handling their daily affairs without assistance, and turned to parents or others only in crisis. They took particular pride in their independence and self-sufficiency (success and autonomy). They were comfortable with who they were, and felt no special need to deny their disability. Indeed, their focus was on their ability rather than on their disability.

Another group, apparently equally comfortable with the quality of their lives, was virtually totally dependent. Although living on their own, these individuals looked to parents for guidance in all aspects of their lives. They were comfortable with this dependence, as were their parents; it was considered necessary. Less mature than the first group described, their interpersonal relationships were more volatile. Nearly half were married, although the marriages were unstable; the rest yearned for heterosexual relationships, but these were incompatible with their family-dependent lifestyle. Less comfortable with their identities, these individuals tended to deny their retardation or to redefine it in a less stigmatizing fashion. Indeed, retarded persons at all levels of adjustment generally seek to avoid being identified as retarded, the earlier-described Roger notwithstanding, and prefer to describe themselves as persons with difficulties in learning.

A third and smaller group was conflicted about its adjustment. Although heavily dependent on family and service agencies, these individuals resented attempts to intervene in their lives. Typically unemployed, they seemed indifferent to work. Their social relationships also were unstable. Particularly defensive about their dependent status, they tended to deny their mental disability. Although they felt stigmatized by their situation, they were not prepared to take constructive steps to alter it. As a group, they were unhappy, a condition that also was true in their adolescence, when, unlike their better-adjusted counterparts, they were much more rebellious. It would appear that their pattern of behavior during adolescence had persisted into adulthood.

Zetlin and Turner summarize their findings with the observation that for most of the people studied, achieving independent living, acquiring possessions, managing their daily affairs, working, and maintaining heterosexual relationships contributed to their self-esteem. Such individuals saw themselves as functioning in the world pretty much like everybody else. Indeed, as an adult, Roger Meyers observed, "Getting married is like coming out of retardation."

In a subsequent study, Zetlin and Turner (1988) describe a group of largely mildly retarded adults who are functioning at a much more dependent level. Residing with their parents, accepting their dependent status as justified by their limitations, seemingly primarily concerned with pleasing their parents, and conveying a childlike endorsement of social rules (e.g., "I can't talk to strangers," "I can't say no dirty words"), the impression is that their continued residence with parents into adulthood has allowed them to maintain a childlike self-image. How the setting in which we function can shape our abilities and self-concept is illustrated in the following self-description of a young adult.

A formerly institutionalized 26-year-old man describes what being retarded has meant to him. Although reported to have an IQ of 49, this man currently functions well beyond that level.

I never thought of myself as retarded . . . but who would want to [avoiding the stigma]. You get a feeling from people around you. . . . You get the feeling that they love you but they are looking down at you. . . .

What is retardation? I guess it's having a problem thinking. Some people think that you can tell if a person is retarded by looking at them. . . . You judge a person by how they look or talk or what the tests show but you can never tell what is inside them. . . .

I don't know. Maybe I used to be retarded. That's what they said anyway. I wish they could see me now [*the former institutional staff*] holding down a regular job [pride] and doing all kinds of things [he was living in a group home at the time]. I bet they wouldn't believe it. (Bogdan and Taylor, 1976, pp. 50 and 51)

As just noted, the settings in which we live and work evoke their own sets of behaviors and expectations. It is only when the settings and expectations change that the possibility for previously unseen potential can emerge.

Moderately to Profoundly Retarded Adults

Although the ranges of moderate to profound retardation cover a wide span of abilities and adaptation, they have in common the probability that a fully independent adjustment will not be attained. Some degree of dependency, at least in the residential domain, is typical. It is, in fact, this segment of the retarded population that in adulthood, as earlier, meets the disability criteria warranting the designation as developmentally disabled.

Within the range of moderate to profound retardation, striking differences in adaptation are found. Moderately retarded adults are often employed, typically in sheltered workshops or day activity programs, although the supported employment thrust of the 1980s is sure to increase their access to jobs in regular work settings. Social relationships are also sought, although these usually do not include marriage and parenthood. For some, leisure time may be primarily spent in solitary activity (Stanfield, 1973). Like their less disabled mildly retarded counterparts, however, these individuals can be expected to eventually acquire relatively complete self-care skills—feeding, dressing, bathing, and toileting.

At the levels of severe and profound retardation, the degrees of dependency are proportionately greater. Sufficiency in self-care is reduced, and there may appear to be little interest in peer relationships, especially in profoundly retarded individuals. Communication skills are very limited, especially in speech; solitary activities may be preferred;

and capacities for productive work are absent without special training. It is interesting to note, however, that experimental training programs have revealed that some profoundly retarded adults, those with mental ages of less than 4 years, can learn to perform simple assembly-type jobs at a level comparable to that of nondisabled workers (Bellamy, Inman, and Yeates, 1978). This type of training takes time and judicious use of rewards (reinforcers), but learning does occur, and in the end, the progress is frequently amazing. The great lesson that I learned from these demonstrations is that our tendency is always to underestimate what retarded or otherwise disabled people can do because it is the disability rather than their abilities that first captures our attention. It is only as we get to know such people better that the strangeness or deficit tends to fade into a more wholistic picture of the person; one that allows us to be aware of what the person can as well as cannot do. This issue is made clear by a disabled person himself, the 26-year-old man who earlier described his sense of what it meant to be retarded. Here he is referring to two of his friends.

> Take a couple of friends of mine. Tommy McCann and P.J. Tommy was a guy who was nice to be with. You could have a nice conversation with him. He was a mongoloid. The trouble was people couldn't see beyond that. If he didn't look that way, it would have been different, but then he was locked into what other people thought he was *(judging him by his appearance)*. Now P.J. was really something else. I've watched that guy and I can see in his eyes that he's aware. He knows what's going on. He can only crawl and he doesn't talk, but you don't know what's inside [an individual's physical and mental disabilities dominate our perception of him or her]. When I was with him . . . I watched him, I know that he knows. (Bogdan and Taylor, 1976, p. 50)

Increasingly, interest has been directed toward the elderly segment of the retarded adult population. It is now seen that these individuals also need access to noninstitutional residential options, day activity, medical services, and such programs as physical and occupational therapy (Janicki and MacEachron, 1984; Krauss and Seltzer, 1986). In the elderly retarded population, persons with Down syndrome appear to be particularly at risk (Silverstein et al., 1988; Zigman et al., 1987), especially after age 50. By their thirties, there is evidence in them of the kinds of abnormal brain changes seen in Alzheimer's disease (Burger and Vogel, 1973), although the behavioral effects are less striking. There does not appear to be the same degree of impairment in memory and personal habits, however, as found in Alzheimer patients with presumably comparable brain abnormalities (Miniszek, 1983; Wisniewski and Rabe, 1986; Zigman et al., 1987). This is most puzzling and deserves to be confirmed, since speculations as to the reasons for the purported difference are unconvincing.

Parent/Care Giver Concerns

Adulthood carries its own special concerns for families or care givers. Movement out of school programs, by law available to all, should be followed by transition into work or day activity programs. However, there is no federal or state law that requires a postschool program, and if none is available or existing ones are full, the young adult is thrown back on the care giver for what is, in effect, full-time supervision. This, of course, will not be true of mildly retarded adults, who can live and function relatively independently, but it will be so at the moderate to profound levels of retardation. For now-older parents, a return to the role that was appropriate in their child's preschool years is likely to be less acceptable and may, ultimately, encourage out-of-home placement. In any case, as parents age, they eventually must consider other care arrangements and plan for their child's future economic, social, and legal protection.

SERVICE NEEDS OF SPECIAL CONCERN

PREVENTION

Drugs and Pregnancy

The effects of fetal exposure to drugs and alcohol are well documented and call for strong educational programs directed toward young adults. Drugs can affect the fetus in a variety of ways, including causing structural malformations, growth retardation, neonatal addiction, alterations of the genitals, and developmental abnormalities (e.g., Gal and Sharpless, 1984). About 15 percent of drug users are at risk (Lipsitt, 1989). Hysteria is not warranted, but prudence and caution are in order.

Chorion Biopsy

It is anticipated that this prenatal diagnostic procedure will eventually supplant amniocentesis. The procedure involves chromosomal study of cells from the outermost fetal membrane, the chorion, and can be done earlier in the pregnancy. Results are also available much more quickly, thus reducing the period of parental anxiety. To the degree that the procedure can be carried out earlier in the pregnancy, earlier and safer abortion is facilitated if prospective parents so choose.

Exposure to Lead

Exposure to high blood levels of lead in a child can lead to severe neurologic and cognitive impairment. In fact, even low to moderate levels of exposure can produce neurobehavioral effects. It has now been shown that blood lead levels heretofore regarded as safe can have an adverse effect on general intelligence (Hawk et al., 1986).

THE PRESCHOOL YEARS

The Right to Live

The "Baby Doe" episodes of recent years reflect the kinds of threats incurred by the child born with probable brain damage and life-threatening health problems (Ellis and Luckasson, 1986; Turnbull, 1986). In 1983, the federal government sought to prevent medical abuse and neglect of newborns through regulations, but these were deemed invalid by the Supreme Court (Turnbull, Guess, and Turnbull, 1988). Thus, parents and physicians may elect to withhold rigorous treatment on the grounds that the future quality of life of the child will be so unsatisfactory that efforts to preserve it should not be made. This decision appears to relate to the expected mental retardation and reveals the extraordinary value that our culture places on intelligence. Other justifications may include the stresses that the child may place on the parents—emotional and even monetary.

Granting the reality of these stresses and our undoubted preference for healthy babies, to choose to allow an infant to die because of likely retardation is to take a societal step in population control whose end cannot be foreseen. The Nazi experience is a chilling reminder of where our capacity to rationalize actions can lead us. The ethical dilemmas posed here are similar in principle to those created by extraordinary life-sustaining advances in medical technology. Given finite economic resources, our society will be increasingly beset with questions of who is to survive. Current discussions of the "rationing of health care" as a means of containing exploding medical costs associated with new technology is an aspect of this dilemma.

Home-Based Infant-Parent Training

One of the great boons to parents of children with serious disabilities is early access to knowledgeable professionals. Parents particularly value professionals who come to their homes and provide guidance and emotional support to them and training for the infant. Physical and occupational therapy for the motor-impaired infant and various forms of sensory, cognitive, and language stimulation are the kinds of activities that can foster development. The federal initiative of 1986 (Public Law 99-457) seeks to encourage these services as well as mandating programs for 3- to 5-year-olds by 1991 if the state is to be eligible for federal assistance in their funding.

Respite Care

Another great aid for parents in coping with the stresses of rearing a handicapped infant or young child at home is access to individuals who provide occasional relief from day-to-day caregiving responsibilities. In a survey of parents of retarded children of all ages, nearly half (47 percent) stated that without respite care they would seriously consider out-of-home placement (Apolloni and Triest, 1983). From the family's perspective, it may be the largest unmet service need (Sherman, 1988). While short-term respite care in the home is the most common type provided, out-of-home short-term respite placement in community or institutional residential settings is also an option. Respite users tend to be parents of children with more severe degrees of retardation and greater behavior problems (Marc and MacDonald, 1988). Older parents tend to be more interested in short-term out-of-home care than younger ones (Lutzer and Brubaker, 1988). In an interesting and successful program, teenagers were recruited and trained as "special sitters" for retarded preadolescents (Edgar, Reid, and Pious, 1988).

Parent and Sibling Counseling

Parents of retarded children need long-term access to a knowledgeable and caring professional as well as to other parents experiencing similar stresses. Sources of this type of assistance include social workers in regional developmental disability programs and parent groups. The latter are often provided for parents whose children are in a developmental preschool or by the local affiliate of the National Association of Retarded Citizens. Sibling groups also can be found and appear to be particularly helpful during the normal sibling's(s') adolescence (Grossman, 1972).

THE SCHOOL YEARS

Mainstreaming and Meeting Curriculum Objectives

In educational parlance, *mainstreaming* refers to serving handicapped students in classes that most nearly approximate those of nonhandicapped children. Apart from educational considerations, there also has been much interest in encouraging social interactions between handicapped and nonhandicapped students (Brinker and Thorpe, 1986).

Educable Student Concerns. For students with mild retardation, mainstreaming has meant at least part-time placement in regular classes rather than the traditional self-contained special classes. Since the educational problems of retarded pupils relate to their disability and not to their placement, such students will continue to need academic assistance, and this is typically provided in a resource class during part of the day. One of the concerns about mainstreaming was the possible loss of the educational goals traditionally stressed in special education (Childs, 1979; Gottlieb, 1981). These goals have been as much social and vocational as academic. Student needs have not changed, but the mechanism for their provision has. Resource classes and distributive (vocational) education must now assume the major responsibility for meeting these goals.

Trainable Student Concerns. For students with upper-level severe and moderate retardation, full-time special class placement continues to be the norm, although some states, e.g., Washington, have insisted on their being mainstreamed as well. Since these students are capable of at least sheltered employment, teachers need to inculcate the requisite work-related social behaviors. These behaviors need not only be taught in a vocational context but can be fostered in all aspects of the educational experience and beginning in the early grades.

Severely/Profoundly Retarded Student Concerns. Previously not served in public schools at all, these students now have access to a number of programs. In smaller population areas, the number of such students may be so small as to not warrant a class as such, and they may be placed in developmental day care centers. While the educational focus of developmental day care programs may be appropriate to goals for severely and profoundly retarded students, at the older ages, such preschool placements may be inappropriate as they convey a childlike image of the now older youngster or adolescent.

Sex Education

Referred to in Chapter 1, (see Self-Esteem Effects in School Age and in Adulthood) here I simply wish to reiterate the importance of sexuality and sex education for retarded individuals (also see Abramson, Parker, and Weisberg, 1988). It is ironic that the very population about whom there is the greatest ambivalence with regard to sex education is the one in greatest need of it. Whether in community or institutional settings, retarded individuals have less opportunity to acquire a realistic understanding of their sexual selves than is true of their nonhandicapped peers. Without proper sex education, these people are at risk for inappropriate behavior and sexual exploitation or interpersonal rejection (Edmonson, 1980).

In a review of sex education for retarded youth, Johnson (1973) points out the need for an instructor who is comfortable with the teaching content and its everyday vocabulary. Gordon (1973), a well-known sex ed-ucator, suggests teaching (1) that masturbation is a normal mode of expression, (2) that all genital sexual behavior is to be expressed in pri-vate, (3) that sexual intercourse between physically mature individuals carries with it the risk of pregnancy (as well as venereal disease and AIDS) and that intercourse before age 18 is inappropriate, and (4) that sexual activity between adults and children is impermissible.[6] Gordon adds that the only way to discourage homosexual activity is to risk het-erosexual expression.

Studies of the impact of sex education on retarded individuals indi-cate a greater readiness to discuss sexual feelings and some increase in masturbation (Kempton, 1978). Of particular interest was a program for trainable young people—ages 12 to 18, IQs of 35 to 54 (Hamre-Nietupski and Williams, 1977). Its emphasis was on providing knowledge about sexuality. The adolescents involved were able to comprehend bodily dis-tinctions, appropriate social behaviors, and concepts of personal hy-giene. Understanding of reproduction was less complete.

Behavior Problems

With the deinstitutionalization thrust of the 1970s and 1980s, a particu-larly visible segment of the retarded population in community settings are those with secondary psychiatric disorders. Discussed in some detail in Chapter 2 (see Mental Health), significant behavioral or personality disorders rank second only to mobility problems as a secondary disabil-ity in mental retardation (Jacobson and Janicki, 1987). A national survey of state services to this dual-diagnosis population revealed widespread discontent with the quality of such services, to some degree, a function of the lack of training in mental retardation on the part of mental health professionals (Jacobson and Ackerman, 1988). Apart from prescribing psychotropic drugs (e.g., Gowdey, Zarfas, and Phipps, 1987), workers in the mental health field have generally avoided serving mentally re-tarded individuals, a problem exacerbated by the intent of mental retar-dation professionals to serve these individuals in community rather than institutional settings.

Within the dual-diagnosis population, problems of aggression are particularly difficult to deal with, and in one state, only a class action suit on behalf of retarded and aggressive young people has moved the mental health authorities to try to serve them. Models for such pro-grams were offered in Chapter 2.

---

[6]Useful training material is found in Kempton and Forman (1976), Edmondson (1980), and Craft (1987).

Apart from the issue of dealing with aggression directed at others, the management of injurious behaviors directed against the self, called self-injurious behavior (SIB), has been especially controversial. Particular concerns have been expressed about the use of treatment procedures that are intended to reduce SIB by punishing the behavior with a response to it that is unavoidably experienced as physically uncomfortable or even painful but not tissue damaging (e.g., Mulick and Kedesdy, 1988). Opponents of punishment stress attempts to understand the condition that tends to evoke it, commonly those of "non-compliance," and then seeking nonpunitive or nonaversive means of altering it. Generally, such measures involve the teaching of alternative behaviors and encouraging their pursuit through the use of rewards, so-called "positive reinforcement" (e.g., LaVigna and Donnellan, 1986).

ADULTHOOD

Day Services

If adulthood, for our purposes, is regarded as commencing with the termination of secondary school, the need for retarded adults is to replace the daily activity of attending school with something else. This typically takes the form of placement in vocational settings and day activity centers (White et al., 1984). Vocational settings (regular competitive employment, supported competitive employment, sheltered workshops, on-the-job training, and work activity centers) primarily serve mildly and moderately retarded individuals. Competitive employment has been largely limited to mildly retarded individuals, although the supported employment initiative will move more moderately retarded persons into such settings (e.g., Wehman, 1988). Sheltered workshops serve both groups about equally. Day activity centers chiefly serve the clearly developmentally disabled segment of the retarded population, those with moderate to profound retardation.

Demonstrating the need for expanded adult services was one study that found that nearly 14 percent had no day program (White et al., 1984). This was predominantly the most impaired segment, those with severe and profound retardation. Of these, nearly half (44 percent) were without any structured daily activity outside their place of residence. The lack of a day placement was variously attributed to lack of availability, health problems, and resident disinterest.

The nonavailability of a day program was epitomized for me by the aged father of a retarded young woman who was seeking assistance in the care of his daughter. The county had a good day activity center, but all the openings in it were filled. It's as if the parents of a kindergarten child had brought her to school to register and were told that all the classroom seats were taken. A caring society should not regard its obligation to its handicapped citizens as ending with high school. Each of us, no matter what our disability, has the right to access to some kind of out-of-home daily activity. It is the most disabled who are least served, and this undoubtedly contributes to some of the behavior disorders they manifest.

Residential Services

If not during adolescence, it will be during the adult years that placement outside the family home becomes more likely. The waning of physical and emotional resources as parents age means that other care givers may eventually be needed. The outcry against earlier abusive institutional care referred to in Chapter 2 (see Residential) and the consequent emphasis on normalization have led to a tremendous growth in community-based residential programs. In 1982, community-based residential programs accounted for about one-third of nonfamily placements, the great majority being in settings serving less than 15 residents (Janicki, Mayeda, and Epple, 1983). These programs also were predominantly housing an adult population, 85 percent of the residents being 18 or older. Along with the mushrooming of community-based residential programs has been a decline in the institutional (public residential facility) population by over 40 percent (see Chapter 2, Residential).

Although concern about the quality of care was the impetus for the deinstitutionalization movement, early mere assertion of the presumed benefits of living in more homelike environments later found support in the research described in Chapter 2 (see Normalization). Two conclusions were drawn: (1) care tends to be more individualized in smaller settings, and (2) community living tends to be associated with gains in adaptive competency.

Community-based residential settings are not without their problems, however. While group homes tend to best serve relatively independent and active young people and family care (foster) homes best serve more sedentary adults, neither is generally prepared to meet the needs of individuals with severe behavior problems. Such persons are more likely to wind up in either mental retardation institutions or psychiatric hospitals. The problem is that the typical range of community-based residential options is too narrow.

An interesting variation on the usual settings involves developing individual residential placements for behaviorally disturbed individuals, autistic as well as retarded. This is done by specifically recruiting and training foster parents to provide a residence for a particular client.[7] The client's behavioral needs are matched with the interests of prospective foster parents. The prospective foster parents have contact with the client and then receive training for a month prior to placement, after which they receive weekly supervision for the first 3 months of placement. The special value of this program is that it takes advantage of existing family homes rather than creating new ones.

The Institutions. A major effect of the growth of community residential programs and of deinstitutionalization has been to change the character of the population of public residential facilities (Scheerenberger, 1982). In particular, the proportion of residents with profound retardation has more than doubled, from 27 percent in the 1960s to 56 percent in the early 1980s. In 1981, in terms of IQ distribution, the levels of retardation in public residential facilities were 7 percent mild, 13 percent moderate, 24 percent severe, and 56 percent profound. Thus 80 percent of this population was in the severely to profoundly retarded range.

Apart from a growing predominance of the more severely impaired in institutions, a second major change has been an increase in the number of patients classified as emotionally disturbed, a whopping 150 percent since the mid-1970s. Attention has already been called to the mental health needs of retarded young people and adults; it is their behavior problems, chiefly aggression, that constitute the single greatest cause of initial institutionalization and of readmission (Hill and Bruininks, 1984; Lakin et al., 1983).

Even with a public residential facility population that has increased in severity of retardation, however, depopulation appears to be continuing, although at a slower pace. In 1981, nearly 12 percent of the public facility residents were moved—nearly half to homes and other, presumably smaller facilities, but also in some numbers to their own homes and to community intermediate-care facilities. Other lesser placements included foster homes, nursing homes, boarding homes, and rest homes. Interestingly, another 4 percent of this population was deemed ready for placement, but there were no alternatives available to them.

Recreation

Apart from a desirable place in which to live and something meaningful to do, retarded adults need the kinds of experiences and pleasures we

---

[7]This concept was outlined in a paper presented at the 1984 annual meeting of the American Association on Mental Deficiency by Marti Cutler, of New Concepts Foundation, 7425 University, Middletown, Wisc. 53562.

call recreation. Chapter 2 (see Recreation) noted that this tends to be the most neglected of the services provided to developmentally disabled persons. The life of the developmentally disabled adult may be inordinately circumscribed by the mental, emotional, or physical impact of the disability. Daily experience may be limited to the place of residence and the day program, and evenings may be restricted to television. Indeed, participation in an outside day program increases use of community recreational resources (Benz, Halperin, and Close, 1986). In some settings there may be little or no opportunity for leisure hour peer experiences. This will be particularly true of adults living at home or in foster family homes. Opportunities for peer experiences are generally greater in group homes. However, under the aegis of a local parks and recreation department, a variety of recreational activities can be provided that greatly enrich the necessarily narrowed lives of these retarded individuals. Indoor activities can include card and table games (Wehman, 1979), creative homemaking, horticulture, and arts and crafts. Outdoor activities can be a mix of vigorous and nonvigorous athletic events, shopping, visiting, gardening and just getting out.

Given increased opportunities for peer interactions, opposite-sex as well as same-sex, retarded young persons and adults will need assistance in their dating relationships. Much attention has been paid here to this aspect of the lives of developmentally disabled people. It is sufficient to reiterate that there is a need for helping them to express their sexual feelings in ways that neither give offense to others nor provide less gratification than we insist upon for ourselves.

Health Services

Within the community-based population of retarded individuals, health services have generally been more available to children than to adults. But four groups of adults living in the community have been found to have special medical needs: those with Down syndrome, elderly individuals, those with severe physical handicaps and seizures, and those with behavioral or psychiatric problems (Rubin, 1987). Ziring (1987) has described an interesting health care program that serves developmentally disabled individuals of all ages through a "developmental disabilities center" at a community hospital. A high level of need was noted in cardiac, endocrine, infectious disease, psychiatric, and genetic areas, with numerous previously undiagnosed conditions identified. The program also provides dental care.

Elderly Persons

Within the population of retarded individuals, no less than in the general population, we can anticipate a rise in the proportion of elderly individuals (Seltzer, 1988). Although society increasingly provides special programs for the nonhandicapped elderly, there is some resistance to broadening this service to include retarded people. The appropriateness of generic aging day programs for retarded individuals has been questioned. Out of this has emerged requests for age-specific social and recreational day programs and for such residential programs as "staffed apartments." As noted in Chapter 2, however, (see The Aged Adult) elderly retarded individuals appear to be making some use of "generic" aging services, those serving the general aged population.

REFERENCES

Achenbach, T. M. (1970). Comparison of Stanford-Binet performance of nonretarded and retarded persons matched for MA and sex. *American Journal of Mental Deficiency, 74,* 488–494.

Abramson, P. R., Parker, T., and Weisberg, S. R. (1988). Sexual expression of mentally retarded people: Educational and legal implications. *American Journal on Mental Retardation, 93,* 328–334.

Alvarez, N. (1989). Discontinuance of antiepileptic medication in persons with developmental disabilities and diagnosis of epilepsy (and commentaries). *American Journal on Mental Retardation, 93,* 593–599, 600–604.

American Psychiatric Association. (1980). *Diagnostic and statistical manual of mental disorders.* Washington, DC: American Psychiatric Association.

Anastasi, A. (1988). *Psychological testing,* 6th Ed. New York: Macmillan.

Anastasi, A., and Levee, R. F. (1960). Intellectual defect and musical talent: A case report. *American Journal of Mental Deficiency, 64,* 695–703.

Anders, T. (1971). Short-term memory for presented supraspan information in nonretarded and mentally retarded individuals. *American Journal of Mental Deficiency, 75,* 571–578.

Apolloni, A. H., and Triest, G. (1983). Respite services in California: Status and recommendations for improvement. *Mental Retardation, 21,* 240–243.

Balla, D., Styfco, S. J., and Zigler, E. (1971). Use of the opposition concept and outer directedness in intellectually average, familial retarded, and organically retarded children. *American Journal of Mental Deficiency, 75,* 663–680.

Barnett, M. L., Press, K. P., Friedman, D., and Sonnenberg, E. M. (1986). The prevalence of periodontitis and dental caries in a Down's syndrome population. *Journal of Periodontology, 57,* 288–293.

Barnett, M. L., Ziring, P., Friedman, D., and Sonnenberg, E. M. (1988). Dental treatment program for patients with mental retardation. *Mental Retardation, 26,* 310–313.

Baroff, G. S. (1959). WISC patterning in endogenous mental deficiency. *American Journal of Mental Deficiency, 64,* 482–485.

Baroff, G. S. (1982). Predicting the prevalence of mental retardation in individual catchment areas. _Mental Retardation, 20,_ 133–135.

Baroff, G. S. (1986). _Mental retardation: Nature, cause, and management,_ 2d Ed. New York: Hemisphere.

Bayley, N. (1970). Development of mental abilities. In P. M. Mussen (Ed.), _Carmichael's manual of child psychology,_ Vol. 1, 3d Ed. New York: Wiley.

Bellamy, G. T., Inman, D. P., and Yeates, J. (1978). Workshop supervision: Evaluation of a procedure for production management with the severely retarded. _Mental Retardation, 16,_ 317–319.

Bellamy, G. T., Peterson, L., and Close, A. (1975). Habilitation of the severely and profoundly retarded: Illustrations of competence. _Education and Training of the Mentally Retarded, 10,_ 174–186.

Belmont, J. M., and Butterfield, E. C. (1971). Learning strategies as determinants of memory deficiencies. _Cognitive Psychology, 2,_ 411–420.

Benson, B. A., Reiss, S., Smith, D. C., and Laman, D. S. (1985). Psychosocial correlates of depression in mentally retarded adults: II. Poor social skills. _American Journal of Mental Deficiency, 89,_ 657–659.

Benz, M., Halpern, A., and Close, D. (1986). Access to day programs and leisure activities by nursing home residents with mental retardation. _Mental Retardation, 24,_ 147–152.

Birch, H. G., Pinuro, C., Atcalde, E., Toca, T., and Cravioto, J. (1971). Relation of kwashiorkor in early childhood to intelligence at school age. _Pediatric Research, 5,_ 579–585.

Blacher, J., Nihira, K., and Meyers, C. E. (1987). Characteristics of home environment of families with mentally retarded children: Comparison across levels of retardation. _American Journal of Mental Deficiency, 91,_ 313–320.

Bogdan, R., and Taylor, S. (1976). The judged, not the judges. _American Psychologist, 31,_ 47–52.

Borkowski, J. G., and Cavanaugh, J. C. (1979). Maintenance and generalization of skills and strategies by the retarded. In N. R. Ellis (Ed.), _Handbook of mental deficiency, psychological theory and research,_ 2d Ed. Hillsdale, NJ: Erlbaum.

Borkowski, J. G., and Turner, L. A. (1988). Cognitive development. In J. F. Kavanaugh (Ed.), _Understanding mental retardation: Research accomplishments and new frontiers._ Baltimore: Paul H. Brookes.

Brinker, R. P., and Thorpe, M. E. (1986). Features of integrated educational ecologies that predict social behavior among severely mentally retarded and nonretarded students. _American Journal of Mental Deficiency, 91,_ 150–159.

Brown, A. L., Campione, J. C., Bray, N. W., and Wilcox, B. C. (1973). Keeping track of changing variables: Effects of rehearsal training and rehearsal prevention in normal and retarded adolescents. _Journal of Experimental Psychology, 101,_ 123–131.

Bruininks, R., McGrew, K., and Maruyama, G. (1988). Structure of adaptive behavior in samples with and without mental retardation. _American Journal of Mental Retardation, 93,_ 265–272.

Burger, P. C., and Vogel, F. S. (1973). The development of the pathologic changes of Alzheimer's disease and senile dementia in patients with Down's syndrome. _American Journal of Pathology, 73,_ 457–476.

Campione, J. C., and Brown, A. L. (1977). Memory and metamemory development in educable retarded children. In R. V. Kail, Jr. and J. W. Hagen (Eds.), _Perspectives on the development of memory and cognition._ Hillsdale, NJ: Erlbaum.

Cattell, R. B. (1963). Theory of fluid and crystallized intelligence: A critical experiment. *Journal of Educational Psychology, 54*, 1–22.

Cattell, R. B., and Horn, J. L. (1978). A check on the theory of fluid and crystallized intelligence with a description of new subtest designs. *Journal of Educational Measurement, 15*, 139–164.

Chamberlin, H. R. (1975). Mental retardation. In T. W. Farmer (Ed.), *Pediatric neurology*, 2d Ed. New York: Harper & Row.

Chess, S., and Hassibi, M. (1970). Behavior deviations in mentally retarded children. *Journal of the American Academy of Child Psychiatry, 9*, 282–287.

Childs, R. E. (1979). A drastic change in curriculum for the educable mentally retarded child. *Mental Retardation, 17*, 299–301.

Cobb, H. V. (1972). *The forecast of fulfillment.* New York: Teacher's College Press.

Corsale, K. (1977). Developmental changes in the use of semantic information for recall. Doctoral dissertation, University of North Carolina at Chapel Hill.

Craft, A. (Ed.) (1987). *Mental handicap and sexuality: Issues and perspectives.* Kent, England: Costello.

Davis, K. (1947). Final note on the case of extreme isolation. *American Journal of Sociology, 52*, 432–437.

Dember, W. N. (1974). Motivation and the cognitive revolution. *American Psychologist, 29*, 161–168.

Detterman, D. K. (1987). Theoretical notions of intelligence and mental retardation. *American Journal of Mental Deficiency, 92*, 2–11.

DiMichael, S. G. (1964). Providing full vocational opportunities for retarded adolescents and adults. *Journal of Rehabilitation, 30*, 11–14.

Dodd, G. (1975). Recognition and reproduction of words by Down's syndrome and non-Down's syndrome retarded children. *American Journal of Mental Deficiency, 80*, 306–311.

Dunst, C. J., Trivette, C. M., and Cross, A. H. (1986). Mediating influences of social support: Personal, family, and child outcomes. *American Journal of Mental Deficiency, 90*, 403–417.

Edgar, E. G., Reid, P. C., and Pious, C. C. (1988). Special sitters: Youth as respite care providers. *Mental Retardation, 26*, 33–37.

Edgerton, R. B., and Bercovici, S. M. (1976). The cloak of competence: Years later. *American Journal of Mental Deficiency, 80*, 485–497.

Edmonson, B. (1980). Sociosexual education for the handicapped. *Exceptional Education Quarterly, 1*, 67–76.

Ellis, N. R. (1969). A behavioral research strategy in mental retardation: Defense and critique. *American Journal of Mental Deficiency, 73*, 557–567.

Ellis, N. R., and Cavalier, A. R. (1982). Research perspectives in mental retardation. In E. Zigler and D. Balla (Eds.), *Mental retardation: The developmental-difference controversy.* Hillsdale, NJ: Erlbaum.

Ellis, N. R., Woodley-Zanthos, P., Dulaney, C. L., and Palmer, R. L. (1989). Automatic-eventful processing and cognitive inertia in persons with mental retardation. *American Journal of Mental Deficiency, 93*, 412–423.

Ellis, J. W., and Luckasson, R. (1986). Denying treatment to infants with handicaps: A comment on *Bowen vs. American Hospital Association. Mental Retardation, 24*, 237–240.

Erickson, E. H. (1968). Identity and identity diffusion. In C. Gordon and K. J. Gergen (Eds.), *The self in social interaction*, Vol. 1. New York: Wiley.

Erlenmeyer-Kimling, L., and Jarvik, L. (1963). Genetics and intelligence: A review. *Science, 142*, 1477–1479.

Ferretti, R. P., and Butterfield, E. C. (1989). Intelligence as a correlate of children's problem solving. *American Journal on Mental Retardation, 95,* 424–433.

Fisher, M. A., and Zeaman, D. (1970). Growth and decline of retardate intelligence. In N. R. Ellis (Ed.), *International review of research and mental retardation,* Vol. 4. New York: Academic Press.

Flavell, J. H. (1963). *The developmental psychology of Jean Piaget.* Princeton, NJ: Van Nostrand.

Fredericksen, N. (1986). Toward a broader conception of human intelligence. *American Psychologist, 41,* 445–452.

Fuller, J. L. (1954). *Nature and nuture: A modern synthesis.* New York: Doubleday.

Gabel, H., McDowell, J., and Cerreto, M. (1983). Family adaptation to the handicapped infant. In S. G. Garwood and R. Fewell (Eds.), *Educating handicapped infants.* Rockville, MD.: Aspen.

Gal, P., and Sharpless, M. K. (1984). Fetal drug exposure: Behavioral teratogenesis. *Drug Intelligence and Clinical Pharmacy, 18,* 186–201.

Glidden, L. M., Valliere, V. N., and Herbert, S. L. (1988). Adopted children with mental retardation: Positive family impact. *Mental Retardation, 26,* 119–125.

Gold, M. W. (1973). Research in the vocational habilitation of the retarded: The present, the future. In N. R. Ellis (Ed.), *International review of research in mental retardation,* Vol. 6. New York: Academic Press.

Gordon, S. (1973). A response to Warren Johnson. In F. F. de la Cruz and G. D. LaVeck (Eds.), *Human sexuality and the mentally retarded.* New York: Brunner/ Mazel.

Gorlin, R. J. (1977). Classical chromosome disorders. In J. J. Yunis (Ed.), *New chromosomal syndromes.* New York: Academic Press.

Gottlieb, J. (1981). Mainstreaming: Fulfilling the promise? *American Journal of Mental Deficiency, 86,* 115–126.

Gowdey, C. W., Zarfas, D. E., and Phipps, S. (1987). Audit of psychoactive drug prescriptions in group homes. *Mental Retardation, 25,* 331–334.

Graham, J., and Poling, J. (1963). Help is a warm puppy. *Ladies Home Journal, 80,* 28.

Grossman, F. D. (1972). *Brothers and sisters of retarded children: An exploratory study.* Syracuse, NY: Syracuse University Press.

Grossman, H. J. (Ed.). (1973). *Manual and terminology and classification in mental retardation* (1st revision). Washington, DC: American Association on Mental Deficiency.

Grossman, H. J. (Ed.). (1977). *Manual on terminology and classification in mental retardation* (2d revision). Washington, DC: American Association on Mental Deficiency.

Grossman, H. J. (Ed.). (1983). *Classification in mental retardation* (3d revision). Washington, DC: American Association on Mental Deficiency.

Guilford, J. P. (1967). *The nature of human intelligence.* New York: McGraw-Hill.

Gunzburg, H. C. (1968). *Social competence and mental handicap.* Baltimore: Williams & Wilkins.

Hamre-Nietupski, S., and Williams, W. (1977). Implementation of selected sex education and social skills to severely handicapped students. *Education and Training of the Mentally Retarded, 12,* 364–372.

Hawk, B. A., Schroeder, S. R., Robinson, G., Otto, D., Mushak, P., Kleinbaum, D., and Dawson, G. (1986). Relation of lead and social factors to IQ of low-SES children: A partial replication. *American Journal of Mental Deficiency, 91,* 178–183.

Henderson, S. E., Morris, J., and Ray, S. (1981). Performance of Down syndrome and other retarded children on the Cratty Gross-Motor Test. *American Journal of Mental Deficiency, 85,* 416–424.

Hill, A. L. (1974). Idiot savants: A categorization of abilities. *Mental Retardation, 12,* 12–13.

Hill, B. K., and Bruininks, R. H. (1984). Maladaptive behavior of mentally retarded individuals in residential facilities. *American Journal of Mental Deficiency, 88,* 380–387.

Hodes, H. H. (1977). Encephalitis. In A. M. Rudolph (Ed.), *Pediatrics,* 16th Ed. New York: Appleton-Century-Crofts.

Hoffman, E. (1971). The idiot savant: A case report and a review of explanations. *Mental Retardation, 9*(4), 18–21.

Hunt, E. (1976). Varieties of cognitive power. In L. B. Resnick (Ed.), *The nature of intelligence.* Hillsdale, NJ: Erlbaum.

Hunt, J. M. (1979). Psychological development: Early experience. *Annual Review of Psychology, 30,* 103–143.

Jacobson, J. W. (1982). Problem behavior and psychiatric impairment in a developmentally disabled population: I. Behavior frequency. *Applied Research in Mental Retardation, 3,* 121–139.

Jacobson, J. W., and Ackerman, L. J. (1989). Psychological services for persons with mental retardation and psychiatric impairments. *Mental Retardation, 27,* 33–36.

Jacobson, J. W., and Janicki, M. P. (1987). Needs for professional and generic services within a developmental disabilities care system. In J. A. Mulick and R. F. Antonak (Eds.), *Transitions in mental retardation, Vol. 2: Issues in therapeutic intervention.* Norwood, NJ: Ablex.

Janicki, M. P., and MacEachron, A. E. (1984). Residential health and social service needs of elderly developmentally disabled persons. *The Gerontologist, 24,* 28–137.

Janicki, M. P., Mayeda, T., and Epple, W. (1983). Availability of group homes for persons with mental retardation in the United States. *Mental Retardation, 21,* 45–51.

Jensen, A. R. (1971). The IQs of MZ twins reared apart. *Behavior Genetics, 2,* 1–10.

Johnson, W. R. (1973). Sex education of the mentally retarded. In F. F. de la Cruz and G. D. LaVeck (Eds.), *Human sexuality and the mentally retarded.* New York: Brunner/Mazel.

Johnston, R. B. (1976). Motor function: Normal development and cerebral palsy. In R. B. Johnston and P. R. Magrab (Eds.), *Developmental disorders: Assessment, treatment, education.* Baltimore: University Park Press.

Jones, K. L., Smith, D. W., Ulleland, C. N., and Streissguth, A. P. (1973). Pattern of malformation in offspring of chronic alcoholic mothers. *Lancet 1,* 1267–1271.

Jordan, T. E. (1967). Language and mental retardation: A review of the literature. In R. Schiefelbusch, R. Copeland, and J. Smith (Eds.), *Language and mental retardation,* New York: Holt, Rinehart and Winston.

Kavanagh, K. T., Kahane, J. C., and Kordan, B. (1986). Risk and benefits of adenotonsillectomy for children with Down syndrome. *American Journal of Mental Deficiency, 91,* 22–29.

Kempton, W. (1978). Sex education for the mentally handicapped. *Sexuality and Disability, 1,* 137–145.

Kempton, W., and Forman, R. (1976). _Guidelines for training in sexuality and the mentally handicapped._ Philadelphia: Planned Parenthood Association of Southeast Pennsylvania.

Kiernan, W. E., McGaughey, M. J., and Schalock, R. L. (1988). Employment environments and outcome for adults with developmental disabilities. _Mental Retardation, 26,_ 279–288.

Kirk, S. A. (1964). Research in education. In H. A. Stevens and R. Heber (Eds.), _Mental retardation: A review of research._ Chicago: University of Chicago Press.

Koller, H., Richardson, S. A., Katz, M., and McLaren, J. (1983). Behavior disturbance since childhood in a five-year birth cohort of all mentally retarded young adults in a city. _American Journal of Mental Deficiency, 87,_ 386–395.

Koluchova, J. (1972). Severe deprivation in twins: A case study of marked IQ change after age 7. _Journal of Child Psychology and Psychiatry, 13,_ 107–114.

Kosterman, C. (1987). Caring for Emily. _Leader_ (Durham, N.C.), 22(9), 10–11.

Krauss, M., and Seltzer, M. M. (1986). Comparison of elderly and adult mentally retarded persons in community and institutional settings. _American Journal of Mental Deficiency, 91,_ 237–243.

Kregel, J., Hill, M., and Banks, P. D. (1988). Analysis of employment specialist intervention time in supported competitive employment. _American Journal on Mental Retardation, 93,_ 200–208.

Kushlick, A., and Blunden, R. (1974). The epidemiology of mental subnormality. In A. M. Clarke and A. D. B. Clarke (Eds.), _Mental deficiency: The changing outlook._ London: Methuen.

LaCampagne, J., and Cipani, E. (1987). Training adults with mental retardation to pay bills. _Mental Retardation, 25,_ 293–303.

Lakin, K. C., Bradley, K. H., Haruber, F. A., Bruininks, R. H., and Heal, L. W. (1983). New admissions and readmissions to a national sample of public residential facilities. _American Journal of Mental Deficiency, 88,_ 13–20.

Lally, M., and Nettlebeck, T. (1977). Intelligence, reaction time and inspection time. _American Journal of Mental Deficiency, 82,_ 273–281.

Landesman-Dwyer, S., Ragozin, A. J., and Little, R. E. (1981). Behavioral correlates of parental alcohol exposure: A four-year follow-up study. _Neurobehavioral Toxicology and Teratology, 3,_ 187–193.

LaVigna, G. W., and Donnellan, A. M. (1986). _Alternatives to punishment: Solving behavior problems with non-aversive strategies._ New York: Irvington Publishers.

Lenneberg, E., Nichols, I., and Rosenberger, E. (1964). Primitive stages of language development in mongolism. _Proceedings of the Association for Research in Nervous and Mental Disorders, 42,_ 119–137.

Lipsitt, L. P. (1989). Fetal development in the drug age. _The Brown University Child Behavior and Development Letter, 5,_ 1–3.

Luftig, R. L. (1988). Assessment of the perceived school loneliness and isolation of mentally retarded and nonretarded students. _American Journal on Mental Retardation, 92,_ 472–475.

Lutzer, V. D., and Brubaker, T. H. (1988). Differential respite needs of aging parents of individuals with mental retardation. _Mental Retardation, 26,_ 13–15.

MacMillan, D. L. (1972). Paired-associate learning as a function of explicitness of mediational set by EMR and non-retarded children. _American Journal of Mental Deficiency, 76,_ 686–691.

Marc, D., and MacDonald, L. (1988). Respite care—Who uses it? _Mental Retardation, 26,_ 93–96.

Mason, M. K. (1942). Learning to speak after six and one-half years of silence. _Journal of Speech Disorders, 7,_ 295–304.

Matson, J. L., DiLorenzo, T., and Andrasik, F. (1983). A review of behavior modification procedures for treating social skill deficits and psychiatric disorders of the mentally retarded. In J. Matson and F. Andrasik (Eds.), *Treatment issues and innovations in mental retardation.* New York: Plenum.

McDevitt, S. C., Smith, D. W., Schmidt, D. W., and Rosen, M. (1978). Deinstitutionalized citizen: Adjustment and quality of life. *Mental Retardation, 16,* 22–24.

McLaren, J., and Bryson, S. E. (1987). Review of recent empidemiological studies of mental retardation: Prevalence, associated disorders, and etiology. *American Journal of Mental Deficiency, 92,* 243–254.

McLean, J. E., Yoder, D. E., and Schiefelbusch, (1972). *Language Intervention with the Retarded.* Baltimore: University Park Press.

McQueen, P. C., Spence, M. W., Garner, J. B., Pereira, L. H., and Winsor, E. J. T. (1987). Prevalence of major mental retardation and associated disabilities in the Canadian Maritime provinces. *American Journal of Mental Deficiency, 91,* 460–466.

Mecham, M. J. (1955). The development and application of procedures for measuring speech improvement in mentally deficient children. *American Journal of Mental Deficiency, 60,* 301–306.

Menchetti, B. M., and Rusch, F. R. (1988). Reliability and validity of the *Vocational Assessment and Curriculum Guide. American Journal on Mental Retardation, 93,* 283–289.

Menolascino, F. J. (1965). Psychiatric aspects of mongolism. *American Journal of Mental Deficiency, 69,* 653–660.

Mercer, J. R. (1973). *Labeling the mentally retarded.* Berkeley: University of California Press.

Merrill, E. C. (1985). Differences in semantic processing speed of mentally retarded and nonretarded persons. *American Journal of Mental Deficiency, 90,* 71–80.

Milar, C. R., and Schroeder, S. R. (1983). The effects of lead on retardation of cognitive and adaptive behavior. In J. L. Matson and F. Andrasik (Eds.), *Treatment issues and innovations in mental retardation.* New York: Plenum.

Miller, L. K. (1987). Developmentally delayed musical savant's sensitivity to tonal structure. *American Journal of Mental Deficiency, 91,* 467–471.

Milunsky, A. (1975). *The prevention of genetic disease and mental retardation.* Philadelphia: Saunders.

Miniszek, N. A. (1983). Development of Alzheimer disease in Down syndrome individuals. *American Journal of Mental Deficiency, 87,* 377–385.

Minnes, P. M. (1988). Family resources and stress associated with having a mentally retarded child. *American Journal on Mental Retardation, 93,* 184–192.

Morishima, A., and Brown, L. F. (1976). An idiot savant case report: A retrospective view. *Mental Retardation, 14*(4), 46–47.

Morishima, A., and Brown, L. F. (1977). A case report on the autistic talent of an autistic idiot savant. *Mental Retardation, 15,* 33–36.

Mulick, J. A., and Kedesdy, J. H. (1988). Self-injurious behavior, its treatment and normalization. *Mental Retardation, 26,* 223–229.

Myers, B. A. (1987). Conduct disorders of adolescents with developmental disabilities. *Mental Retardation, 25,* 335–340.

Nahmias, A. J., and Tomeh, M. D. (1977). Herpes simplex virus infections. In A. M. Rudolph (Ed.), *Pediatrics,* 16th Ed. New York: Appleton-Century-Crofts.

National Institutes of Health (1986). *Hope through research.* Washington, DC: U.S. Government Printing Office, Publication No. 86-309.

Needleman, H. L., Gunnoe, C., Leviton, A., Reed, R., Peresie, H., Maher, C., and Barrett, B. S. (1979). Deficits in psychologic and classroom performance of children with elevated dentine lead levels. *New England Journal of Medicine, 300,* 689–695.

Olshansky, S. (1962). Chronic sorrow: A response to having a mentally defective child. *Social Casework, 43,* 190–193.

Papania, N. (1954). A qualitative analysis of vocabulary responses of institutionalized mentally retarded children. *Journal of Clinical Psychology, 10,* 361–365.

Paulson, M. J., and Stone, D. (1973). Specialist-professional intervention: An expanding role in the care and treatment of the retarded and their families. In G. Tarjan, R. K. Eyman, and C. E. Meyers (Eds.), *Sociobehavioral studies in mental retardation.* Washington, DC: American Association on Mental Deficiency.

Pawlarcyzk, D., and Beckwith, B. E. (1987). Depressive symptoms displayed by persons with mental retardation: A review. *Mental Retardation, 25,* 325–330.

Payne, J. S. (1971). Prevalence survey of severely mentally retarded in Wyandotte County, Kansas. *Training School Bulletin, 67,* 220–227.

Payne, J. S., and Patton, J. R. (1981). *Mental retardation.* Columbus, OH: Merrill.

Phibbs, R. H. (1977). The newborn infant. In A. M. Rudolph (Ed.), *Pediatrics,* 16th Ed. New York: Appleton-Century-Crofts.

Piaget, J. (1952). *The origins of intelligence in children,* 2d Ed. New York: International Universities Press.

Plomin, R. (1988). The nature and nurture of cognitive abilities. In R. J. Sternberg (Ed.), *Advances in the psychology of human intelligence,* Vol. 4. Hillsdale, NJ: Erlbaum.

President's Committee on Mental Retardation (1967). *A first report on the nation's progress and remaining great needs in the campaign to combat mental retardation.* Washington, DC: U.S. Government Printing Office.

Ramey, C., and Landesman, S. (In press.) Prevention of intergenerational intellectual retardation. *Intelligence.*

Reid, A. H. (1972a). Psychoses in adult mental defectives: I. Manic-depressive psychosis. *British Journal of Psychiatry, 120,* 205–212.

Reid, A. H. (1972b). Psychoses in adult mental defectives: II. Schizophrenia and paranoid psychoses. *British Journal of Psychiatry, 120,* 213–218.

Reiss, S. (1982). Psychopathology and mental retardation: Survey of a developmental disabilities mental health program. *Mental Retardation, 20,* 128–132.

Reiss, S., and Benson, B. A. (1985). Psychosocial correlates of depression in mentally retarded adults: I. Minimal social support and stigmatization. *American Journal of Mental Deficiency, 89,* 331–337.

Resnick, L. B., and Glaser, R. (1976). Problem solving and intelligence. In L. B. Resnick (Ed.), *The nature of intelligence.* Hillsdale, NJ: Erlbaum.

Reynolds, W. M., and Baker, J. A. (1988). Assessment of depression in persons with mental retardation. *American Journal on Mental Retardation, 93,* 93–103.

Richardson, S. A. (1978). Careers of mentally retarded young persons: Services, jobs and interpersonal relations. *American Journal of Mental Deficiency, 82,* 349–358.

Richardson, S. A., Koller, H., Katz, M., and McLaren, J. (1981). A functional classification of seizures and its distribution in a mentally retarded population. *American Journal of Mental Deficiency, 85,* 457–466.

Robinson, N. M., and Robinson, H. B. (1976). *The mentally retarded child: A psychological approach,* 2d Ed. New York: McGraw-Hill.

Rohwer, W. D., Jr. (1968). Mental mnemonics in early learning. *The Record (Teachers College), 70,* 213–216.

Rubin, I. L. (1987). Health care needs of adults with mental retardation. *Mental Retardation, 25*, 201–206.

Rusch, F. R., Schutz, R. P., Mithaug, D. E., Stewart, J. E., and Mar, D. E. (1982). *Vocational assessment and curriculum guide.* Seattle: Exceptional Education.

Ryckman, D. B., and Henderson, R. A. (1965). The meaning of a retarded child for his parents: A focus for counselors. *Mental Retardation, 3*, 4–7.

Sattler, J. M. (1974). *Assessment of children's intelligence.* Philadelphia: Saunders.

Scarr-Salapatek, S. (1975). Genetics and the development of intelligence. In F. D. Horowitz (Ed.), *Review of child development research*, Vol. 4. Chicago: University of Chicago Press.

Scarr, S., and Weinberg, R. A. (1976). IQ test performance of black children adopted by white families. *American Psychologist 31*, 726–739.

Scheerenberger, R. C. (1982). Public residential services (1981): Status and trends. *Mental Retardation, 20*, 210–215.

Schiefelbusch, R. L., and Lloyd, L. L. (1974). *Language perspectives—Acquisition, retardation, and intervention.* Austin, TX: PRO-ED.

Schiff, M., Duyme, M., Dumaret, A., Stewart, J., Tomkeiwicz, S., and Feingold, J. (1978). Intellectual status of working-class children adopted early into upper-middle-class families. *Science, 200*, 1503–1504.

Schlanger, B. B. (1953). Speech measurements of institutionalized mentally handicapped children. *American Journal of Mental Deficiency, 58*, 114–122.

Segal, J. J. (1971). *Imagery: Current cognitive approaches.* New York: Academic Press.

Sells, C. J., and Bennett, F. C. (1977). Prevention of mental retardation: The role of medicine. *American Journal of Mental Deficiency, 82*, 117–129.

Seltzer, M. M. (1988). Structure and patterns of services utilization by elderly persons with mental retardation. *Mental Retardation, 26*, 181–185.

Sherman, B. R. (1988). Predictors of the decision to place developmentally disabled family members in residential care. *American Journal of Mental Retardation, 92*, 344–351.

Siegel, G. M. (1962). Interexaminer reliability for mean length of response. *Journal of Speech and Hearing Research, 5*, 91–95.

Silverstein, A. B. (1968). WISC subtest patterns of retardates. *Psychological Reports, 23*, 1061–1062.

Silverstein, A. B., Herbs, D., Miller, F. J., Nasuta, R., Williams, D. C., and White, J. F. (1988). Effects of age on the adaptive behavior of institutionalized and noninstitutionalized individuals with Down syndrome. *American Journal on Mental Retardation, 92*, 455–460.

Skeels, H. M., and Dye, H. B. (1939). A study of the effects of differential stimulation on mentally retarded children. *Proceedings and Addresses of the Sixty-Third Annual Session of the American Association on Mental Deficiency, 44*, 114–130.

Skeels, H. M., and Harms, I. (1948). Children with inferior social histories: Their mental development in adoptive homes. *Journal of Genetic Psychology, 72*, 283–294.

Skodak, M., and Skeels, H. M. (1949). A final follow-up study of one hundred adopted children. *Journal of Genetic Psychology, 75*, 85–125.

Spearman, C. E. (1923). *The nature of intelligence and the principles of cognition.* London: Macmillan.

Speer, G. S. (1940). The mental development of children of feebleminded and normal mothers. *NSSE, Thirty-Ninth Yearbook*, Pt. II, 309–314.

Spradlin, J. E. (1963). Language and communication of mental defectives. In N. R. Ellis (Ed.), *Handbook of mental deficiency.* New York: McGraw-Hill.

Springer, N. S. (1987). From institution to foster care: Impact on nutritional status. *American Journal of Mental Deficiency, 91*, 321–327.

Stanfield, J. S. (1973). Graduation: What happens to the retarded child when he grows up? *Exceptional Children, 39*, 548–552.

Sternberg, R. J. (1980). Sketch of a componential subtheory of human intelligence. *Brain and Behavioral Sciences, 3*, 573–614.

Sternberg, R. J. (1981). The nature of intelligence. *New York University Education Quarterly, 12*, 10–17.

Sternberg, R. J., and Powell, J. S. (1983). Comprehending verbal comprehension. *American Psychologist, 38*, 878–893.

Terman, L. M., and Merrill, M. A. (1973). *The Stanford-Binet intelligence scale, third revision* (with 1972 tables by R. L. Thorndike). Boston: Houghton-Mifflin.

Thompson, M. M. (1963). Psychological characteristics relevant to the education of the mongoloid child. *Mental Retardation, 1*, 148–151, 185–186.

Thorndike, R. L., Hagen, E. P., and Sattler, J. M. (1986). *Stanford-Binet Intelligence Scale (4th Ed.)*. Chicago: Riverside.

Thurstone, L. L. (1938). Primary mental abilities. *Psychometric Monographs*, No. 1 (special issue).

Turnbull, H. R., III (1986). Incidence of infanticide in America: Public and professional attitudes. *Issues in Law and Medicine, 1*, 363–389.

Turnbull, H. R., III, Guess, D., and Turnbull, A. P. (1988). Vox populi and Baby Doe. *Mental Retardation, 26*, 127–132.

Turnure, J. E. (1970a). Distractibility in the mentally retarded: Negative evidence for an orienting inadequacy. *Exceptional Children, 37*, 181–186.

Turnure, J. E. (1970b). Children's reactions to distractors in a learning situation. *Developmental Psychology, 2*, 115–122.

Tymchuk, A. J., Andron, L., and Rahbar, B. (1988). Effective decision-making/problem-solving training with mothers who have mental retardation. *American Journal on Mental Retardation, 92*, 510–516.

Walker, K. P., and Gross, F. L. (1970). IQ stability among educable retarded children. *Training School Bulletin, 66*, 181–187.

Webster, T. G. (1970). Unique aspects of emotional development in mentally retarded children. In F. J. Menolascino (Ed.), *Psychiatric approaches to mental retardation*. New York: Basic Books.

Wechsler, D. (1967). *Manual for the Wechsler Preschool and Primary Scale of Intelligence*. New York: The Psychological Corporation.

Wechsler, D. (1974). *Manual for the Wechsler Intelligence Scale for Children, Revised*. New York: The Psychological Corporation.

Wechsler, D. (1981). *WAIS-R Manual: Wechsler Adult Intelligence Scale, Revised*. New York: Harcourt, Brace, Jovanovich.

Wehman, P. (1979). *Curriculum design for the severely and profoundly handicapped*. New York: Human Sciences Press.

Wehman, P. (1988). Supported employment: Toward equal employment opportunity for persons with severe disabilities. *Mental Retardation, 26*, 357–361.

Wehman, P., and Kregel, J. (Eds.) (1989). *Supported employment and transition: Focus on excellence*. New York: Human Sciences Press.

White, C. C., Hill, B. K., Lakin, K. C., and Bruininks, R. H. (1984). Day programs of adults with mental retardation in residential facilities. *Mental Retardation, 22*, 121–127.

Willerman, L. (1979). Effects of families on intellectual development. *American Psychologist, 34*, 923–929.

Wisniewski, K. E., and Rabe, R. A. (1986). Discrepancy between Alzheimer-type neuropathology and dementia in people with Downs syndrome. In H. M. Wisniewski and A. Snider (Eds.), *Mental retardation: Research, education, and technology transfer*. New York: New York Academy of Sciences.

Wolfensberger, W. (1988). Common assets of mentally retarded people that are commonly not acknowledged. *Mental Retardation, 26*, 63–70.

Yoder, D. E., and Miller, J. F. (1972). What we may know and what we can do: Input toward a system. In J. E. McLean, D. E. Yoder, and R. L. Schiefelbusch (Eds.), *Language intervention with the retarded*. Baltimore: University Park Press.

Yoeli, M., and Scheinesson, G. P. (1976). Infections in residential institutions. In J. Wortis (Ed.), *Mental retardation and developmental disabilities: An annual review VIII*. New York: Brunner/Mazel.

Zetlin, A. G., and Turner, J. L. (1985). Transition from adolescence to adulthood: Perspectives of mentally retarded individuals and their families. *American Journal of Mental Deficiency, 89*, 570–579.

Zetlin, A. G., and Turner, J. L. (1988). Salient domains in the self-conception of adults with mental retardation. *Mental Retardation, 26*, 219–222.

Zigler, E. (1966). Research on personality structure in the retardate. In N. R. Ellis (Ed.), *International review of research in mental retardation*, Vol. 1. New York: Academic Press.

Zigler, E. (1969). Developmental vs. difference theories of mental retardation and the problem of motivation. *American Journal of Mental Deficiency, 73*, 536–556.

Zigler, E., and Balla, D. (1982). Introduction: The developmental approach to mental retardation. In E. Zigler and D. Balla (Eds.), *Mental retardation: The developmental-difference controversy*. Hillsdale, NJ: Erlbaum.

Zigler, E., and Seitz, V. (1982). Social policy and intelligence. In R. J. Sternberg (Ed.), *Handbook of human intelligence*. Cambridge, England: Cambridge University Press.

Zigman, W. B., Schupf, N., Lubin, R. A., and Silverman, W. P. (1987). Premature regression in adults with Down syndrome. *American Journal of Mental Deficiency, 92*, 161–168.

Ziring, P. R. (1987). A program that works. *Mental Retardation, 25*, 207–210.

CHAPTER 4

Autism

OVERVIEW

Autism is a developmental disorder of early childhood that profoundly affects social and emotional behavior, language, cognition, activities, and interests. Variously labeled as *infantile autism, childhood autism,* and *Kanner's syndrome,* in current psychiatric nomenclature (*DSM-III-R,* 1987[1]) it is termed *autistic disorder.* This chapter explores (1) the essential features of autistic disorder, (2) its prevalence and theories of causation, (3) its adaptive effects in early childhood, the school-age years, and adulthood, and (4) its special-service needs.

NATURE OF AUTISM

HISTORICAL AND CURRENT VIEWS

In 1943, Leo Kanner, an American child psychiatrist, described a group of 11 children who showed a pattern of behaviors he called "early infantile autism" (Kanner, 1943). Their chief characteristics were (1) extreme aloofness and disinterest in people, (2) impairment in language, (3) an intense need for sameness, and (4) a fascination with objects rather than people.

This behavioral picture of autism was confirmed by later researchers (e.g., Creak, 1961; DeMyer, 1979; Goldfarb, 1970; Hingtgen & Bryson, 1972; Rutter, 1978; Schopler, 1983; Wing, 1985) and is largely reflected in the current diagnostic criteria of *DSM-III-R.* The current criteria are (1) onset usually by age 3, (2) a pervasive lack of responsiveness to others, (3) abnormalities of communication, and in both verbal and nonverbal forms, and (4) a very narrow range of interests and activities that tend to be pursued in a rigid and compulsive fashion.

The severity of the social and communication abnormalities together with much odd and seemingly bizarre behavior led people to view autistic children as psychotic, and some early workers, including Kanner (Schopler, 1983), regarded autism as a childhood version of schizophrenia (e.g., Bender, 1947; Goldfarb, 1961) or did not distinguish between them (Creak, 1961). Subsequent research has not indicated any relationship between autism and schizophrenia. A follow–up study found that, unlike schizophrenics, autistic children rarely developed delusions and hallucinations as adults (Rutter, 1970). In the current psychiatric nomen-

---

[1] *Diagnostic and Statistical Manual of Mental Disorders,* 3d Ed. Revised (Washington, D.C.: American Psychiatric Association, 1987).

clature, autism is classified as a pervasive developmental disorder rather than as a psychosis or a mental illness.

Apart from the issues of psychosis and mental illness, there has been much confusion between autism and mental retardation. Autistic children are also commonly mentally retarded, and both populations include children who show odd, stereotyped movements, e.g., body rocking and hand and arm waving. Although these movements are particularly prominent in nonautistic children with severe or profound levels of retardation (Baumeister, 1978), they are also found in blind children. Like autistic individuals, severely retarded and/or blind children tend to twist and turn their hands near their eyes, are often attracted to bright lights, and frequently engage in body rocking. As in autism as well, retarded and/or blind children seem to prefer sensory experiences of touch, taste, and smell (Wing and Attwood, 1987). While all three disability groups—retarded, autistic, and blind children—share this behavior, it is only the autistic child who is unable to develop normal affectional relationships. It is the social distance of the autistic child that sets him or her apart, not the motor behavior.

The communication problems of the autistic child also have some similarity to developmental language disorders—the so-called childhood aphasias (Wing, 1985). This is particularly true when the understanding of speech is especially impaired. However, while children with receptive and expressive language disorders do not develop normal speech, there is at least the *desire* to communicate, in nonverbal as well as verbal ways. It is only the autistic child who does not spontaneously use gestures in the absence of speech. Autistic children also show poorer judgment than aphasic children (Lincoln et al., 1988).

CHARACTERISTIC BEHAVIORS

This section elaborates on each of the major aspects of autism and also indicates other behaviors commonly observed.

Age of Onset

About two-thirds of autistic children appear to have been abnormal from birth, with another one-third having autism arise following a period of normal development (Lotter, 1966, 1967). The disorder is usually recognized by age 2½ (Rutter, 1978; Short and Schopler, 1988; Volkmar, Stier, and Cohen, 1986) although the current nomenclature allows for its possible occurrence up to school age (*DSM-III-R*). Onset by age 2½ appears to be associated with more severe impairment than a later onset

(Dahl, Cohen, and Provence, 1986; Volkmar, Cohen, and Paul, 1986; Short and Schopler, 1988).

In the infant one may observe abnormal sleep patterns, extreme irritability and difficulty in comforting, lack of responsiveness to parental affection, and by the end of the first year, delay in language development (DeMyer, 1979). In contrast to the highly irritable infant, some are extremely placid. By the second year, the more conspicuous symptoms appear.

A minority of the children have a history of apparently normal development and an onset of symptoms in the second or third year, sometimes following illnesses that involve brain infection, e.g., encephalitis. Variability in age of onset is one indication that no single factor can be viewed as the cause of autism. Less than a tenth of the cases occur after 3 years (Hoshimo et al., 1982; Lotter, 1966; Short and Schopler, 1988; Volkmar, Stier, and Cohen, 1985).

Social (Interpersonal) Abnormalities

Aloofness, distance (both social and emotional), and a seeming lack of interest in other human beings are the hallmarks of autism (e.g., Baron-Cohen, 1988; Schopler and Mesibov, 1986; Volkmar, 1987; Hobson, 1989). Here is one mother's description of her son, Peter, as an infant:

> More troubling was the fact that Peter didn't look at us, or smile. . . . [autistic children tend to avoid looking at others' faces, so called gaze aversion]. While he didn't cry, he rarely laughed, and when he did, it was at things that didn't seem funny to us. He didn't cuddle but sat upright in my lap even when I rocked him [avoidance of physical contact is common though some enjoy roughhouse play]. We thought it was hilarious when my brother, visiting us when Peter was 8 months old, observed . . . "that kid has no social instincts whatever" [an extremely insightful observation about the autistic child]. Although Peter was a first child, he was not isolated. I frequently put him in his playpen in front of the house where the school children stopped to play with him as they passed [the children showed a normal interest in him; he did not respond] (Eberhardy, 1967, p. 2581).

Another aspect of the social and emotional distance of autism is the nature of the interaction when the child is involved with people. People are treated quite literally as if they were inanimate objects rather than feeling human beings. When the child wants his or her parent, for example, to get something not within reach, the child will take the parent's wrist, not hand, and move it to the object as if the hand were a tool. There is also little or no reaction to the distress of others. Autistic children seem to lack normal feelings of compassion or identification with other people. Hobson (1989) attributes this to an innate inability to enter into emotional touch with others.

The unresponsiveness to normal parental affection can be devastating to parents. Parental needs for intimacy are frustrated by a child who seems to have little interest in or desire for parental affection. In terms of the personhood model presented in Chapter 1, the autistic child is unique in the lack of the need for intimacy.

Communication (Language) Abnormalities

The language difficulties of the autistic child occur both in understanding speech and in its use (Baltaxe, 1977; Baron-Cohen, 1988, Cunningham, 1968; Schopler and Mesibov, 1985; Ricks and Wing, 1976; Tager-Flusberg, 1985). There may be a total failure to develop functional speech; language may consist only of inarticulate grunts and sounds sporadically punctuated by clearly expressed words that have no relevance to the situation in which they occur. Indeed, the very imitation of speech or speech sounds may be difficult for the autistic child (Yoder and Layton, 1988). While estimates vary, as many as half of all autistic children never develop functional speech (Eisenberg, 1956; Rutter, 1972; Rutter, Greenfield, and Lockyer, 1967). And this occurs despite normal hearing (Hingtgen and Bryson, 1972). Indeed, autistic children may be so indifferent to speech, as well as to other sounds, that parents suspect a hearing loss (Rutter, 1972). A recent study does suggest, however, that a chronic conductive (middle ear) loss may be present in a significant minority (Smith et al., 1988), but it is the autistic child's selective response to sounds that reveals the general intactness of hearing.

Of those who acquire speech, three-quarters have a prolonged period of echolalia (Rutter, 1972), the immediate or delayed parroting of words and phrases used by others (Rutter, 1965). Curiously, echoed speech will often accurately reflect and mimic that of its original user, evidence for normal hearing, but the spontaneous speech of the same child will be much poorer in quality. Together with echoing one often hears pronoun reversals; that is, the child refers to himself as *you* rather than as *I*. For example, in indicating desire for a preferred food, the child might say, "You want cookie" instead of "I want a cookie." When pronoun reversal occurs in the context of an apparently understood communication, it may simply represent the literal feedback of what the child hears. After all, he or she is referred to in the question "Do you want a cookie" as "you."

The literalness with which words are interpreted is illustrated by the child who always referred to her dog's dinner plate as a "dish." When asked to put some food in the dog's bowl, she was completely confused. In autism, things can only have one label. The concept of a synonym seems to be unknown. A more bizarre example is that of the child who instead of first saying "No" would say, "Don't throw it out of the window!" He had come to connect that event with the idea of "no" but didn't use the word (Ricks and Wing, 1976; Wing, 1985).

Despite these difficulties, by about age 5, many autistic children are able to understand at least single brief expressions, e.g., "Put on your hat," and show improvement in functional speech. Their spontaneous language, however, tends to be telegraphic in quality. As in the young child, connective words are not used, and even word order may be confused. Moreover, even where speech is grossly normal in sentence length and structure, its sound quality will be odd. It may be lacking in normal speech tone variations and have a monotonous or even robot-like quality.

But language problems are not confined to speech alone. There is a fundamental deficiency in the understanding of language. It is as if the child were listening to a foreign language. And not only are the words not understood, but there is little sensitivity to the meaning that is conveyed by change in voice quality or accompanying gestures. In the nonverbal realm there is comparable difficulty in understanding the meaning conveyed by facial expressions and the gestures that accompany speech (Baron-Cohen, 1988; Bartak, Rutter, and Cox, 1975; Curcio, 1978; Ohta, 1987; Wetherby and Prutting, 1984).

In autism, then, there is a fundamental difficulty in understanding and using the most basic aspects of communication. The autistic child seems to be unaware of the very idea of communication and may not even use simple gestures (Curcio, 1978). Where attempts to communicate are seen in autistic children without functional language, they tend to be indirect, expressed in crying, temper tantrums, self-hitting, or even echolalic speech. With regard to echolalia, studies suggest that it can serve as an indirect way of expressing requests, protests, and affirmations (Prizant and Duncan, 1981; Prizant and Rydell, 1984). Direct expressions of what one wants or does not want are simply not present or are limited to requests for objects or actions. Autistic children do not use speech to request information or to comment on what others have said (Wetherby and Prutting, 1984).

With normal modes of communication often absent, the attempt to teach communication through either speech or sign language is a major educational objective. What follows is a description that epitomizes the communication difficulty:

> The child did not respond to attempts to engage him in conversation. At times he gave clear indication of understanding simple speech, especially when it related to something he enjoyed—a food, a favored object, or a routine. The child stays in his own little world and indicates interest in others

only when in physical distress or if there is something to be sought or avoided. His mode of communication is rudimentary—a cry, a tantrum, a leading of the parent by the back of the hand (Allen et al., 1971, p. 313). [The highly selective word understanding is characteristic of autism and is best understood as a conditioned response to the sound (word) connected with a preferred object or activity.]

Activities and Interests

In the language sphere, we have discussed the extraordinary narrowing of word understanding. A similar kind of restrictiveness is found in the autistic child's activities and interests. Whereas the normally developing child seeks a blend of the novel and the familiar, the autistic child craves sameness. Novelty is not the spice of life in autism. In relentless fashion, the child spends long periods of time in activities that are repetitive, compulsive, indeed, ritualistic in quality. Whatever is enjoyed is performed in a rigid and unchanging fashion. A sense of the lengths to which the pursuit for sameness can go is seen in the child who insisted that the wood that was used to build a fire in the fireplace always be laid out in exactly the same manner.

While change is disturbing, sometimes a radical change may be accepted without upset. Thus one child reacted calmly to a move to a new house but became frantic when given a new bedcover. Another responded with a tantrum to any new clothes.

The narrow interest range of autistic children has been noted, as has the almost obsessional intensity of their activities. For example, a child may spend hours lining up objects on the floor or playing the same record, or parts of it, over and over.

In adolescence one encounters odd interests. There may be fascination with travel schedules or telephone numbers. One child insisted that he be read to from the telephone book. This preoccupation with an activity or a topic may lead to endless questions, but the questions are not really intended to obtain information. Rather, they seem to be intended to obtain a standard answer. Perhaps this is what passes for social interaction in autism.

Autistic young people tend to be collectors, but their collections are usually not of things others would want to collect or even value. Leaves, pieces of string, empty containers, even pieces of concrete all may be collected and prized with the same intensity as valued stamps or coins.

Another idiosyncratic behavior is seen in the use of toys (Rutter, 1972; Wing, 1985). A toy is not played with as intended, e.g., as in pulling a toy wagon, but it may be enjoyed for its sensory properties. The child may like the smooth texture of its surface or enjoy watching the spinning of its wheels. There seems to be a special interest in watching things spin, and autistic children enjoy whirling themselves around, seemingly without getting dizzy.

Another striking feature of autistic play, and one discussed later as well, is its apparent lack of fantasy or pretend quality (Wing, 1985). Autistic children do not participate in games in which the players pretend to be someone or something else.

Cognitive Functioning

Autism affects not only social development, language, and interests, it also influences intellectual development. The confusion and overlap with mental retardation have already been noted. Kanner (1943) recognized the frequent presence of intellectual impairment in autistic children, but he assumed that their basic cognitive capacities were intact, only disguised by the disorder. He noted that the children's faces appeared intelligent, in contrast to the stigmatic appearance of some retarded children, and that they often displayed unusual rote memory ability. It also had been observed that in some children, in contrast to language difficulties, there could be normal levels of functioning in such nonlanguage areas as assembling the pieces of a puzzle.

Intelligence Test Findings. Kanner's presumption of an underlying normal cognitive capacity could have been confirmed if dramatic changes in ability were commonplace. This is not the case. Although the degree of deviance in many children does lessen by school age, the majority still function in the retarded range (Lotter, 1966; Chess, 1971; DeMyer et al., 1974; Lincoln et al., 1988). Even more significant is the degree of intellectual impairment. From one-half to two-thirds of all autistic children fall in the below-50 IQ range (DeMyer et al., 1974; Chess, 1971; Schopler, 1983; Jacobson and Janicki, 1983; Lotter, 1966; Rutter and Lockyer, 1967; Wing and Gould, 1979). Only one study is reported in which less than half were retarded (Steinhausen et al., 1983). The severer levels of retardation tend to be found in children with some neurologic abnormality; such children also have the poorest prognosis for major changes in general adjustment (Carr, 1976).

The accuracy of mental tests and IQ determinations in these children has been questioned on the grounds that their aloofness, lack of language, and general disinterest would severely limit their capacity to cooperate in intelligence testing. While such assessments would be impossible in the extremely withdrawn or highly negativistic child, it has been shown that cooperation improves when tasks are presented that are within the child's ability level (Alpern, 1967; DeMyer, Norton, and Barton, 1971; Schopler, 1976). Testing must include nonlanguage as well as language items, however.

Unusual Concreteness of Thought. Like retarded children, autistic children function better on nonlanguage or visual and visual-motor tasks. These tasks are more concrete in the sense that they have a meaning that can be readily apprehended at a purely sensory perceptual level. The assembly of a jigsaw puzzle, for example, involves vision, seeing the pieces that need to be put together. Of course, it is not necessary to depend on vision; a blind child or a blindfolded child also could assemble a puzzle by the sense of touch. Most of our knowledge originates from our senses, our "windows" on the world, but language is not a sense. Words, whether spoken or written, are symbols for what they represent. The word *puzzle* is not a puzzle, it is only the language equivalent of a puzzle. And it is precisely in this nonsensory domain, that of language and word meaning, that the autistic child is disadvantaged. Words are interpreted literally, as if they *were* what they stand for; this was illustrated earlier in the *dish-plate* confusion in the section on language.

Concreteness is also reflected in the type of humor autistic children prefer. They enjoy slapstick comedy, which is a visual experience, and they are mystified by humor that involves a play on words or double meaning. Similarly, autistic children do not understand proverbs; they interpret proverbs literally and lack appreciation for metaphor. Thus the child is described who when asked if he'd "lost his tongue" began anxiously to search for it (Ricks and Wing, 1976).

"Splinter" Skills: Islets of Intelligence. Within a cognitive picture reflective of retardation, poor language understanding, and concreteness, sometimes one finds areas of relatively normal or even superior ability in autistic children. Frequently, they show relative superiority in visual or visual-motor ability, and this is reflected in their tendency to achieve higher scores on the nonlanguage parts of intelligence tests (Bartak, Rutter, and Cox; Lincoln et al., 1988). In one study of 155 children (DeMyer et al., 1974), the mean Verbal IQ was 35 as contrasted with a Performance IQ of 53, a difference of 18 points. A difference of more than 15 points denotes a real difference in the abilities sampled by the two types of intelligence test items (Wechsler, 1974). The average overall IQ of this group was only 45. An even greater difference was found in a high-functioning population (Lincoln et al., 1988). On the WISC-R, with an average Full Scale IQ of 69, there was a 24-point difference between the two scales, 60 IQ on the Verbal and 84 IQ on the Performance. The subtests that most clearly reflected this difference were Block Design and

Object Assembly on the Performance Scale and Vocabulary and Comprehension on the Verbal Scale.

It is in the rote memory sphere that unusual ability may be seen in autism. The same child who has little understanding of language may in delayed echolalia reveal good recall for words heard earlier (Ricks and Wing, 1976). Since what is recalled has no apparent meaning for the child, memory in some fashion operates like a tape recorder—it stores what it hears and reproduces it unchanged. But this kind of automatic and out-of-consciousness memory may have little utility in daily functioning. Thus the child in school might memorize facts but be unable to explain what has been memorized.

In addition to good rote recall, on rare occasions one also encounters such an extraordinary and idiosyncratic ability as calendar calculating. I once tested a pair of identical twins who were both autistic and retarded.[2] Although they could tell on what day of the week a particular date would fall, they could not solve arithmetic problems involving amounts of less than 10. And while they had speech, they could not explain how they had learned to calendar count. It was an ability totally unrelated to all other aspects of their cognitive functioning, an example of what was referred to in Chapter 3 as a savant.

Odd Movements (Stereotypic) and Self-Injurious Behavior

A striking and bizarre-appearing behavior seen in autistic children is rhythmic and repetitive body movements (Rutter and Lockyer, 1967; Wing, 1985). Body rocking and hand flapping are common, along with twiddling, flicking, and flapping of objects. Autistic children may jump, walk on tiptoe, or spin themselves. These movements tend to intensify when the child is excited or is gazing at something that absorbs his or her attention. They've been referred to previously in connection with retarded children. Some of them are thought to be forms of self-stimulation, activities pursued for their inherently pleasurable quality. You and I also engage in such behaviors, for example, rocking in a rocking chair or twisting our hair, but these activities are much more pronounced in autism.

Of these motor behaviors, those which involve the actual hitting of the self are of particular concern. Autistic children may strike their own heads or bite or even kick themselves. These blows can draw blood and do tissue damage. To literally protect the children from themselves, pro-

---

[2]One of the twins was shown on "Sixty Minutes." I had tested him when he was 12, and some 30 years later he still had not mastered simple arithmetic, although his calendar-calculating ability was still intact.

tective devices are commonly employed, such as football helmets for children who bang their heads and restraints to limit hand and limb action for hitters and kickers. More controversial has been the use of various forms of physically discomforting and even painful stimuli administered immediately following self-hitting—a kind of punishment intended to discourage it. These so-called aversion treatment procedures have evoked widespread concern. Though purportedly effective, at least in the short run, their inherently punitive and pain-inducing nature is offensive to many mental health professionals.

Fears and Emotions

Autistic children may show unusual fears—fears of things that ordinarily evoke no emotions or that are usually enjoyed (Achenbach, 1974; Wing, 1972, 1985). Balloons, friendly dogs, or riding in buses may frighten the child. One autistic infant would scream at the sight of a teapot, not stopping until it was removed from sight. Loud noises can be distressing; some children keep their fingers in their ears as if to reduce sound. Others show fears of such ordinarily neutral moving objects as vacuum cleaners, egg beaters, tricycles, and elevators. These fears also can be persistent, creating problems for the family when the object of the fear is not easily avoided. One little girl was made uncomfortable by a new pair of shoes; thereafter, she screamed and refused to talk if her parents put shoes on her.

Some children are continually tense and frightened, while others seem blithely indifferent, even to things that ought to frighten them. A boy is described who enjoyed the sound of squealing car tires (Wing, 1972). He would run in front of cars to produce the desired squeal; surely a short-lived hobby! It is presumed that the child who is indifferent to real danger simply does not understand the risks.

Emotional states can change dramatically in autism. A change in routine or the loss of a preferred object can turn the quiet and remote child into a bundle of fury, but the tantrum can end as quickly as it began—in Wing's (1985) words, "as if a tap had been turned off."

Apart from periodic upsets, some autistic children seem to be in perpetual states of disturbance, commencing with birth itself. There may be prolonged screaming during both day and night, and, especially upon awakening, the child cannot be comforted. The motion of a rocking baby carriage or of a moving automobile may end the screaming, but it frequently resumes when the motion ends. Presumably the pleasure of motion or kinesthetic sensation underlies some of the preferred stereotypic activities, e.g., body rocking.

Fortunately for the families, in the majority of autistic children, the intensity of behavioral upset diminishes by school age. They tend to become more social and better behaved. Adolescence, however, may see a renewal of difficulty; some autistic adolescents become very aggressive, while others lapse into states of apathy.

Unusual Sensory Reactions

A number of behaviors suggest some alteration in the basic senses. Already noted was the sticking of fingers in the ears as if to shut out sound. An autistic adult with good language reported that in childhood, all his sensations were magnified. Smells as well as sounds seemed more intense (Grandin and Scariano, 1986).

On the other hand, some behaviors suggest a dulling of the sense of pain. Besides those children who engage in self-injurious behavior, there are some who seem indifferent to temperature. Such children may run out of doors in icy weather without apparent discomfort. At present, however, there is no research evidence to support a higher pain or temperature threshold in autism.

Apart from unusual sensory reactions, autistic children may use their senses differently than normal children. While all infants with intact senses explore the world through touch, taste, and smell, as well as through sight and hearing, autistic children tend to continue to stress the use of touch, taste, and smell to a degree not found in sighted children. Autistic children may behave as if they were recognizing people through smell and touch—smelling people's hands or exploring with their hands other people's features. It is as if these children cannot make sense of what they see. In this respect, autistic children often have difficulty in understanding visual gestures, although, admittedly, their use of the visual mode is usually greater than their use of the auditory one.

Seizures

Attention has thus far been called to resource deficits of autistic children in the cognitive, communicative, and personality spheres. However, health problems also exist. In a follow-up study of autistic children in early adolescence, at about age 12 (DeMyer et al., 1973), 14 percent had a seizure history. By young adulthood, studies have found from a quarter to a third so affected (Brask, 1970; Lotter, 1978; Rutter, Greenfield, and Lockyer, 1967; Deykin and MacMahon, 1980).

An increased risk of autism also appears to be present in tuberous sclerosis, a neurologic disorder that often includes epilepsy and mental retardation.

Psychiatric Disorders

Although autism is distinguished from major forms of mental illness by its age of onset and behavioral manifestations, during adolescence and adulthood recognizable psychiatric disorders can occur. These include depression (Wing and Wing, 1976), catatonic excitement or posturing, and undifferentiated psychosis with delusions and/or hallucinations. These reactions are seen as stress-related and clear rapidly with its removal (*DSM-III-R*, 1987).

Patterns of Behavior in Autistic Children, Youths, and Adults

Within the autistic population, three subgroups have been distinguished seemingly largely on the basis of their interpersonal behavior. The three groups are—aloof, passive, and active-but-odd (Wing and Attwood, 1987; Wing and Gould, 1979). Aloofness, in early childhood, may persist into adulthood or transmute into one of the other two patterns. On the other hand, children who originally were either passive or active-but-odd generally do not become more aloof. The major characteristics of each are summarized in the following subsections.

Aloof. Relatedness. Avoid social contact and even physical proximity; may seek brief contact for preferred foods or activity, but separate easily; aloofness is especially marked with peers; approximates the classical, or Kanner's, depiction of autism.

Communication. Tends to be much impaired; either the child is mute or speech is noncommunicative; equally deficient in nonverbal communication—little or no attempt to communicate through facial expression, gesture, or body movement; poor eye contact and seeming avoidance of same (gaze aversion); absence of normal social gestures, e.g., waving and nodding; face may lack expression.

Activities and Interests. Narrow interests; repetitive and stereotyped in play, e.g., forms of self-stimulation; interest in the sensory properties of objects rather than in their function; ritualistic play in childhood may be replaced by odd collections and routines.

Cognition. Lacking in imagination, do not engage in fantasy or pretend play; visuospatial abilities tend to surpass verbal ones, although in those children with more severe degrees of cognitive impairment, no "islets of ability" may be evident; the level of cognitive impairment (degree of retardation) is likely to be greatest in those in whom aloofness persists into adulthood.

Odd Movements and Self-Injurious Behavior. Prominent stereotypic movements; may see tiptoe walking and springy gait in childhood; most likely to show self-injurious behavior.

Fears and Emotions. Unusual fears or lack of appropriate ones; inexplicable mood changes; dejected postures and unexplained tears.

Sensory Reactions. In early childhood, may ignore, be distressed, or fascinated with sound, light, cold, touch, pain, vibration, or movement; children have been reported with acute appendicitis or broken bones who gave no sign of discomfort (Wing & Attwood, 1987).

Physiological Peculiarities. Excessive fluid consumption; irregular eating and sleeping; marked weight fluctuations; occasional unexplained sweating, irregular breathing, and rapid pulse.

Behavior Problems. Temper tantrums, aggression, physical destructiveness, restlessness, screaming; socially embarrassing behaviors, e.g., public disrobing, taking things that do not belong to them, entering strangers' homes.

Passive. *Relatedness.* Do not initiate interaction except for need gratification, but do accept approaches of others without protest and may even appear to enjoy some interactions; can be led to participate in games and activities, although the involvement is passive in nature.

Communication. Functional speech, although with characteristic abnormalities; may have large vocabularies and express self grammatically; may be fascinated by long words; speech likely to be stilted in quality.

Activities and Interests. Although little or no imaginative play, there may be some imitating of other children's activities, e.g., bathing and feeding a doll; play is lacking in spontaneity, narrow and repetitive; routines are less resistive to interference.

Cognition. Tends to be less impaired than the aloof child; visuospatial superiority over verbal skills is more apparent; some may be able to function in regular classrooms (presumably not significantly impaired intellectually); routines can take the form of memorizing facts about a topic, although there is little understanding of its meaning; may show some appreciation of humor, enjoying slapstick or even a childish play on words.

Odd Movements and Self-Injurious Behavior. May be only minimally present; similarly self-injurious behavior is likely to be less of a problem than in the aloof child.

Sensory Reactions. Minimal or absent.

Physiological Peculiarities. Minimal or absent.

Behavior Problems. Have the fewest behavior problems; less disturbed by the presence of others and by change.

Active-But-Odd. *Relatedness.* Unlike the other two groups, these children initiate interactions but in a peculiar, naive, and one-sided manner; interests are reflected in persistent questions; they talk *at* a person, but exchanges are intended neither to foster intimacy nor to share information; verbal approaches and possibly associated physical clinging may be so persistent as to distress others.

Communication. Most functional speech of the three groups, although there is delay of language onset in childhood and some of the usual language abnormalities; may show an unusual pattern of speech development, with first words occurring in the context of complete sentences; speech is repetitive, long-winded, and there is lack of understanding of colloquialisms; may initiate interactions without usual preparatory remarks; speech is monotonous in tone or shows unusual inflections, poor breath and volume control; may lack associated gestures and emotions; during speech there may be exaggerated and inappropriate movements of face and limbs; gaze is inappropriate, either averted or too fixed.

Activities and Interests. There may be some pretend play, although it is repetitive and stereotyped in quality, e.g., building and rebuilding the same objects, pretending to be an animal, an object, or a TV character; may be preoccupied with bizarre or frightening subjects; may have a repetitive fantasy that has a delusional quality, e.g., Jessy, a later-described "middle functioning" autistic adult.

Cognition. Intellectual functioning tends to be higher than in aloof group, but no comparison is drawn with the passive one; strength tends to be in rote memory; includes individuals with moderate and severe retardation.

Odd Movements and Self-Injurious Behavior. Typical stereotypy is present in early years and then disappears; no comment is offered concerning self-injurious behavior, but it is presumably less common than in the aloof group.

Fears and Emotions. May show much anxiety.

Sensory Reactions. If present, they usually fade with age.

Physiological Peculiarities. None noted.

Behavior Disorders. Behavior problems are common; irrelevant comments and repetitive questioning can include socially inappropriate and embarrassing themes; apparent unawareness of effects of comments on others; odd approaches can turn into pestering and then to tantrums and aggression; inappropriate behavior can create minor legal problems, e.g., taking books that deal with the child's interests without understanding the need to pay for them; may carry out experiments involving potential danger to self and others without apparent awareness of hazards, e.g., testing the effects of chemicals on unsuspecting relatives!

PREVALENCE AND CAUSATION

PREVALENCE

The majority of studies of the prevalence of autism both in the U.S. and elsewhere report frequencies of about 4 to 5 per 10,000 or about 1 in 2000 in the general population [Gillberg, 1974 (Sweden); Hoshimo et al., 1982 (Japan); Lotter, 1966 (England); Wing et al., 1976 (England); Steinhausen et al., 1983 (West Germany)]. The 4-to-5-per-10,000 rate is seen as representing about equal numbers of children with the classical clinical picture—the aloof child—and those with the other forms. Only one study is reported with a much lower rate, a frequency of 0.7 per 10,000 [Treffert, 1970 (American)].

When the usual criteria for diagnosis are expanded to include children with *some* autistic features, e.g., impairments in social interaction, repetitive and stereotyped play, or problems in the understanding and use of language, verbal and nonverbal, the number more than doubles (Wing, 1985).

Gender

Males are much more likely to be affected and in a ratio of 3 or 4 to 1 (*DSM-III-R*, 1987).

CAUSATION

Earlier Perspective

Earlier workers tended to attribute autism to the effects of inadequate parenting. Although Kanner regarded the aloofness of the autistic child as biological in origin, as does Hobson (1989), he characterized the parents as highly intellectual and emotionally remote (Kanner, 1943, 1949). Kanner's colleague, Eisenberg (1957), saw these qualities in the fathers rather than in the mothers. Kanner appears to have taken the view that the child's inborn difficulty in developing emotional attachments was aggravated by unresponsive parents. Subsequent research, however, has not supported the presumption of parental inadequacy. Studies of both parental personalities (Creak and Ini, 1960; Rutter, Bartak, and Newman, 1971; Koegel et al., 1983) and parental childrearing practices (DeMyer et al., 1974; Gillies, Mittler, and Simon, 1963; Pitfield and Oppenheim, 1964) found no distinguishing characteristics from parents of nonautistic children. A review of this literature (Cantwell, Baker, and Rutter, 1978; Morgan, 1988) led to the conclusion that pathologic family factors were not a sufficient cause for the development of autism, a conclusion also strongly held by Schopler (1983), who regards parents as potential cotherapists in the treatment of their autistic child rather than as sources of their child's difficulty.

Current Perspective

Current workers tend to view autism as caused by some form of organic brain abnormality (DeMyer et al., 1973; Golden, 1987; Ornitz, 1989; Schopler, 1983; Wing, 1976), but there is little agreement as to its specific nature.

Related Brain Findings. *Epilepsy.* One of the striking observations suggestive of organic brain abnormality is the much increased frequency of epilepsy. From a third to a quarter of autistic children are so affected by adulthood.

Ventricular Enlargement. Neuroradiologic studies utilizing the pneumoencephalograph and computerized tomography (CT scan) have found enlargement of the ventricles of the brain in some autistic children (Damasio et al., 1980; Hauser, DeLong, and Rosman, 1975). *Although the majority do not show such abnormality,* in those who do, the more common finding is of enlargement of the left lateral ventricle. The ventricles are the chambers in the brain through which flow cerebrospinal fluid, and their enlargement, in the absence of hydrocephaly, indicates reduced brain tissue in the adjacent areas. This could have been either present at birth or be the result of a later brain insult and tissue atrophy. The limited nature of this finding as an "explanation" for autism is seen in another neuroradiologic study of children with the classical Kanner picture in whom there was no evidence of brain disease (Prior et al., 1984). In a similar vein, Rumsey et al. (1988) concluded that the macroscopic brain anatomy is normal in many autistic individuals, especially those without an apparent neurological basis for their disorder.

Hemispheric Lateralization. Possibly related to temporal lobe deficiency is the finding of an atypical pattern of cerebral hemisphere specialization

(Dawson, 1982, 1983; Prior and Bradshaw, 1979). Autistic young people appear to be less lateralized for language in their left hemispheres. Language stimuli produce a greater than expected level of electrical activity in their right hemispheres, even though the right hemisphere is typically dominant for visuospatial functioning rather than for language. There is also the suggestion of an interference with left hemisphere function as a result of an overactivation of right hemisphere activity (e.g., Dawson et al., 1988). That, indeed, the right cerebral hemisphere exerts an unusually prominent influence in autism is suggested by the frequent superiority of autistic individuals in visuospatial areas as opposed to language, as well as their frequent enjoyment of music. Both are right hemisphere functions.

Vestibular Dysfunction. Researchers have found a diminished nystagmus response in autistic children, the movement of the eye in response to spinning (Ornitz and Ritvo, 1968). This may explain their enjoyment of spinning themselves without getting dizzy. The vestibular mechanism is found in the brainstem, and based on sleep studies in autism, the investigators hypothesized disruptions in the waking state in autism that would affect levels of general excitability.

Autism Following Brain Infection. Of particular interest is the sudden emergence of autistic-like behaviors in previously normal children who have suffered an acute brain infection, e.g., encephalitis. In a study describing three such children (DeLong, Bean, and Brown, 1981), the symptom picture was by no means classical—neither aloofness nor ritualistic behaviors were prominent. The children were irritable, hyperactive, showed some toe-walking, and were impaired in language and relatedness. Of the three, only one made a complete recovery.

Another brain infection, congenital rubella, generally of early prenatal origin, is associated with an increased risk of autism (Chess, 1971). A follow-up study of 17 of these children found surprising improvement, about a third achieving complete recovery. In some there were increased symptoms with time. The study suggested that a chronic viral infection of the brain could cause autistic symptoms. As with the aforementioned seizure and neuroradiologic findings, however, the great majority of autistic children show no clinical evidence of brain infection.

Prenatal and Perinatal Findings. With the majority of autistic children apparently abnormal from birth, the elusive nature of whatever genetic or prenatal factors might play a role is illustrated in a massive study of 30,000 pregnancies reported by Golden (1987). Of these, 14 resulted in autism—incidentally, a prevalence rate of 4.7 per 10,000. The only abnormality in these pregnancies was an increased frequency of midtrimester bleeding in the mother. The bleeding was mild, apparently lacking medical significance, and it was concluded that neither events during pregnancy nor at delivery play a major role in autism.

Genetic Findings. Twin studies have been employed in examining traits that might be inherited. These studies involve comparing the degree of similarity of identical twins with regard to the trait in question with that of same-sex fraternal twins. Where the trait is heritable, identical twins will be more similar than fraternal ones. Two twin studies have been reported in autism (Folstein and Rutter, 1977; Ritvo et al., 1985). Both show much higher rates of concordance (both affected) in identical twins. A limitation of the Ritvo study, in particular, is that it is not based on a truly representative sample of twins. There is an overrepresentation of identical twins, a common problem when populations are self-selected [an observation also made by Folstein and Rutter (1988) in a recent review of the twin data]. Suggestive of some genetic contribution, both sets of researchers also call attention to an increased risk of cognitive or language impairment in either the unaffected twin or a sibling. Based on the study of their discordant identical twin pairs, Folstein and Rutter concluded that brain injury in infancy with or without a genetic predisposition could cause autism. While this may very well be true, the pregnancy and perinatal study just described found no evidence for significant prenatal or perinatal abnormalities in the 14 pregnancies associated with autism. Similarly, a comparative study of obstetrical complications in autistic and nonautistic children with roughly comparable average IQs (54 autistic, 61 nonautistic) found no evidence of less optimal prenatal, perinatal, and neonatal conditions in the autistic group (Hagerman et al., 1986; Levy, Zoltak, and Saelen, 1988).

Two other findings suggest a possible genetic influence. First, about 2 percent of the siblings of autistic children are similarly affected (Folstein and Rutter, 1988; August, Steward, and Tsai, 1981), a risk far in excess of that of the general population. Second, some association is reported between the form of mental retardation known as fragile X syndrome and autism (Bregman, Leckman, and Ort, 1988; Brown et al., 1982). Fragile X was described in Chapter 3 and refers to an abnormality on the X chromosome. An X-chromosome abnormality in autism would at least be consistent with the excess of males, and a review of that literature suggests that about 8 percent of autistic males will have the fragile X chromosomal anomaly (Bregman et al., 1987).

Biochemical Findings. Numerous studies have failed to find any consistent biochemical abnormalities in autism, although there is some indication of an elevated level of the neurotransmitter serotonin in a significant minority (Ritvo et al., 1985).

Theorized Brain Dysfunctions. Given the absence of clearcut brain findings, theories of the cause of autism reflect reasoning by analogy. The behaviors seen in autism have some similarities to those found in neurologically intact children with developmental language disorders and in neurologically impaired adults (adults with brain damage). Given current understanding of brain-behavior relationships, e.g., the importance of the left temporal lobe in the understanding of spoken language, the theories that have been proposed translate autistic behavior into their presumed neurologic equivalents.

Abnormality of the Inner (Medial) Portion of the Frontal and Temporal Lobes and of the Corpus Striatum. This theory (Damasio and Maurer, 1978) is based on some of the sensory and motor abnormalities found in autism. It does not attempt to explain the social deficit.

Temporal Lobe Dysfunction. In addition to their role in the understanding of spoken (and written) language, the inner or medial portions of the temporal lobes include structures important in learning and memory, i.e., the hippocampus. Given the prominence of the receptive language impairment in autism, it is natural to assume that there must be a deficiency in the brain's language-processing centers. Hauser, DeLong, and Rosman (1975) theorize that lesions of the left medial temporal lobe early in life impair left hemisphere functions that affect language and social interaction. These authors distinguish between mild and severe degrees of autism. In the milder form, the right hemisphere (including the right temporal lobe) is intact. This hemisphere has a great effect on visuospatial functioning—hence the relatively good visuospatial abilities, even when language is much impaired. The selective impairment of the left hemisphere in milder cases would mean that information and understanding known through the right hemisphere, the "visual" part of the brain, would not be available to its language-processing partner, the left hemisphere. This theory allows for the islets of normal functioning or splinter skills seen in autism. In the severer degrees of impairment, it is presumed that both temporal lobes (and both hemispheres) are damaged.

Reasoning in similar fashion from the research literature, Hetzler and Griffin (1981) conclude that the main features of autism are consistent with temporal lobe dysfunction, and in both hemispheres. These authors note that in addition to their role in language, the temporal lobes are tied to memory (and learning) by means of the hippocampus and to emotions by means of the limbic system.

Disorder of Sensory Modulation and Directed Attention. While most investigators have focused on the receptive language area of the brain, Ornitz (1989) continues to call attention to the abnormal response to general stimulation seen in autism. Stimuli may be ignored that would catch a normal person's attention (a gunshot), or the autistic person appears to be especially sensitive to stimuli. This was mentioned in the earlier section on unusual sensory reactions. In earlier work by Ornitz and Ritvo (1968), the attempt was made to relate the autistic child's arousal state to a vestibular abnormality; now the focus shifts to the right cerebral hemisphere and its control of directed attention. *Directed attention* refers to the capacity both to be aroused by a novel stimulus and to give it the attention it deserves.

Reasoning from known brain-behavior relationships, several areas of the brain are presumed abnormal in autism. These are (1) the arousal and alertness center in the brainstem, the reticular system; (2) the brain system that controls emotional and motivational aspects of behavior, the limbic system; and (3) the parietal lobes, a contributor to the understanding of visual stimuli. Unlike other theorists, Ornitz regards the nonlanguage hemisphere, the right hemisphere, as the probable site of the basic abnormality in autism. The right hemisphere is thought to be dominant for directed attention and for the understanding of nonverbal forms of emotional expression. The latter feature hearkens back to the autistic person's difficulty in "reading" the emotional behavior of others.

Summary. Although numerous theories have been offered to explain the presumed biological abnormality(ies) in autism, we are still left with only speculation. Autism appears to be a disorder of multiple origins, and it may be either prenatal or postnatal in origin. The attempt to clarify its etiology is one of the fascinating problems in science.

ADAPTIVE BEHAVIOR

INFANCY AND EARLY CHILDHOOD

The First Year of Life

Although autism may be evident in the very first year of life, a retrospective survey of 29 parents of autistic adults (DeMyer, 1979) revealed that their child's first year tended to be the least disturbing. In looking back, these parents recognized a variety of peculiarities—motor, social, language, and temperament. The most characteristic abnormality was a delay in the appearance of the first word. While 70 percent of normal infants produce their first word by 12 months, only 15 percent of the autistic children had done so.

Ages 1 to 5

It is during the second year, toddlerhood, that autism becomes apparent; new abnormal behaviors emerge and existing ones worsen. Rocking and headbanging, less deviant in the first year, now cause concern. Growth in language, a hallmark of the second year, fails to occur. Even more distressing is the occasional disappearance of words that were present. The social unresponsiveness of the hitherto crib-confined and less mobile infant assumes a more ominous aspect. The now-walking child can actively withdraw and socially isolate himself or herself. And this developing mobility may add a messy or destructive dimension to the child's activity.

The second year sees a worsening of problems that center around physiologic functions—eating, sleeping, and toileting. Food intake may be very limited in both amount and variety, and there may be difficulty in chewing, swallowing, or sucking. Use of utensils can be delayed. In contrast to normally developing young children, nearly half of the autistic children studied were still eating with their fingers at age 4. Sleep disturbances also were common. While normal infants may awaken during the night, autistic children frequently roam the house or sit and rock. Toilet training also is delayed. While their siblings were usually fully trained by age 4, less than half (45 percent) of the autistic children were. And there were frequently toilet-related problems—chronic constipation, diarrhea, and fecal smearing.

The autistic child's social behavior also typically worsens in the second year. About a third of the children studied had been seen as socially responsive in their first year, but by the end of the second, virtually all were quite withdrawn.

Some sense of the disruptiveness and parental frustration that can arise is evident in this mother's description of her attempts to control and discipline her child:

> When he first started acting the way he does—messing in everything he can reach, pulling down drapes—I thought it was just a phase. I scolded but didn't spank too much. He kept getting into things [possibly "hyperactive"] and began to bite, punch, and hit himself. [self-injurious behavior] . . . We started spanking him a lot but it didn't do any good. He just ignored it. . . . you couldn't set him in a chair—he either jumped off right away or sat twiddling his hands [a stereotypical movement]. I didn't want to send him to his room, he was too withdrawn any how. . . . *he doesn't seem to understand what punishment means*—he goes right ahead doing the same thing over and over. You just can't reach him. He doesn't understand praise. We finally realized

that spanking doesn't do any good and we've stopped completely except when he's doing something . . . dangerous like getting into the street or pushing the baby downstairs. We really don't know what to do [graphic description of parental bewilderment and the need for assistance]. (DeMyer, 1979, p. 116)

It is during the early childhood years that fears arise. An autistic adolescent characterized his childhood as consisting of two emotional states, terror and confusion (Bemporad, 1979). The world was fearsome. Sensory experiences were intensified, noises were unbearably loud, and smells were overpoweringly strong. And nothing was constant. Daily experiences were strange and unpredictable. Could this be the source of the intense need for sameness? Other children frightened this child. He was afraid of being hurt by them, and he couldn't predict their behavior.

We can only imagine what it would be like to live a constant state of bewilderment and fear. Fortunately, by about age 4, anxiety begins to abate, as do fears. The autistic child becomes less withdrawn and more sociable. A mother describes the change in her child's response to Christmas presents:

When her autistic son had his second Christmas she already knew that he didn't care much about anything. But neither she nor her husband were prepared for a total lack of interest in Christmas presents! The father would open the boy's gifts but he ignored them. The same thing happened every year until he was five when he startled them with a smile at some of his presents. The mother tells us how she cried her heart out when her child couldn't even enjoy Christmas. (DeMyer, 1979)

Summary

It is during early childhood that autistic behavior peaks in intensity. The age period of 2 to 4 is especially trying for parents, but behavior tends to improve as the child nears school age. By age five, they are more responsive, less disturbed by change, less fearful, and generally just better behaved. Improvement in language, however, is less certain (Wing, 1972).

With respect to language, by school age, language and cognitive level are good predictors of future adaptation. Children who at age 5 still lack functional speech and whose mental development is at less than the 3-year level have a lower expectation for significant improvement in their future functioning (DeMyer et al., 1973; Rutter, 1970). Less change is seen also in those whose autism seems to be associated with some organic brain disorder. This is not true, however, in the case of an acute brain infection, from which there can be complete recovery.

THE SCHOOL-AGE YEARS

The improvement frequently seen by school age tends to be maintained in later childhood, although in adolescence new problems often emerge (Mesibov, 1983; Bristol and Schopler, 1983). In the behavioral domain, oft-present hyperactivity lessens, although it may be replaced by equally undesirable states of inertia and apathy (Ando and Yoshimura, 1979; Rutter, 1970). With regard to aggression, no consistent increase or decrease in adolescence is reported (Ando and Yoshimura, 1979; Rutter, 1970), although parents seem to perceive the management of their autistic adolescent children as more difficult (Bristol, 1984, Holroyd et al., 1975). Undoubtedly, the increased size and strength of the developing youth is a factor here. Improvements are seen in self-help skills, e.g., toileting and eating (Ando, Yoshimura, and Wakabayashi, 1980; Rutter, 1970; Rutter, Greenfield, and Lockyer, 1967), and there tends to be a lessening of ritualistic and compulsive behaviors. Most extreme in the early school years, these behaviors tend to diminish in intensity with adolescence and adulthood (Rutter, 1970; Rutter, Greenfield, and Lockyer, 1967). Sensory experiences also appear to be less troubling (Garfin, McCallon, and Cox, 1988).

The social (interpersonal) sphere is of particular interest. At least in higher-functioning and nonretarded autistic young people, there is often a desire for friendship, one that is likely to be frustrated by the young person's peculiarities. A lack of empathy, poor communication, and little social savvy present continuing barriers to the development of friendships. Indeed, autistic young people may be unaware of what a "friend" is, equating acquaintanceship with friendship (Dewey and Everard, 1974). Confusion about friendship will be seen in a young woman, Jessy, who is described later. However, there can be an awakening to their differences from others and the initiation of attempts to do something about them (Kanner, Rodriguez, and Ashenden, 1972). In addition, sometimes the more striking features of the disorder may disappear in adolescence, although these young people continue to be reserved, lacking in understanding of the feelings of others, and socially awkward.

The language area may see some important changes in the school years. Of the half who eventually develop some functional speech, about one-fifth acquire it after age 5. This is particularly true of those with relatively good visual understanding (Rutter, Greenfield, and Lockyer, 1967).

Autistic features continue to be prominent in cognition. Scores on intelligence tests (IQs) are usually not very different from those found earlier (DeMyer et al., 1973, Rutter, 1970), although there may be marked deterioration in those who develop seizures in adolescence (Rutter, 1970). IQ scores will, of course, indicate scholastic potential, but even when an autistic child has relatively good cognitive abilities, learning problems still exist. Autistic children tend to do better in arithmetic than in reading (Ando, Yoshimura, and Wakabayashi, 1980; Rutter and Bartak, 1973), a reflection of their difficulties with language. After all, the written word is merely the visual form of the spoken one.

Of interest is the presence of autistic thinking even in young people with college ability. They may have difficulty in separating the trivial from the crucial aspects of a problem (Bemporad, 1979). This is perceived to be a manifestation of the literality of their thinking. Their attention is drawn to that which is the most obvious. They cannot see the forest for the trees.

In light of the persistent social problems of autistic young people, it is not surprising that the sexual area is also a source of difficulty. In one study, only 1 of 64 autistic adolescents had a heterosexual friendship (Rutter, Greenfield, and Lockyer, 1967), also seen in adults, and marriage itself is rare (DesLauriers, 1978). Parents of autistic males report that their sons appear to have a low drive for intercourse, although masturbation is commonly noted. Indeed, frequent and sometimes public masturbation is a major source of parental concern (Bristol and Schopler, 1983). Parents also express fear of the possible exploitation of their daughters (DeMyer, 1979).

It is not surprising that masturbation should be, perhaps, the sexual behavior of choice. The typical autistic adolescent "learns by unfortunate experience that it is safer not to yield to the impulses to follow, touch, or speak to a person he (she) finds attractive. When even tentative expressions of yearning cause trouble, it is no wonder that most autistic persons eventually decide that sexual fulfillment is not for them" (Dewey and Everard, 1974). For most, the consequence of this is celibacy (Adams and Sheslow, 1983).

During the latter part of adolescence (and adulthood), vocational considerations loom. In the past, at least, very few, perhaps not more than 5 percent of autistic young people, found employment (Lotter, 1974; Rutter, Greenfield, and Lockyer, 1967). However, autistic young people have greater job potential than hitherto realized. Given a work setting that accepts their limitations and capitalizes on their abilities, e.g., attention to detail, compulsiveness, and tolerance for routine, these young people can be productively employed.

Within the school-age population, the focus will be on the autistic adolescent, since it is at this age that problems may arise that threaten the person's already precarious adjustment. DeMyer (1979) has distinguished three levels of adjustment in autistic adolescents—higher, middle, and lower. These also tend to carry over into adulthood, and each is now discussed.

The Higher-Functioning Adolescent

Aaron is 13, but he's progressed a long way from the isolated child he was at 5. Then he could only relate to adults and only if they read telephone numbers to him! He had no interest in peers. He had some speech but he couldn't "converse"; nor could he play a "pretend" game. By 13, his speech had improved; he could now converse but in a stilted manner. He gets along well with adults but is still friendless. The degree of his interpersonal alienation is reflected in his relationship to his older brother; he was like a non-family adult to him! Lonely, and longing for peer companionship, he didn't understand that his preoccupation with mathematics and geography "turned off" peers. Math had replaced the telephone book!

This same lack of "social sense" was evident in experiences at a therapeutic summer camp. He couldn't distinguish between peer teasing directed at him and peer laughter unrelated to him. This certainly has a paranoid quality.

In school, though interested in sports, he was poorly coordinated. His teachers thoughtfully capitalized on his math interest by letting him keep statistics for the basketball team and moving the yard marker at football games.

He has benefited from summer camp experiences and gained better control of his emotions. His temper tantrums have decreased and he's less withdrawn. He still is more comfortable with adults. He'll try new games but is very sensitive about losing. (Adapted from DeMyer, 1979) [*The need for "success" and the wish to avoid criticism do not seem to be diminished by autism.*]

The Middle-Functioning Adolescent

This level is illustrated by Jessy, a young woman whose history has been described by her mother (Parke, 1967, Parke, 1983). This section presents Jessy's functioning during school age, and Jessy will be discussed again in the description of the adult adaptation of autistic individuals.

Her symptoms were evident before age 2. She was emotionally remote, neither used nor understood speech, was extremely sensitive to change, and rocked. Though cognitively behind, it became evident that she functioned better in the visuo-spatial sphere. As a child she could match shapes and colors, could do jigsaw puzzles, and had an early understanding of numbers.

The "visual" sphere was important to her. At school age her speech was still extremely limited and art became a stimulus to communication. Between the ages of 8 and 14, she produced literally thousands of pictures that she stapled into "books." They represented adventures of herself, her family, and "little imitation people." Her mother would spend hours with her talking about her preoccupation with these "little people." She notes that speech was still too much of an effort to be evoked by ordinary events but could be elicited around her "bizarre obsession."

At 14 she was in high school, as a special student, and there involved herself with their fine arts department. Though a good art student, she never had the interest in formal art that was reflected in her earlier spontaneous drawings. As a student she had difficulty in understanding what she read but did better in math. Her speech was minimal and understandable only to those familiar with it. She spoke in a low halting manner and had difficulty in both finding the words to express her thoughts and in stringing them together to make a sentence. [These are also the kinds of problems found in nonautistic individuals with either developmental or acquired speech disorders.]

Her social relationships were minimal. Eating alone in the school cafeteria didn't bother her; she had little understanding of her classmates' conversations and concerns. She did have an apparently asexual relationship with a student who she referred to as her "boyfriend."

During adolescence there was dramatic change in her behavior. Always passive and needing to be encouraged to perform chores, overnight her attitude changed with the fortuitous discovery that the clicking sounds of a golf counter were highly rewarding. The counter was being used in a "behavior modification" program as a means of recording the frequency of the behavior being encouraged. But it turned out that the clicks accompanying the recording of behavior were themselves reinforcing! It was the clicking sounds rather than the intended reward that dramatically increased the behavior that they were trying to teach!

Incredibly, she hadn't learned to greet people until she was 14! In the behavior modification program she was taught to greet her teacher with a "Hello, Mrs. Jones." Saying "hello" earned her one point on the counter, eye contact a second, and "Mrs. Jones," a third. People at school were astonished at suddenly being greeted by someone who had always ignored them!

She graduated high school and, to the surprise of her mother, also passed a competency exam, although the reading portion was hard for her. (Adapted from Parke, 1983)

The Lower-Functioning Adolescent

Kirk, at 15, is a tall, handsome youth with a disarming smile. He has a younger sister. His father recalls that Kirk cried incessantly as an infant, clung to his mother, rocked, and was tense and utterly miserable. He slept poorly. His development for the first two years was not considered unusual; he was somewhat delayed in walking but had some speech. Following the birth of his sister, he "kind of disintegrated." He lost the speech he had, regressing to muteness, and spent his time in hours-long headbanging, spinning of a wheel, and listening to fractions of recorded music.

Kirk illustrates the difficulty of trying to attribute autism to any one cause. Apparently abnormal from birth, though not glaringly so, implying a biological causality, there is also evidence of a psychological influence. Seemingly very dependent on his mother, recall the "clinging," the loss of his mother's full attention at the birth of his sister may have been stressful for him; hence the regression. This regression caused the disorder to appear primarily psychological in origin and led to the entry of all family members into psychotherapy. The pain of this period and the kinds of stresses that autism can place on parents is graphically described by the father.

". . . for a while with two psychiatrists and one psychologist directing our lives, our stately urban home became a mental institution with three patients and an increasingly bewildered housekeeper who quietly cared for Kirk. My sister . . . mercifully took our youngest to live with her while we were immersing ourselves deeper and deeper in painful guilt feelings [prompted by the therapists' presumption that our poor parenting caused Kirk's behavior]. Meantime, Kirk's behavior continued to deteriorate; bewildered by play therapy to which he could not respond and drugged by phenothiazines which were prescribed to improve his hyperactivity. [*His lack of response to a therapeutic procedure that requires imagination and pretense is understandable; it is the kind of activity that is foreign to an autistic child.*] Finally, our pediatrician convinced us to send Kirk to an out-of-state "day" treatment center. [*Possibly none were available in their state. The treatment center offered a program of behavior therapy and special education, which is still the most common treatment procedures in day or residential settings. The family discontinued psychotherapy and, after the father sold his share of the family business, they followed Kirk and bought a farm near the treatment center. This is an example of how loving and concerned parents are willing to uproot themselves to help their child.*] He was finally toilet trained at age 7 and learned to dress . . . himself with relative ease. [*A study of 6-year-old autistic and retarded Japanese children found that less than half, 11 out of 24, were fully toilet trained at that age. However, most were toilet trained by age 14.*]

Kirk made progress in the "day" program; he ate and slept well and his mood was better. Crying spells and fierce temper tantrums were infrequent, and there was more eye contact. There was also improvement in his speech. He had earlier moved from muteness to echolalic speech and now began to use a little functional language. He was a passive participant in group activities; again, very characteristic of the autistic adolescent. He enjoyed going to the zoo and riding a bicycle, but there were still major abnormalities. He exhibited inappropriate sexual behavior—frequent masturbation and rubbing his genitals against men and women. This lack of awareness of the social taboos regarding public expressions of sexuality is another common problem. (Adapted from Melone and Lettick, 1983.) Other persisting autistic behaviors were rocking, licking of books and objects, and listening to fragments of repetitive recorded music.

In spite of the family turmoil, Kirk's parents view themselves as better off than many other families of autistic youth. But they're concerned about the future. As with other parents of autistic adolescents, expectations for change lessen and they begin to consider placing their child in some out-of-home setting. The never-ending responsibilities take their toll, and relief may be eventually sought from the care of youth who will "remain forever a child in an adult's body." (Adapted from DeMyer and Goldberg, 1983, p. 236)

ADULTHOOD

The quality of the adjustment in adolescence tends to carry over into adulthood (DeMyer, 1979), and for the great majority of autistic individuals, adulthood is marked by continued dependency. Earlier studies found few autistic adults in regular employment (Rutter, 1970; Rutter, Greenfield, and Lockyer, 1967; Wing and Wing, 1976), with the remainder in either sheltered workshops or day activity programs. With the recent national initiative in supported employment, however, the numbers of autistic persons in the regular work force will be much increased. The great majority are, nevertheless, likely to need some form of permanent residential care either in the family home or in some other supervised setting. Group homes especially for autistic adolescents and adults are becoming available, although autistic adults also may be found in settings serving retarded individuals.

Although most autistic adults do not achieve full independence, those who do show what is possible, and it is they who can give us some inkling of what autism is like from the inside. In light of the usual prominence of language and communication difficulties, such "personal" descriptions are much to be valued.

Higher-Functioning Autistic Adults

This category refers to the small proportion of the adult autistic population, about 15 percent, whose general intelligence is grossly normal. These individuals have made satisfactory school progress, e.g., graduation from high school or even college (e.g., Grandin and Scariano, 1986), and may have some awareness of their own behavior difficulties. These individuals also are capable of employment, but only in settings and jobs that do not require good communication and interpersonal skills, judgment, and flexibility. While one of Kanner's early patients eventually worked as a bank teller and Jack, who will be described shortly, is a piano tuner, such individuals are more likely to be employed in unskilled and routinized jobs (Dewey, 1983, Lettick, 1983). The greatest challenge to the autistic adult, however, is to be able to live independently. Managing their own daily affairs is a perpetual challenge and requires ready access to someone who can help whenever the unexpected occurs (Dewey, 1983). Within the category of higher-functioning adults, then, will be those who, though working, are not necessarily living on their own—still residing in the family home or in some other kind of setting in which someone else has ultimate responsibility, e.g., a boarding home, a family care home, or a group home. One such individual, living independently, but needing periodic assistance, illustrates the typical lack of social know-how in dealing with problem situations, here a residential and a vocational one (Dewey, 1983).

> Jack, a high school graduate, is employed as a piano tuner. At 22, with his first steady job and a car, he moved out of the family home. His initial choice of a place to live and his rationale for it illustrate the quality of his thinking. Proudly inviting his family to his new abode they were shocked to find him living in a miserable furnished room in a rundown hotel.
>
> "We all (parents and 3 siblings) crowded into his living room. It was so

hot that the temperature was surely more than 100. . . . when we mentioned the heat, Jack explained that his radiator was stuck in the open portion. To remedy that, he kept his single window wide open. This, he pointed out proudly, provided him with a handy refrigerator on the outside ledge and an effective stove for cooking on the surface of his sizzling metal radiator. The room had a single bed, a wooden chair, and a dresser, but no closet. He had hung his clothes on nails. Most of his other possessions were in cartons on the floor." (Adapted from Dewey, 1983, pp. 300–301). [Whereas most of us would seek lodgings by using newspapers, real estate agencies, or word of mouth, Jack had no understanding of how to go about finding a residence.] He decided that renting a single room would be best, logically the cheapest place to live. From family trips, he knew that the name of a place which rents rooms is a hotel. He went to the shabbiest hotel he could find . . . [it would be less costly]. Once he made that choice, he did not question the price which was quoted for a room, nor ask to see the place in advance. That seemed like rude behavior [!]. For the same reason he did not criticize the room which was given to him [clearly ill-prepared for dealing with life other than in heaven!].

Another episode that illustrates his unawareness of the "ways of the world" occurred in connection with his job. He had tuned the piano for a family that lived some distance from town and was invited to remain overnight. He wanted to leave in the morning and, apparently, expected to be paid although his employer often sent bills. Money was not mentioned and he felt it rude to ask so he simply remained. He was served breakfast and took a swim in the neighboring lake. He returned for lunch, had supper, and remained another night! All because the customer made no mention of money and he felt it was rude to ask. On the third day [!] he decided he must be rude and asked to be paid so he could leave. The customer replied, "Don't you think we're about even, with all the meals?" Humiliated, Jack settled on a low fee and left. He was unhappy about the lost time and income, and wanted to know what he did wrong. His mother served as his "instructor" in the ways of the world. She indicated that he must have had some hints that his remaining at the house was inappropriate. He apparently had recognized some distress in his "hosts" but attributed it to "family tensions."

Terry, another higher-functioning young adult, tells us something about his language difficulty, especially at the speech level:

When I was a 3-year-old I felt awful because I could not talk and for that reason I screamed for hours when frustrated. I was becoming able to talk at 4½ . . . but was not able to talk correctly. . . . A doctor once showed me a tape recorder, and he and I recorded a . . . conversation and played it back. I was fascinated but was disgusted to hear the poor sounds of speech on my ·side . . . compared with the doctor's words. This made me wish I could talk as correctly as other people. (Adapted from DeMyer, 1979, pp. 232–233)

A third higher-functioning adult has some awareness of the nature of his social difficulties: "I lack intuitive capacity . . . which makes it difficult to perceive the subtleties that other people find easy. . . . I tried to learn . . . what other situations called for." (Imagine trying to *learn* the automatic give-and-take of human relationships.) This epitomizes what Baron-Cohen (1988) characterizes as a persistent inability to participate in a mutually reciprocal social interaction.

The Middle-Functioning Autistic Adult

This category largely refers to those autistic adults with significant cognitive impairment—from borderline intelligence to mild retardation. These individuals will have major learning problems in school and in their postschool years, and because of their autistic behavior, will always need some degree of supervision. If employed, it must be in a carefully structured setting or a sheltered workshop. This category also includes persons with higher-level cognitive abilities but autistic behaviors whose severity requires more or less permanent supervision.

Paul, in his early 20s, lives at home. He has been in special schools and in adult day programs. Following a family move he became fearful of going out and no longer attends a day program.

Paul also illustrates the language problem in autism but at the receptive as well as expressive level. As a child he made no response to verbal commands but would respond when they were communicated visually—through gesture and mime. Communicating with him as if he was deaf, his parents used gestures as well as words. His vocabulary grew, but like that of the deaf child, it lacked words that have no inherent meaning and served as "connectives," e.g., the, but, to. He also had much difficulty in understanding words that convey "ideas" as opposed to "things"; the "abstract" versus the "concrete."

Paul began to use words at 4 but they were poorly articulated. He learned to say "no" but not "yes," indicating "yes" by repeating what he heard—echoing! He sometimes reversed pronouns, referring to himself as "you" but more often as "Paul." It was not until his 20s that he began to use "I"! His speech has improved in intelligibility as has his understanding, but words must be carefully tailored for him. In the fullest sense, English for him is a foreign language!

Paul also epitomizes the "passive" autistic person. Though never aloof he has developed few social relationships. His main characteristic is passivity—a lack of initiative. He's mildly retarded but has some reading ability though his arithmetic is stronger, again, characteristic of autism. Never a behavior problem, he readily participates in organized social and recreational activities. He enjoys music; again, common in autism, and he has an intense interest in bus routes. He is said to know these *in detail!* (Adapted from Wing, 1976)

Our second "middle functioning" adult is Jessy, the individual we first met as an adolescent. Though her intelligence test scores are reported to be in the normal range (Parke, 1983), her unusual ideas suggest the need for some degree of supervision. We meet her first at 20 and then at 24.

At 20 she lived with her parents, both college teachers, in a home from which her siblings had departed. Though devoted to her parents and enjoying visits of her siblings, her life was still solitary. Earlier, her parents had tried to provide some companionship for her by bringing a young woman to live in the home. She was to be both a friend and a teacher. On one occasion Jessy observed an exchange of money between them and concluded that friends are "hired"!

At 24, still at home, she has a half-time job in the mailroom of the college where her parents teach. Her job involves sorting mail, processing telephone billings, and, amazing to her mother, answering the telephone. Recall that in childhood her speech was intelligible only to those familiar with it. Her co-workers accept her for both her abilities and disabilities. They make allowances "for the peculiarities of an efficient and reliable worker [good work habits], especially one with a child's simplicity and attractiveness [naivete]."

The unusual ideation to which we've referred includes several themes, one of which involves discomfort in situations in which she is expected to say "thank you." Under such circumstances she averts her eyes and mumbles in discomfort. She knows that politeness is appropriate but if she says one of the "politenesses," she'll see the "hangman." He's a little fellow who hangs from trees or is pinned to a clothesline and who jumps higher or lower according to "forms of politeness" (see Fig. 4-1). She also has a fantasy about a "family" that lives in kitchen appliances, the "little people" referred to earlier. These phenomena suggest hallucinatory and delusional ideation and, along with depression and anxiety, are said to be found in some autistic adolescents. (Adapted from Wing, 1983) Much more normal artistic representations are found in paintings distributed by her family as Christmas cards. They show real talent in the representation of form and the use of color.

The Lower-Functioning Autistic Adult

This category includes individuals with more than mild retardation (IQs below 50) or those with such severe behavior problems as to require continuous supervision. These adults are unlikely to be permanent residents in the family home and will eventually reside in special settings.

Bobby, in his late 30s, has been institutionalized. As a child it was noted that he was unresponsive to sound though his hearing was intact. He also seemed insensitive to pain. Originally sent to a school for the deaf, he was returned to the family home as "unreachable." He is described by his mother as physically strong, active, and negative—certainly a lethal combination! He enjoyed jigsaw puzzles but didn't know how to play with toys. Language is limited to single words, labels for specific objects. In fact, he does not really use speech for communicating, indicating his wants by grunts and gestures.

He is most burdened by a bizarre compulsive routine. When he would walk down the stairs at home this would trigger repeated walking up and down the stairs. When going through a door he'd open and close it endlessly. These are the kinds of strange compulsive rituals seen in schizophrenia. He was finally institutionalized when his aged and widowed mother could no longer care for him (Adapted from DeMyer, 1979). Assuming that he is not typically aggressive or dangerous to others, under current residential options he might also have been placed in a community setting.

FIGURE 4-1. Drawing by Jessy at age 16.

SERVICES

PRESCHOOL AGE

Diagnostic and Family Assistance

The formal diagnosis of autism is usually not made before age 2 (Wing, 1985) and more often later in childhood (Marcus and Schopler, 1987). The child may have had prior contact with professionals who, even if they recognized the disorder, were reluctant to share this with the parents, a reluctance stemming from uncertainties about the diagnosis itself, lack of awareness of treatment possibilities, and a wish to protect the parents from facing such a potentially catastrophic disorder (Marcus, 1977). Clearly, what parents and child do need is access to knowledgeable professionals, persons who can help the parents understand (1) the nature of their child's difficulties, (2) the child's abilities as well as his or her impairments, (3) the child's general developmental level and (4) who can provide guidance with regard to appropriate education and management. The evaluation also could lead to medical recommendations for such problems as constipation, hyperactivity, or poor sleeping. While the diagnosis is not likely to answer the question of *why* the child is autistic, the assumption of an organic basis can relieve parents of any presumption that *they* are its cause (Marcus and Schopler, 1987).

I have been privileged to observe the diagnostic procedure in North Carolina's statewide TEACCH autism program, one in which parents are seen as therapeutic partners in management of the child. Not aspiring to the cure of a disability that is seen as organic and chronic, the goal of the program is educational in nature. They seek to enable the child to function in the family home and to allow both parents and child to live as normally as possible.

Respite Care[3]

Parents of autistic and other chronically disabled children need relief from the responsibilities of 24-hour care through access to both respite and preschool programs (DeMyer and Goldberg, 1983). The need for periodic respite from the kind of care giving that an autistic child might require is painfully evident in the experience of this father of a 4-year-old:

> I think both of us are at our wits end. We haven't had a vacation in 4 years. A month ago we said that no matter what, we were going to visit some people we'd known in school. We planned to stay a weekend. We took Sue's bed

---

[3]Described in Chapter 2.

and everything we could think of to make her feel at home. After a terrible night, she screamed a day and a night, we packed up at 5 in the morning and left. Everybody was wrung out. How much can one family take? (De-Myer, 1979, p. 111)

A study of parental perceptions of the stressfulness of raising an autistic child indicated that the most stress related to the child's limited capacity for self-control and for prudent and cooperative behavior, especially in unfamiliar situations (Milgrim and Atzil, 1988).

Health and Mental Health Services

Because of the severity of their reactions to strange settings and people, autistic children may never have had a complete medical examination or dental care (Marcus and Schopler, 1987). In Great Britain, a special traveling van offers dental services in its local area (Wing, 1985).

With reference to autistic behavior disorders themselves, no psychotropic drug has been found that specifically benefits the autistic child, although the drug fenfluramine appears to reduce hyperactivity and stereotypic movements in higher-functioning children (DeVerglas, Banks, and Guyer, 1988).

Day Care[4]

With the 1986 federal legislation strengthening support for preschool programs, as well as creating a new initiative for those serving infants and toddlers (Public Law 94-457), expanded access for autistic children to preschool programs can be expected. Autistic children may be found in centers serving normal and/or retarded children (Wing and Wing, 1976) and, in major population areas, in programs specifically for them.

SCHOOL AGE

General Educational Considerations

With federal legislation requiring the provision of educational services to all handicapped children (Public Law 94-142), autistic children are now served by our public schools. The kind of class setting in which an autistic child is placed will depend on his or her cognitive functioning and general behavior. Whatever the school placement, stress should be placed on the need for effective communication between parents and teachers (Marcus and Schopler, 1987).

---

[4]Described in Chapter 2.

Language. A major focus in the education of these children is on language, the goal being to help the child acquire some *functional* means of communication. This has taken a variety of forms: the teaching of speech itself, as, for example, to "mute" children through the conditioning techniques of behavior modification (e.g., Lovaas et al., 1973), the teaching of American sign language as a nonverbal alternative to speech (e.g., Bonvillian, Nelson, and Rhyne, 1981), the simultaneous teaching of signs and speech (Gains et al., 1988), or the teaching of the use of "communication boards" or other pictorial means of communication. The behavioral approach has included the training of appropriate speech utterances, as in the case of the echolalic child, but the child's learning seems to be situation-specific; that is there is little tendency to incorporate what has been learned into spontaneous speech (e.g., Paul, 1987). There is also the suggestion that just reinforcing *attempts* at speech in nonverbal children, e.g., naming objects, rather than reinforcing speech quality per se, can be effective in encouraging its use (Koegel, O'Dell, and Dunlap, 1988).

Sign language instruction has been directed toward the teaching of functional signs, with or without associated speech (Schuler and Baldwin, 1981), and virtually all autistic children can learn to understand and use at least some signs (Carr et al., 1978; Salvin et al., 1977); they are "visual" rather than auditory symbols. While the use of signs or other forms of nonverbal communication, such as picture boards, can increase communication skills, it should be understood that the language problems in autism are not confined only to speech. Autistic individuals can be almost as impaired in the use and understanding of nonverbal speech forms as in speech itself (Paul, 1987).

Social Skills. Another important educational domain is social skills, the teaching of appropriate social behaviors. Also much in vogue in the field of retardation, this teaching area has three components: (1) modeling of the appropriate behavior by the instructor, (2) practice by the student, and (3) feedback (Mesibov, 1983). While such methods may reduce the degree of aberrant social behavior, they cannot be expected to produce the kind of sensitivity and effortless reciprocity that characterizes normal social interactions.

Wing (1983) describes a young man who had been taught to knock on a door before entering: ". . . this young man came into the office of the director of the unit . . . without tapping on the door. After being reminded, he apologized politely, turned around, and tapped on the inside of the door." We recognize that he was carrying out an act without understanding why. In my view, the teaching of social skills without emphasizing the "why" produces behaviors that can be only caricatures of what is expected. Admittedly, this is a huge challenge to would-be educators. In Wing's view, the best approach is to teach as many social rules as possible and in as simple, concrete, and safe a form as possible. The difficulty of the task lies in the subtle nature of the rules that underlie social interaction. As Wing notes, even more so than with language, the rules vary with the situation, and unlike mathematics, cannot be stated in absolute form. Together with the teaching modalities mentioned earlier, social skills instructors include such practices as (1) acting out everyday social encounters with the autistic person taking different roles (role playing), (2) videotaping interactions, real or acted, and (3) regular group discussions of daily experiences in a setting that can provide feedback and constructive suggestions.

Vocational Skills. Although prior studies have found only a very small proportion of autistic adults in regular competitive employment, e.g., 4 percent in an English population (Wing and Wing, 1976), the current emphasis on techniques for placing developmentally disabled individuals into regular job settings, so-called supported employment, is sure to increase this number. Similarly, this emphasis will increase the number of sheltered workshop employees who can make the transition to nonsheltered employment.

Admittedly, the nonsheltered employment settings appropriate to persons with autism will be narrower than those available to nondisabled individuals. In particular, autistic individuals will generally function best in relatively routinized activities and where neither language nor skill in dealing with people are necessary. It should be added that complete separation from other people is unlikely, and the autistic individual therefore has to be prepared to deal with even the modified expectancies of future coworkers and supervisors, especially the latter.

Within the school experience can be found activities that begin to teach work skills to autistic young people (Fredericks et al., 1983). And even when retardation is present, as it usually is, the schools can prepare them for functioning in either sheltered workshops or day activity programs. In the English study cited earlier, 11 percent of autistic individuals were in sheltered workshops and 19 percent were in day programs (Wing and Wing, 1976). And here again, the educational focus should be on inculcating the kinds of work habits that underlie all forms of employment, vocational skills per se being of lesser importance.

Residential Services

It is during adolescence, if not before, that many families begin to consider out-of-home placement for their autistic child. The stresses that autism often imposes on families have been sensitively portrayed by Bristol and Schopler (1983), together with the kinds of support services that parents seek. One of these involves residential options to the family home, e.g., group homes and sheltered communities.

Within autism, concerns exist regarding whether settings should (1) include people with other disabilities or serve only those with autism, (2) be in a more rural or "protected" settings as opposed to the community, and (3) should include a wide range of severity of autism or be limited to a particular degree (Wing, 1983). These questions tend to resolve themselves in terms of severity, with the more specialized, protected, and homogeneous settings serving those least able to integrate with others, whether autistic or nonautistic.

Recreation

With inactivity a common behavior in adolescence, there is need to expose autistic young people to recreational activities in which they might become interested. These will usually be physical and visual in nature, although in the auditory mode, music is often enjoyed. Swimming is a frequent preference, along with cartoons, puzzles, and slapstick comedy. Wehman (1983) offers guidelines for developing recreational skills that mirror those taught to other developmentally disabled populations.

ADULTHOOD

The service needs of the autistic adult will relate to the chronicity and severity of cognitive, communicative, and social problems. In the past, autistic adults were commonly institutionalized; for example, 64 percent of Rutter's follow-up about population, typically severely and profoundly retarded, were in various forms of institutional care (Wing and Wing, 1976). But the high proportion living in such settings probably relates to an earlier dearth of noninstitutional services that could have supported more adaptive levels of functioning.

In the residential sphere, Marcus and Schopler (1977) propose that, by early adulthood, autistic persons should be afforded the opportunity to leave the family home, like their normal siblings, and live either semi-independently or in more supervised settings.

The need of the post-school-age autistic individual for meaningful ways in which to pass each day will require access to vocational, day, and recreational services. And in the case of the older autistic adult, parents must plan for the care of their dependent child when they can no longer perform this function. This will entail such legal considerations as estate planning and guardianship (Frolik, 1983).

REFERENCES

Achenbach, T. M. (1974). *Developmental psychopathology.* New York: Ronald.

Adams, W. V., and Sheslow, D. V. (1983). A developmental perspective of adolescence. In E. Schopler and G. B. Mesibov (Eds.), *Autism in adolescents and adults.* New York: Plenum.

Allen, J., DeMeyer, M. K., Norton, J. A., Pontius, W., and Yang, E. (1971). Intellectuality in parents of psychotic, subnormal and normal children. *Journal of Autism and Childhood Schizophrenia, 1,* 311–326.

Alpern, G. D. (1967). Measurement of "untestable" autistic children. *Journal of Abnormal Psychology, 72,* 478–496.

American Psychiatric Association (1987). *Diagnostic and statistical manual of mental disorders,* 3d Ed. Rev. *(DSM-III-R).* Washington, DC: American Psychiatric Association.

Ando, H., and Yoshimura, I. (1979). Effects of age on communication skill levels and prevalence of maladaptive behaviors in autistic and mentally retarded children. *Journal of Autism and Developmental Disorders, 9,* 83–93.

Ando, H., Yoshimura, I., and Wakabayashi, S. (1980). Effects of age on adaptive behavior levels and academic skill levels in autistic and mentally retarded children. *Journal of Autism and Developmental Disorders, 10,* 173–184.

August, G. J., Stewart, M. A., and Tsai, L. (1981). The incidence of cognitive disabilities in the siblings of autistic children. *British Journal of Psychiatry, 138,* 416–422.

Baltaxe, C. (1977). Pragmatic deficits in the language of autistic adolescents. *Journal of Pediatric Psychology, 2,* 176–180.

Baron-Cohen, S. (1988). Social and pragmatic deficits in autism: Cognitive or affective. *Journal of Autism and Developmental Disorders, 18,* 379–402.

Bartak, L., Rutter, M. J., and Cox, A. (1975). A comparative study of infantile autism and specific developmental receptive language disorder: I. The children. *British Journal of Psychiatry, 126,* 127–147.

Baumeister, A. A. (1978). Origins and control of stereotyped movements. In C. E. Meyers, (Ed.), *Quality of life in severely and profoundly mentally retarded people: Research foundation for improvement.* Washington, DC: American Association on Mental Deficiency.

Bemporad, J. R. (1979). Adult recollections of a formerly autistic child. *Journal of Autism and Developmental Disorders, 9,* 179–197.

Bender, L. (1947). Childhood schizophrenia: Clinical study of one hundred schizophrenic children. *American Journal of Orthopsychiatry, 17,* 40–56.

Bonvillian, J. D., Nelson, K. E., and Rhyne, J. M. (1981). Sign language and autism. *Journal of Autism and Developmental Disorders, 11,* 125–137.

Brask, B. H. (1970). A prevalence investigation of childhood psychosis. Paper presented at the 16th Scandanavian Congress of Psychiatry.

Bregman, J. D., Dykens, E., Watson, M., Ort, S. I., and Leckman, J. F. (1987). Fragile-X syndromes: Variability of phenotypic expression. *Journal of the American Academy of Child and Adolescent Psychiatry, 26,* 463–471.

Bregman, J. D., Leckman, J. F., and Ort, S. I. (1988). Fragile X syndrome: Genetic predisposition to psychopathology. *Journal of Autism and Developmental Disorders, 18,* 343–354.

Bristol, M. M. (1984). Family resources and successful adaptation to autistic children. In E. Schopler and G. B. Mesibov (Eds.), *The effects of autism on the family.* New York: Plenum.

Bristol, M. M., and Schopler, E. (1983). Stress and coping in families of autistic adolescents. In E. Schopler and G. B. Mesibov (Eds.), *Autism in adolescents and adults.* New York: Plenum.

Brown, W. T., Jenkins, E. C., Friedman, E., Brooks, J., Wisniewski, K., Raguthu, S., and French, J. (1982). Autism is associated with the fragile-X syndrome. *Journal of Autism and Developmental Disabilities, 12,* 303–308.

Cantwell, D. P., Baker, L., and Rutter, M. (1978). Family factors. In M. Rutter and E. Schopler (Eds.), *Autism: A reappraisal of concepts and treatment.* New York: Plenum.

Carr, J. (1976). The severely retarded autistic child. In L. Wing (Ed.), *Early childhood autism.* New York: Pergamon.

Carr, E., Binkoff, J., Koldginsky, E., and Eddy, M. (1978). Acquisition of sign language of autistic children: I. Expressive labeling. *Journal of Applied Behavior Analysis, 11,* 489–501.

Chess, S. (1971). Autism in children with congenital rubella. *Journal of Autism and Childhood Schizophrenia, 1,* 33–47.

Creak, M. (1961). Schizophrenia syndrome in childhood. Progress report of a working party (April 1961). *Cerebral Palsy Bulletin, 3,* 501–504.

Creak, M., and Ini, S. (1960). Families of psychotic children. *Journal of Child Psychology and Psychiatry, 1,* 156–175.

Cunningham, M. A. (1968). A comparison of the language of psychotic and nonpsychotic children who are mentally retarded. *Journal of Child Psychology and Psychiatry, 9,* 229–244.

Curcio, F. (1978). Sensorimotor functioning and communication in mute autistic children. *Journal of Autism and Childhood Schizophrenia, 8,* 281–292.

Dahl, E. K., Cohen, D. J., and Provence, S. (1986). Clinical and multivariate approaches to the nosology of pervasive developmental disorder. *Journal of the American Academy of Child Psychiatry, 25,* 170–180.

Damasio, A. R., and Maurer, R. G. (1978). A neurological model for childhood autism. *Archives of Neurology, 35,* 777–786.

Damasio, H., Maurer, R. G., Damasio, A. R., and Chui, H. C. (1980). Computerized tomographic scan findings in patients with autistic behavior. *Archives of Neurology, 37,* 504–510.

Dawson, G. (1982). Cerebral lateralization in individuals diagnosed as autism in early childhood. *Brain and Language, 15,* 353–368.

Dawson, G., Finley, D., Phillips, J., Galpert, L., and Lewy, A. (1988). Reduced P3 amplitude of the event-related brain potential and its relationship to language ability in autism. *Journal of Autism and Developmental Disorders, 18,* 493–504.

DeLong, G. R., Bean, S. C., and Brown, F. R. (1981). Acquired reversible autistic syndrome in acute encephalopathic illness in children. *Archives of Neurology, 38,* 191–194.

DeMyer, M. K. (1979). *Parents and children in autism.* New York: Wiley.

DeMyer, M. K., Barton, S., Alpern, G. D., Kimberlin, C., Allen, J., Yang, E., and Steele, R. (1974). The measured intelligence of autistic children. *Journal of Autism and Childhood Schizophrenia, 4,* 42–60.

DeMyer, M. K., Barton, S., DeMyer, W. E., Norton, J. A., Allen, J., and Steele, R. (1973). Prognosis in autism: A follow-up study. *Journal of Autism and Childhood Schizophrenia, 3,* 199–246.

DeMyer, M. K., and Goldberg, P. (1983). Family needs of the autistic adolescent. In E. Schopler and G. B. Mesibov (Eds.), *Autism in adolescents and adults.* New York: Plenum.

DeMyer, M. K., Norton, J. A., and Barton, S. (1971). Social and adaptive behaviors of autistic children as measured in a structured psychiatric interview. In D. W. Churchill, G. D. Alpern, and M. K. DeMyer (Eds.), *Infantile autism: Proceedings of the Indiana University Colloquium.* Springfield, IL: Thomas.

DeMyer, M. K., Pontius, W., Norton, J. A., Barton, S., Allen, J., and Steele, R. (1974). Parental practices and innate activity in normal, autistic, and brain-damaged infants. *Journal of Autism and Childhood Schizophrenia, 2,* 49–66.

DesLauriers, A. M. (1978). The cognitive-affective dilemma in early infantile autism: The case of Clarence. *Journal of Autism and Childhood Schizophrenia, 8,* 219–229.

DeVerglas, G., Banks, S. R., and Guyer, K. E. (1988). Clinical effects of fenfluramine on children with autism: A review of the research. *Journal of Autism and Developmental Disorders, 18,* 297–308.

Dewey, M. A. (1983). Parental perspective of needs. In E. Schopler and G. B. Mesibov (Eds.), *Autism in adolescents and adults.* New York: Plenum.

Dewey, M. A., and Everard, M. P. (1974). The near normal autistic adolescent. *Journal of Autism and Childhood Schizophrenia, 4,* 348–356.

Deykin, E., and MacMahon, B. (1980). The incidence of seizures among children with autistic symptoms. *American Journal of Psychiatry, 10,* 1310–1312.

Eberhardy, F. (1967). The view from the couch. *Journal of Child Psychology and Psychiatry, 8,* 257–263.

Eisenberg, L. (1956). The autistic child in adolescence. *American Journal of Orthopsychiatry, 112,* 607–613.

Eisenberg, L. (1957). Fathers of autistic children. *Journal of Orthopsychiatry, 27,* 715–724.

Folstein, S., and Rutter, M. (1977). Infantile autism: A genetic study of 21 twin pairs. *Journal of Child Psychology and Psychiatry, 18,* 297–321.

Folstein, S., and Rutter, M. J. (1988). Autism: Familial aggregation and genetic implications. *Journal of Autism and Developmental Disorders, 18,* 3–30.

Fredericks, H. D., Buckley, J., Baldwin, V. L., Moore, W., and Stremel-Campbell, K. (1983). The educational needs of the autistic adolescent. In E. Schopler and G. B. Mesibov (Eds.), *Autism in adolescents and adults.* New York: Plenum.

Frolik, L. A. (1983). Legal needs. In E. Schopler and G. B. Mesibov (Eds.), *Autism in adolescents and adults.* New York: Plenum.

Gaines, R., Leaper, C., Monahan, C., and Weickgenant, A. (1988). Language learning and retention in young language-disordered children. *Journal of Autism and Developmental Disorders, 18,* 281–296.

Garfin, D. G., McCallon, D., and Cox, R. (1988). Validity and reliability of the childhood autism rating scale with autistic children. *Journal of Autism and Developmental Disorders, 18,* 367–378.

Gillberg, C. (1984). Infantile autism and other childhood psychoses in a Swedish region: Epidemiological aspects. *Journal of Child Psychology and Psychiatry, 25,* 35–43.

Gillies, S., Mittler, P., and Simon, G. B. (1963). Some characteristics of a group of psychotic children and their families. *British Psychological Society Conference Proceedings.* Reading, England: British Psychological Society.

Golden, G. S. (1987). Neurological functioning. In D. J. Cohen, A. M. Donellan, and R. Paul (Eds.), *Handbook of autism and pervasive developmental disorders.* New York: Plenum.

Goldfarb, W. (1961). *Childhood schizophrenia.* Cambridge, MA: Harvard University Press.

Goldfarb, W. (1970). Childhood psychosis. In P. H. Mussen (Ed.), _Carmichael's manual of child psychology._ New York: Wiley.

Grandin, T., and Scariano, M. M. (1986). _Emergence: Labeled autistic._ Novato, CA: Arena.

Hagerman, R. J., Jackson, A. W., Levitas, A., Rimland, B., and Braden, M. (1986). An analysis of autism in fifty males with fragile-X syndrome. _American Journal of Medical Genetics, 23,_ 359–374.

Hauser, S. I., DeLong, G. R., and Rosman, N. P. (1975). Pneumographic findings in the infantile autism syndrome: A correlation with temporal lobe disease. _Brain, 98,_ 667–688.

Hetzler, B. E., and Griffin, J. L. (1981). Infantile autism and the temporal lobe of the brain. _Journal of Autism and Developmental Disorders, 11,_ 317–329.

Hingtgen, J. N., and Bryson, C. Q. (1972). Recent developments in the study of early childhood psychoses: Infantile autism, childhood schizophrenia and related disorders. _Schizophrenia Bulletin, 5,_ 8–53.

Hobson, R. P. (1989). Beyond cognition: A theory of autism. In G. Dawson (Ed.), _Autism: New perspectives on diagnosis, nature and treatment._ New York: Guilford.

Holroyd, J., Brown, N., Wikler, L., and Simmons, J. Q. (1975). Stress in families of institutionalized autistic children. _Journal of Community Psychology, 3,_ 26–31.

Hoshimo, Y., Kumashiro, H., Yashima, Y., Tachibana, R., and Watanabe, M. (1982). The epidemiological study of autism in Fukushima-Ken. _Folia Psychiatrica et Neurologica Japonica, 36,_ 115–124.

Jacobson, J. W., and Janicki, M. P. (1983). Observed prevalence of multiple developmental disabilities. _Mental Retardation, 21,_ 87–94.

Kanner, L. (1943). Autistic disturbances of affective contact. _Nervous Child, 2,_ 217–250.

Kanner, L. (1949). Problems of nosology and psychodynamics in early childhood autism. _American Journal of Orthopsychiatry, 19,_ 416–426.

Kanner, L., Rodriguez, A., and Ashenden, B. (1972). How far can autistic children go in matters of social adaptation? _Journal of Autism and Childhood Schizophrenia, 2,_ 9–33.

Koegel, R. L., O'Dell, M., and Dunlap, G. (1988). Producing speech use in nonverbal autistic children. _Journal of Autism and Developmental Disorders, 18,_ 525–538.

Koegel, R. L., Schreibman, L., O'Neill, R. E., and Burke, J. C. (1983). The personality and family-interaction characteristics of parents of autistic children. _Journal of Consulting and Clinical Psychology, 51,_ 683–692.

Lettick, A. L. (1983). Benhaven. In E. Schopler and G. B. Mesibov (Eds.), _Autism in adolescents and adults._ New York: Plenum.

Levy, S., Zoltak, B., and Saelen, T. (1988). A comparison of obstetrical records of autistic and nonautistic referrals for psychoeducational evaluations. _Journal of Autism and Developmental Disorders, 18,_ 573–581.

Lincoln, A. J., Courchesne, E., Kilman, B. A., Elmasian, R., and Allen, M. (1988). A study of intellectual abilities in high-functioning people with autism. _Journal of Autism and Developmental Disorders, 18,_ 505–524.

Lotter, V. (1966). Epidemiology of autistic conditions in young children: I. Prevalence. _Social Psychiatry, 1,_ 124–137.

Lotter, V. (1967). Epidemiology of autistic conditions in young children: II. Some characteristics of the parents and children. _Social Psychiatry, 1,_ 163–173.

Lotter, V. (1974). Social adjustment and placement of autistic children in Middlesex: A follow-up study. *Journal of Autism and Childhood Schizophrenia, 1,* 11–32.

Lotter, V. (1978). Follow-up studies. In M. Rutter and E. Schopler (Eds.), *Autism: A reappraisal of concepts and treatment.* New York: Plenum.

Lovaas, O. I., Koegel, R., Simmons, J., and Stevens-Long, J. (1973). Some generalizations and follow-up measures on autistic children in behavior therapy. *Journal of Applied Behavior Analysis, 6,* 131–165.

Marcus, L. (1977). Patterns of coping in families of psychotic children. *American Journal of Orthopsychiatry, 47,* 388–399.

Marcus, L. M., and Schopler, E. (1987). Working with families: A developmental perspective. In D. J. Cohen, A. M. Donnellan, and R. Paul (Eds.), *Handbook of autism and pervasive developmental disorders.* Silver Springs, MD: Winston.

Melone, M. B., and Lettick, A. L. (1983). Sex education at Benhaven. In E. Schopler and G. B. Mesibov (Eds.), *Autism in adolescents and adults.* New York: Plenum.

Mesibov, G. B. (1983). Current perspectives and issues in autism and adolescence. In E. Schopler and G. B. Mesibov (Eds.), *Autism in adolescents and adults.* New York: Plenum.

Milgrim, N. A., and Atzil, M. (1988). Parenting stress in raising autistic children. *Journal of Autism and Developmental Disorders, 18,* 415–424.

Morgan, S. B. (1988). The autistic child and family functioning: A developmental-family systems perspective. *Journal of Autism and Developmental Disorders, 18,* 263–280.

Ohta, M. (1987). Cognitive disorders of infantile autism: A study employing the WISC, spatial relationship conceptualization, and gesture imitations. *Journal of Autism and Developmental Disorders, 17,* 45–62.

Ornitz, E. M. (1989). Autism at the interface between sensory and information processing. In G. Dawson (Ed.), *Autism: New perspectives on diagnosis, nature and treatment.* New York: Guilford.

Ornitz, E. M., and Ritvo, E. R. (1968). Neurophysiologic mechanisms underlying perceptual inconstancy in autistic and schizophrenic children. *Archives of General Psychiatry, 19,* 22–27.

Parke, C. C. (1967). *The siege.* New York: Harcourt, Brace & World.

Parke, C. C. (1983). Growing out of autism. In E. Schopler and G. B. Mesibov (Eds.), *Autism in Adolescents and Adults.* New York: Plenum.

Paul, R. (1987). Communication. In D. J. Cohen, A. M. Donellan, and R. Paul (Eds.), *Handbook of autism and pervasive developmental disorders.* Silver Springs, MD: Winston.

Pitfield, M., and Oppenheim, A. N. (1964). Child rearing attitudes of mothers of psychotic children. *Journal of Child Psychology and Psychiatry, 5,* 51–57.

Prior, M. R., and Bradshaw, J. L. (1979). Hemisphere functioning in autistic children. *Cortex, 15,* 73–81.

Prior, M. R., Tress, B., Hoffman, W. L., and Boldt, D. (1984). Computed tomographic study of children with classic autism. *Archives of Neurology, 41,* 482–484.

Prizant, B. M., and Duncan, J. F. (1981). The functions of immediate echolalia in autistic children. *Journal of Speech and Hearing Disorders, 46,* 241–249.

Prizant, B. M., and Rydell, P. J. (1984). Analysis of functions of delayed echolalia in autistic children. *Journal of Speech and Hearing Research, 27,* 183–192.

Ricks, D. M., and Wing, L. (1976). Language, communication and the use of symbols. In L. Wing (Ed.), *Early childhood autism,* 2d ed. New York: Pergamon.

Ritvo, E. R., Freeman, B. J., Mason-Brothers, A., Mo, A., and Ritvo, A. M. (1985). Concordance for the syndrome of autism in 40 pairs of afflicted twins. *American Journal of Psychiatry, 142,* 74–77.

Rumsey, J. M., Creasey, H., Stepanek, J. S., Dorwart, R., Patronis, N., Hamburger, S. D., and Duara, R. (1988). Hemispheric asymmetries, fourth ventricular size, and cerebellar morphology in autism. *Journal of Autism and Development Disorders, 18,* 127–137.

Rutter, M. J. (1965). Speech disorders in a series of autistic children. In A. W. Franklin (Ed.), *Children with communication problems.* London: Pitman.

Rutter, M. J. (1970). Autistic children: Infancy to adulthood. *Seminars in Psychiatry, 2,* 435–450.

Rutter, M. J. (1972). Psychiatric causes of language retardation. In M. Rutter and J. A. M. Martin (Eds.), *The child with delayed speech.* London: Heinemann.

Rutter, M. J. (1978). Diagnosis and definition of childhood autism. *Journal of Autism and Developmental Disorders, 8,* 139–161.

Rutter, M. J., and Bartak, L. (1973). Special educational treatment of autistic children, a comparative study: II. Follow-up findings and implications for services. *Journal of Child Psychology and Psychiatry, 14,* 241–270.

Rutter, M. J., Bartak, L., and Newman, S. (1971). Autism: A central disorder of cognition and language. In M. Rutter (Ed.), *Infantile autism: Concepts, characteristics and treatment.* London: Churchill.

Rutter, M. J., Greenfield, D., and Lockyer, L. (1967). A five to fifteen year follow-up study of infantile psychosis: II. Social and behavioural outcome. *British Journal of Psychiatry, 113,* 1183–1199.

Rutter, M. J., and Lockyer, L. (1967). A five to fifteen year follow-up study of infantile psychosis: I. Description of the sample. *British Journal of Psychiatry, 113,* 1169—1182.

Salvin, A., Routh, D., Foster, R., and Lovejoy, K. (1977). Acquisition of modified American sign by a mute autistic child. *Journal of Autism and Childhood Schizophrenia, 7,* 359–371.

Schopler, E. (1976). Towards reducing behavior problems in autistic children. In L. Wing (Ed.), *Early childhood autism,* 2d ed. New York: Pergamon.

Schopler, E. (1983). New developments in the definition and diagnosis of autism. In B. B. Laney and A. E. Kazdin (Eds.), *Advances in clinical child psychology,* Vol. 6. New York, Plenum.

Schopler, E., and Mesibov, G. B. (Eds.). (1985). *Communication problems in autism.* New York: Plenum.

Schopler, E., and Mesibov, G. B. (Eds.). (1986). *Social behavior in autism.* New York: Plenum.

Schuler, A. L., and Baldwin, M. (1981). Non-speech communication and childhood autism. *Language, Speech and Hearing Services in the Schools, 12,* 246–258.

Short, A. B., and Schopler, E. (1988). Factors relating to age of onset in autism. *Journal of Autism and Developmental Disorders, 18,* 207–216.

Smith, D. E. P., Miller, S. D., Stewart, M., Walter, T. L., and McConnell, J. V. (1988). Conductive hearing loss in autistic, learning disabled, and normal children. *Journal of Autism and Developmental Disorders, 18,* 53–65.

Steinhausen, H. C., Gobel, D., Breinlinger, M., and Wohleben, B. (1983). A community survey of infantile autism. Paper presented at the 30th Annual Meeting of the American Academy of Child Psychiatry, San Francisco.

Tager-Flusberg, H. (1985). Psycholinguistic approaches to language and communication in autism. In E. Schopler and G. B. Mesibov (Eds.), *Communication problems in autism.* New York: Plenum.

Treffert, D. A. (1970). Epidemiology of infantile autism. *Archives of General Psychiatry, 22,* 431–438.

Volkmar, F. R. (1987). Social development. In D. J. Cohen, A. M. Donellan, and R. Paul (Eds.), *Handbook of autism and prevasive developmental disorders.* New York: Wiley.

Volkmar, F. R., Cohen, D. J., and Paul, R. (1986). An evaluation of *DSM-II* criteria for infantile autism. *Journal of the American Academy of Child Psychiatry, 25,* 190–197.

Volkmar, F. R., Stier, D. M., and Cohen, D. J. (1986). Age of recognition of pervasive developmental disorder. *American Journal of Psychiatry, 142,* 1450–1452.

Wechsler, D. (1974). *Manual for the Wechsler Intelligence Scale for Children—Revised.* New York: Psychological Corporation.

Wehman, P. (1983). Recreation and leisure needs: A community integration approach. In E. Schopler and G. B. Mesibov (Eds.), *Autism in adolescents and adults.* New York: Plenum.

Wetherby, A. M., and Prutting, C. A. (1984). Profiles of communicative and cognitive-social abilities in autistic children. *Journal of Speech and Hearing Research, 27,* 364–377.

Wing, J. K., and Wing, L. (1976). Provision of services. In L. Wing (Ed.), *Early childhood autism,* New York: Pergamon.

Wing, L. (1972). *Autistic children: A guide for parents and professionals.* New York: Brunner/Mazel.

Wing, L. (1976). Case histories of three young autistic adults. In L. Wing (Ed.), *Early childhood autism.* New York: Pergamon.

Wing, L. (1976). Epidemiology and theories of etiology. In L. Wing (Ed.), *Early childhood autism.* New York: Pergamon.

Wing, L. (1983). Social and interpersonal needs. In E. Schopler and G. B. Mesibov (Eds.), *Autism in adolescents and adults.* New York: Plenum.

Wing, L. (1985). *Autistic children,* 2d Ed. New York: Brunner/Mazel.

Wing, L., and Attwood, A. (1987). Syndromes of autism and atypical development. In D. J. Cohen, A. M. Donnellan, and R. Paul (Eds.), *Handbook of autism and pervasive developmental disorders,* Silver Springs, MD: Winston.

Wing, L., and Gould, J. (1979). Severe impairments of social interaction and associated abnormalities in children: Epidemiology and classification. *Journal of Autism and Developmental Disorders, 9,* 11–29.

Wing, L., Yeates, S. R., Brierly, L. M., and Gould, J. (1976). The prevalence of early childhood autism: Comparison of administrative and epidemiological studies. *Psychological Medicine, 6,* 89–100.

Yoder, P. J., and Layton, T. L. (1988). Speech following sign language training in autistic children. *Journal of Autism and Developmental Disorders, 18,* 217–229.

CHAPTER 5

Cerebral Palsy

OVERVIEW

This chapter examines (1) the nature of cerebral palsy and its three major variants, (2) its prevalence and causation, (3) its associated or secondary disabilities, (4) the adaptive problems it creates in infancy, school age, and adulthood, and (5) its special service needs.

NATURE OF CEREBRAL PALSY

Cerebral palsy is a nonprogressive neuromuscular disorder of movement and balance (Capute, 1975; Cruickshank, 1976; Thompson, Rubin, and Bilenker, 1983; Levitt, 1982). Its symptoms do not reflect an active illness but rather are the residual effects of damage to brain cells in the cortex and cerebellum, usually occurring prenatally or at birth. The disorder is not limited to movement and balance. It also commonly produces other disabilities—intellectual, speech, perceptual, sensory, and health. Indeed, of the various developmental disabilities, none other is likely to be so multidisabling. This is epitomized in the child who is exposed to the rubella virus during the first 3 months of prenatal life. A not uncommon consequence is the combination of motor paralysis (palsy), blindness, deafness, epilepsy, and mental retardation. Fortunately, the development of a rubella vaccine has made this disorder preventable; nor is the impairment in cerebral palsy usually of this magnitude.

FORMS OF CEREBRAL PALSY

Within the clinical picture of cerebral palsy are seen a variety of movement abnormalities, typically grouped into three categories—spasticity, dyskinesias, and ataxia. In addition to variations in movement abnormalities, there are also different combinations of limb involvement, primarily legs, or arms and legs, or limited to one side of the body.

SPASTICITY

Nature

The spastic form of cerebral palsy is the most common variant, accounting for about half of all affected persons (40 to 60 percent) (Cruickshank, 1976; Denhoff, 1976; Hopkins, Bice, and Colton, 1954). Indeed, the term *spasticity* is sometimes used as synonymous with cerebral palsy itself. In spasticity, movement is slow, effortful, and restricted in range, although, on occasion, it is jerky and explosive. Difficulty of movement is due to the tendency of limb muscles to contract (flex) when an extending motion is attempted (Denhoff, 1976). In effect, the muscle inhibits the very movement intended.

Limb Involvement

Spasticity may involve all four limbs (quadriplegia); all limbs but primarily the legs (diplegia); three limbs, a rare form (triplegia); only the legs (paraplegia); only the limbs on one side of the body, with the arm usually more affected than the leg (hemiplegia); and only one limb (monoplegia). Of these, hemiplegia is the most common, representing about a third of persons with spasticity.

Severity

In addition to limb involvement, spasticity is also categorized by severity, from mild to severe.

Mild. In its mild form, there may be only imprecision in fine motor movements (Denhoff, 1976) and an awkward gait, walking with arms extended for balance (Thompson, Rubin, and Bilenker, 1983).

Moderate. At the moderate level, there is difficulty with both gross motor and fine motor movements, and the neuromuscular abnormality also affects the clarity of speech. The characteristic body posture is shown in Figure 5-1b. This degree of severity does not interfere with carrying out most activities of daily living.

Severe. At the severe level of involvement, there is an inability to walk, to use one's hands, and to articulate intelligible speech (Denhoff, 1976). In the severest form, the individual may be unable to sit unsupported or even to hold up his or her head. It is here that we see the use of various assistive or "prosthetic" devices—braces for legs, crutches, and wheelchairs. The person so affected requires the support of others to carry out the most basic activities of daily living.

DYSKINESIAS

Dyskinesias are a group of motor disorders in which movements are uncontrolled and purposeless. They disappear during sleep and intensify under stress (Denhoff, 1976; Shapiro et al., 1983). Three subtypes are found—athetoses, rigidity, and tremor.

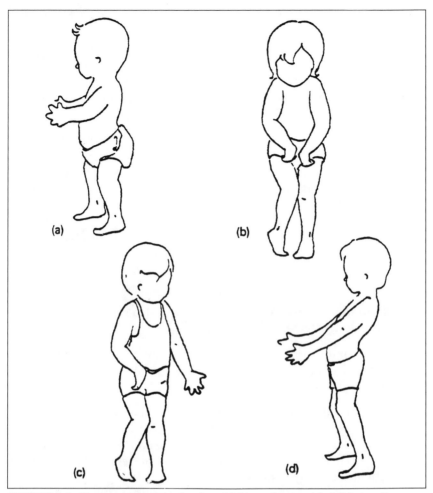

FIGURE 5-1. Postures in cerebral palsy. (*a*) *Normal* year-old child standing. (*b*) The young *spastic diplegic* child standing. This posture is one of flexion. His head "pokes" forward and up to compensate for the lack of extension in his trunk and hips. His arms are usually bent and press down and forward at the shoulders. His legs turn in and are held together; his standing base is very narrow, making balance difficult and in many cases impossible. Some children do manage to get the foot of one leg flat on the floor as illustrated, but in doing so they bend the hips even more and the whole of the pelvis is pulled back on that side. (*c*) The young *hemiplegic* child standing. His posture is asymmetrical; all his weight is on his good leg. The affected arm bends and turns in at the shoulder, which presses down, and his trunk bends on that side. The leg is stiff and turns in at the hip, the pelvis is pulled up and back; his foot is stiff, and the ankle does not bend, so that he takes weight only on the toes and ball of his foot. In some cases, the head is also pulled towards the affected side. (*d*) Typical position adopted by the *athetoid* child. His arms are held forward to overcome the extension of his hips and to prevent him falling backwards. (From *Handling the Young Cerebral Palsied Child at Home*, 2nd. ed., by Nancie R. Finnie. Copyright © 1974 by Nancie R. Finnie, F.C.S.P. Reprinted by permission of the publisher, E. P. Dutton, a division of Penguin Books USA Inc.)

Athetosis

The most common of the dyskinesias, athetosis accounts for approximately one-fifth (15 to 20 percent) of all cases of cerebral palsy (Denhoff, 1976), although its frequency appears to be diminishing (Paneth et al., 1981). Movements are relatively slow, wormlike, and writhing in quality. If they are jerky, the movements are called *choreic* and *choreoathetoid*. Athetoid movements are especially prevalent in the fingers and wrists, but they also occur in the face. In walking, gait is lurching and stumbling. The typical standing position is that shown in Figure 5-1*d*.

Rigidity

As in spasticity, movement is impeded, but unlike spasticity, where relaxation of the muscle releases movement as in the springing free of a jackknife blade, in rigidity, resistance to movement is continuous and "lead pipe" in quality. Rigidity is seen in about 13 percent of all cases of cerebral palsy.

Tremor

Tremor is a movement that is rhythmic and pendulum-like. A distinction is drawn between tremors associated with movements that are intentional, nonintentional, and constrained (Denhoff, 1976). This is a rare form of cerebral palsy, accounting for only about 3 percent of all cases (Hopkins, Bice, and Colton, 1954).

ATAXIA

Ataxia is primarily a disorder of balance, but it also includes some general incoordination (Denhoff, 1976). Gait is unsteady; the person walks with a high step as if on stilts. Hand movements are awkward, with a tendency to either overreach or underreach (Levitt, 1982). Ataxia represents less than 10 percent of cerebral palsy, estimates varying of from 2 to 9 percent (Hopkins, Bice, and Colton, 1954; Denhoff, 1976).

MIXED FORMS

Although three separate groups of movement disorders are recognized, the frequently diffuse nature of cortical damage (Taft and Matthews, 1983) often results in combinations of movement disorders, of which spasticity with athetosis, ataxia, or rigidity are the most common.

PREVALENCE AND CAUSATION

PREVALENCE

About 4 in 1000 persons (0.4 percent) in the general population have cerebral palsy (Brent and Harris, 1976; Cruickshank, 1976). Rates at birth varying from 1 to 6 per 1000 persons have been reported both in the United States and in Great Britain (Asher and Schonell, 1950; Henderson, 1961; Perlstein, 1949; Rutter, Graham, and Yule, 1970; Taft, 1984). Approximately half of all cases are present at birth (congenital). Together with those caused by illness in either childhood or early adolescence, the highest prevalence is found in the 10- to 14-year age range (Cruickshank, 1976).

At particular risk is the low-birth-weight child (premature) (less than 2000 gm or 4½ lb at birth), in whom the prevalence is about 10 times greater, about 4 per 100 persons; or 4 percent (Stanley and English, 1986). Of the various forms of cerebral palsy, spastic diplegia is the one most often associated with prematurity (Alexander and Bauer, 1988).

CAUSATION

Cerebral palsy can result from brain lesions occurring prenatally, perinatally, and postnatally. Prenatal factors appear to account for just under half of all cases, the remainder being caused equally by perinatal and postnatal ones. Apart from the risk to low-birth-weight children, other high-risk pregnancies are those of mothers who are retarded and where the baby is malformed (Nelson and Ellenburg, 1986).

PRENATAL CAUSES

Exposure during pregnancy to viral infections transmitted through the placenta is a prominent cause. The potentially devastating effects of the rubella virus on the fetus were mentioned earlier. Additional intrauterine infections that can produce the disorder are cytomegalovirus and toxoplasmosis (Taft and Matthews, 1983). Other prenatal causes include exposure to drugs, therapeutic as well as "recreational," and Rh incompatibility disease (Drillien, 1974; Heinonen, Slone, and Shapiro, 1977; Taft and Mathews, 1983).

The two most common effects of these prenatal insults are reduced oxygen to brain cells (hypoxia) and intracranial bleeding. These lead to cortical and subcortical abnormalities, the most frequent being a smaller brain, diminished "white matter" (the myelin sheath that surrounds nerve cell fibers that transmit, i.e., axons, and receive, i.e., dendrites, impulses from other cells), enlargement of the cerebral ventricles (the chambers through which flows the cerebrospinal fluid) (Banker and Bruce-Gregoris, 1983), and a damaged basal ganglia and/or cerebellum. Injury to the basal ganglia affects posture and the coordination of voluntary movements and occurs particularly in the athetoid form. Damage to the cerebellum affects balance and occurs primarily in ataxia. In spasticity, there will be damage to the motor portion of the cortex, those nerve cells involved in voluntary movement.

Perinatal Causes

Complications of the birth process itself have long been considered a major cause of cerebral palsy. Birth injury may result from interference with the fetus' oxygen supply due to either constriction of the umbilical cord or bleeding around the brain ventricles, and it is the low-birth-weight (less than 4.4 lb) and small-for-gestation-age fetus that is at particular risk (Stanley and English, 1986). Almost 40 percent of children with cerebral palsy have a history of low birth weight (Scherzer and Mike, 1974). Indeed, serious oxygen deprivation in the fetus can itself predispose to bleeding in the brain (Towbin, 1970). A respiratory disease in the first week of life also can cause cerebral palsy (Powell et al., 1988a, 1988b).

Postnatal Causes

Brain infection and head trauma are the two main postnatal causes of cerebral palsy (Thompson and O'Quinn, 1979). The infections of concern are meningitis, encephalitis, and brain abscess. In head injury, cerebral palsy is associated with subsequent intracranial bleeding. With reference to head injury, a study of children served by United Cerebral Palsy centers revealed that in better than a third of the children (34 percent), the injury resulting in the disorder was associated with child abuse (Cohen and Warren, 1987) a grim picture of "parenting."

ASSOCIATED DISORDERS

The multidisabling nature of cerebral palsy, one of its hallmarks, is revealed in its effects on capacities (resources) other than motor. These are now described.

COGNITIVE

Three kinds of cognitive problems are found—intellectual, perceptual, and attentional.

Intellectual Problems

Large-scale studies reveal a consistent picture of significant intellectual impairment in cerebral palsy. Taking into account motor disabilities that can interfere with a child's responding, especially those affecting speech, intelligence test findings indicate that about half of children with cerebral palsy function in the mentally retarded range, with rates in major studies varying from 45 to 59 percent (Hohman and Freedheim, 1958; Hopkins, Bice, and Colton, 1954; Crothers and Paine, 1959; Schonell, 1956). In the largest study, involving 1000 children (Hopkins, Bice, and Colton, 1954), 600 males and 400 females, the average IQ was 69, with two-thirds scoring in the IQ range of 53 to 86.

Within the retarded range, the proportions at each level of severity are estimated as mild (IQ 55 to 69), 34 percent; moderate (IQ 40 to 54), 28 percent; severe (IQ 25 to 39), 21 percent; and profound (IQ 0 to 24), 17 percent. This distribution differs strikingly from that of the total mental retardation population in that it has a much higher proportion of persons with more than mild retardation. This is attributed to the fact that all persons with cerebral palsy have an organic brain disorder, while the majority of the retarded population, those with "cultural familial" or "psychosocial" causation, have no clear evidence of organic brain damage. The latter terms refer to individuals from families in which retardation is also present in at least one parent and in one or more siblings (Grossman, 1983).

Apart from the relatively high rate of retardation, how does the non-retarded segment fare? Table 5-1 shows the findings in two studies that describe the cerebral palsied population in terms of intelligence ranges. The comparable proportions in the general population also are shown. The table reveals that children with cerebral palsy fall within all IQ ranges, but there are fewer in the average and above average to superior ranges. Only 28 percent were in these two ranges as compared with 76 percent of the general population. Given the relationship between IQ and school achievement, academic learning problems can be anticipated in nearly three-quarters of the children. Moreover, even those with average or above average IQs may have difficulties owing to an increased frequency of visual-perceptual disorders. These are described later. With regard to cognitive assessment, an adaptation of the Wechsler Adult Intelligence Scale-Revised (WAIS-R) has been developed for per-

Table 5-1. IQ levels in two large studies of children with cerebral palsy (Adapted from Cruickshank, 1976)

Intelligence level*	IQ range	Percent in general population	Percent in Bice and Cruickshank (1966)	Percent in Miller Rosenfeld (1952)
Above average to superior	100+	26.2	6.9	4.5
Average	90–109	49.4	21.6	23.0
Low average	80–89	16.2	11.4	11.0
Borderline	70–79	6.0	11.3	11.5
Retarded	Below 70	2.2	48.8	50.0

*The descriptive levels and IQ ranges are drawn from the Wechsler Intelligence Scale for Children-Revised (WISC-R).
Source: Adapted from Cruickshank, 1976.

sons with either limited or absent speech or motor functions (McCarty et al., 1986).

Age and Intelligence. An interesting and unusual finding is the tendency for IQ scores to increase over time (Cruickshank, Bice, and Wallen, 1957; Klapper and Birch, 1967). It is speculated that one effect of diminished mobility is a deprivation of stimulation and general experience, in part reflected in frequently noted naiveté, and that with increasing experience, the child's basic intellectual capacities emerge. In a sense, early mobility-limited sensory deprivation is gradually reduced. Clearly, caution is needed in projecting future learning potential in an immobilized young child, and there is the need for ensuring as much stimulation as possible, TV being one obvious medium.

In general, IQs in children in the below 50 and 90 plus ranges tend to be stable over time, the greatest changes occurring in the 51 to 89 range. It is speculated that these changes, either declines or elevations, may be due to age-related changes in the content of intelligence tests as these relate to the child's special deficits (Klapper and Birch, 1967).

Forms of Cerebral Palsy and Intelligence. The risk of cognitive impairment is greatest in ataxia and rigidity. In the two most frequent forms, spasticity and athetosis, there is little difference in cognitive impairment (Bice and Cruickshank, 1966; Katz, 1955). In spasticity, however, the risk is highest in those with all limbs affected (quadriplegia) (Shapiro et al., 1983).

Severity of Motor Impairment and Intelligence. There appears to be little relationship between the severity of motor impairment and intelligence (Neuman, 1983), although, as just noted, the wider the limb involvement, the greater the risk.

Intelligence and Response to Physical Therapy. A review of this research literature (Parette and Hourcade, 1984a) indicates some relationship between intelligence and the response to physical therapy in young children. Nonretarded children typically showed greater gains than retarded ones. Nevertheless, even with this difference, the majority of mildly retarded children appear to be able to eventually attain "walking" with a lesser expectancy for more severely retarded ones. It has been suggested that a lesser level of motivation in the more retarded child might account for some of the differences in response to therapy associated with intelligence level.

Perceptual Problems

Perceptual disorders in cerebral palsy are frequent, especially in those with spasticity (Cruickshank, Bice, and Wallen, 1957). Most often present are visual and visual-motor difficulties, although tactile problems also occur (Abercrombie, 1964). In one study (Miller and Rosenfeld, 1952), perceptual disorders were found in more than a third of those with spasticity (39 percent), but in only 8 percent of those with athetosis.

The perceptual problems do not involve acuity (e.g., impaired vision or poor tactile sensitivity), but rather reflect impaired understanding of what is being experienced in a particular sensory mode. These are the same kinds of modality-specific learning disorders found in some learning-disabled and autistic individuals. In the visual-motor realm, such persons have difficulties in motor planning and execution (apraxia), that is, in imitating movements that are clearly seen and understood at the receptive sensory level. This is apparent in a statement of frustration by a cerebral palsied child at poor attempts at copying. She complains, "Why can't I make my hand do what my eyes see?" This is, of course, only an extreme example of what we all experience, although to varying degrees. In drawing, for example, although all of us can see the object that we wish to represent, only those with special talent are able to direct their hands to accurately portray what the eyes see.

Together with visual-motor problems, there is vulnerability to figure-ground confusion. We are all familiar with "hidden figure" games in which objects to be found are camouflaged by their background so as to be relatively invisible (see Fig. 5-2). Not only are such games more difficult for some cerebral palsied children, but even recognition of shape, color, and size against normal backgrounds may present problems (Cruickshank, Bice, and Wallen, 1957; Dolphin and Cruickshank, 1951; Klapper and Werner, 1950). These figure-ground difficulties also have been observed in the tactile (Dolphin and Cruickshank, 1951) and auditory (Laraway, 1985) spheres.

Within the population with spasticity, these visual disorders occur more often in those with bilateral or at least left-side motor involvement (Wedell, 1961). This is consistent with our understanding of the importance of the right hemisphere in visual types of activities, a left-side motor impairment denoting right-hemisphere damage. In block-design reproductions, for example, left-hemisphere damage (right-side motor involvement) may lead to errors in detail, but the general form, or *gestalt*, is retained. Right-hemisphere damage (left-side motor involvement), however, can result in the total loss of a figure's general configuration. An educational implication of this kind of figure-ground

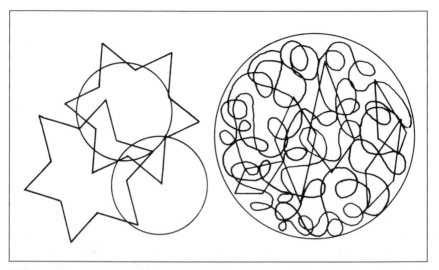

FIGURE 5-2. Two items from the figure-ground test of the Frostig Developmental Test of Visual Perception. The child is asked to outline the two stars and the "kites." (From Abercrombie, 1964. Used with permission of the Spastics Society, London, England.)

confusion is that in teaching situations, the figure should be emphasized, for example, through color or size (or both).

Abercrombie (1964) has devoted particular attention to visual and visual-motor problems in children with cerebral palsy. She sees them as deficient in their understanding of spatial relationships and notes the potential impact of this problem on school-related activities (e.g., writing and drawing) as well as on even the more basic self-care skills of feeding and dressing. Suggestions regarding activities designed to aid in the development of spatial and temporal understanding are found in the Soviet literature (e.g., Simonova, 1981).

Reference has been made to tactile as well as to visual and visual-motor difficulties. Apart from figure-ground confusion, also seen is a basic difficulty in recognizing objects only by touch; this is called *astereognosis*. In those with spastic hemiplegia (involvement of only one side), the difficulty is limited to the hand on the impaired side. An astonishing story of a developmental astereognosis is told by the neurologist Sacks (1984) of a congenitally blind and cerebral palsied woman who throughout her life had had other people do things for her to such an extent that she had made little use of her hands. At the age of 60, this woman could recognize nothing by touch and regarded her hands as useless appendages. In fact, the woman's hands did prove to be functional, as she learned to recognize objects by touch when encouraged to do so. Eventually, she was able to use her hands to sculpt. Clearly, hand use should be encouraged whenever possible, especially for a blind cerebral palsied person, for whom touch becomes a key sensory avenue to experiencing the world.

Attention-Deficit Disorders

Limited attention span and easy distractibility are also found in cerebral palsy (Burks, 1960; Cruickshank, Hallahan, and Bice, 1956; Dolphin and Cruickshank, 1951; Fassler, 1970; Levitt, 1982; Mastikova, 1982). This familiar duo is sometimes accompanied by hyperactivity, a frequent correlate of attentional problems. A child so affected is extremely restless and may be erratic and unpredictable. This trio of behaviors is commonly found in children with organic brain involvement (Cruickshank and Paul, 1971), irrespective of motor difficulties. Other behaviors associated with organicity in children are impulsivity, easy emotionality, and tendencies to inappropriately persist in a behavior that is no longer adaptive (perseveration).

Cerebral palsy children also have difficulty in listening (Finnie, 1975), and stress is placed on the need to give special clarity to verbal communications. In connection with the aforementioned figure-ground confusion, background noise also can be a contributor to problems in listening (Laraway, 1985).

LANGUAGE

Impaired speech is pervasive in cerebral palsy and, in one view (Shapiro et al., 1983), is its most disabling aspect. More than two-thirds are so affected (68 percent), including virtually all of those with athetosis and about half of those with spasticity (Hopkins, Bice, and Colton, 1954). Difficulties in articulation are especially prominent (Byrne, 1959; Irwin, 1972; Largo et al., 1986; Lencione, 1976) and largely result from neuromuscular abnormalities in the organs of speech (Yost and McMillan, 1983). Omission of sounds and substitutions of one sound for another are the most frequent errors (Irwin, 1972). The term applied to impaired articulation due to brain abnormality is *dysarthria*.

Forms of Cerebral Palsy and Quality of Speech

Spasticity. In spasticity, speech is labored and indistinct. Sounds are omitted or distorted, particularly consonant blends, such as *sk* or *tsh*. Changes in pitch occur. Such changes are abrupt and uncontrolled, and voice quality may be husky, gutteral, and tense. Vowel sounds are hypernasal, and speech is frequently accompanied by excessive salivation.

Within the spastic population, the diplegic subgroup is the least affected (Ingram, 1964).

Athetosis. In athetosis, distortion or inconsistency of speech sounds is caused by the continuous involuntary movements and by speech-related airflow irregularities. Speech difficulties are found with sounds that are produced by expelling air, such as *p, b,* and *d,* and those which require a steady flow of air, such as *s, sh,* and *th.* Airflow problems are attributed to the proximity of an impaired movement-related brain structure in athetosis, the basal ganglia, to the respiration center in the brain, the hypothalamus. There is reduced airflow, and the voice lacks force. In addition to airflow irregularities, there may be neuromuscular problems in the larynx, the voice-producing mechanism itself.

Ataxia. In ataxia, speech has a mechanical quality and is accompanied by spasmodic breaks and pauses. Speech may fade away as if a spring-driven mechanism needed rewinding.

FIGURE 5-3. Sample communication board and head pointer. (From *Mental Retardation: Nature, Cause, and Management,* 2nd ed., by George S. Baroff. Copyright © 1986. Used with the permission of Hemisphere Publishing Corp., a subsidiary of Harper & Row, Publishers, Inc.)

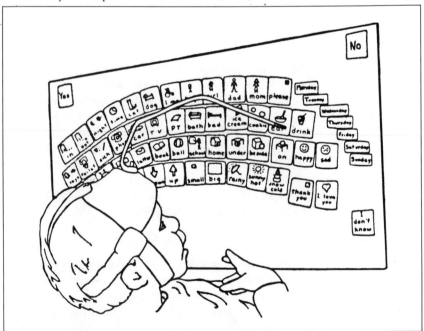

Remediation

Speech and language therapy is encouraged in the cerebral palsied child in the very first year of life, even before first words emerge (Kirk and Gallagher, 1976; Yost and McMillan, 1983). Speech and occupational therapists can stimulate speech-related muscles involved in feeding and babbling. They also can try to eliminate drooling and a protruding tongue. Gain in control of swallowing reduces drooling (e.g., Koheil et al., 1987). Pediatricians should be alert to hypernasal or cleft-palate speech; it can be modified by a prosthetic device that elevates the palate. During school age, speech therapy may involve treatment of articulation and voice-quality disorders together with general stimulation of language itself—vocabulary, grammar, and sentence structure (e.g., Malofeyev, 1985).

Even with early intervention and lengthy therapy, however, some children will remain nonverbal or have speech that is unintelligible (Wolfe, 1950; Yost and McMillan, 1983). For these, alternative modes of communication must be developed, so-called augmentative communi-

FIGURE 5-4. Electronic touch talker. (*Courtesy of Prentke Romich, Co., Wooster, Ohio.*)

cation. One form of visually based communication system is the *communication board*, which is a portable board that contains pictures, words, or symbols that permit communication through pointing with one's finger or with a head pointer, if necessary (see Fig. 5-3). Electronic communication boards now can provide an auditory equivalent for the visual symbol (see Fig. 5-4) and speech representation as well (e.g., Tarnowski and Drabman, 1986).

HEALTH, SENSORY, AND PHYSICAL PROBLEMS

The multidisabling nature of cerebral palsy has been discussed in terms of movement, balance, cognition, and speech difficulties. Its common related health problems are now described.

Epilepsy

Nearly a third (25 to 35 percent) of cerebral palsied children have epilepsy, with the highest frequencies in those with spastic hemiplegia and quadriplegia (Crothers and Paine, 1959; Hopkins, Bice, and Colton, 1954; Shapiro et al., 1983). Both generalized and partial seizures are found. (For a description of epilepsy, see Chapter 6.)

Orthopedic Deformities

Excessive muscle tone tends to pull joints into abnormal positions and eventually creates deformities of foot and ankle, spine, hip, and knee (Makley and Kim, 1983; Shapiro et al., 1983; Thompson, 1983). These deformities often require orthopedic surgery, and repeated operations are the fate of some children. In adults, the most common intervention involves surgery to correct spinal curvature caused by "pulling" muscles. Other treatment procedures consist of exercise and prostheses (e.g., splints and braces).

Visual Problems

More than a quarter (about 28 percent) of cerebral palsied children have visual problems, most often strabismus or squint, an eye-muscle abnormality (Donlon, 1976; Shapiro et al., 1983). Both general visuospatial functioning and depth perception are affected. Such visual difficulties are more frequent in spasticity than in athetosis (Levitt, 1982). Other eye problems are nystagmus (rhythmical oscillation of the eyeballs), amblyopia (dimness of vision or partial loss of sight), optic atrophy, refractive errors, and blindness (Mitchell, 1983). Acuity deviations and muscle imbalances are correctible with glasses, but safety lenses should be standard. In addition, stabilizing frames can correct for head movements (Donlon, 1976). Nystagmus is more difficult to treat, while blindness due to brain-caused visual-field defects (e.g., hemianopia) is not correctible.

Hearing Problems

From 13 to 20 percent of cerebral palsied children have some amount of hearing loss (Colton, 1954; Nober, 1976), with from 6 to 16 percent actually suffering deafness (Shapiro et al., 1983). Hearing loss is particularly common in athetosis (Morris, 1973), where it is chiefly caused by kernicteris (Shapiro et al., 1983), a disorder involving red blood cell deficiency in the newborn. Hearing loss is usually sensorineural in nature, although conductive loss, a middle ear problem, also occurs.

Hearing loss, either present at birth or originating in infancy, interferes with the development of speech. This is why children who are born deaf require special training in order to speak. Treatment is tied to the degree of impairment (hard-of-hearing or deaf) and consists of amplifying sound through hearing aids, training sound discrimination, and teaching speech reading. Conductive loss, more so than sensorineural, benefits from amplification. It is ironic that children whose speech is already affected by neuromuscular and breathing problems must face further difficulties caused by hearing loss. Indeed, motor and cognitive disabilities may mask the presence of a hearing impairment; it may not be detected until as late as age 4 (Shapiro et al., 1983). It is recommended that these children should be fitted with hearing aids as soon as possible, even in the first few months of life (Nober, 1976). Early amplification creates an awareness of sound and speech and is crucial to later language development.

Respiratory Problems

The severely impaired child in particular is vulnerable to respiratory problems (Schleichkorn, 1983). Overcoming the common cold or flu can be extremely difficult. Children with cerebral palsy should be taught breathing exercises so as to increase their breathing capacity and reduce the likelihood of lung infections (Rothman, 1978).

Mortality

The variety of medical problems can affect life span with mortality related to the severity of disability (Eiben and Crocker, 1983).

PERSONALITY: TEMPERAMENT, EMOTIONS, CHARACTER

The focus of this section is on the personality aspects of cerebral palsy. The question may be asked as to whether the disorder produces any behaviors that can be regarded as intrinsic to it.

General Observations

Apart from the earlier-mentioned behaviors associated with organicity, most workers see no particular pattern of adjustment as intrinsic to cerebral palsy (Cruickshank, Hallahan, and Bice, 1976; Nussbaum, 1962; Phelps, 1948). To the contrary, commonly seen behaviors in childhood and adolescence are viewed as the *effects* of the experiences of these individuals, with the attitudes of family, peers, and teachers being particularly significant (e.g., Denhoff and Holden, 1954; Parette and Hourcade, 1984b). Moreover, in the postschool years, attitudes remain important—of parents with regard to their child's degree of self-sufficiency, of potential service providers, of employers, of recreational workers, and of the community at large. All these affect overall adjustment.

What is apparent is that it is generally not disability as such that leads to psychopathology in those with cerebral palsy, but rather the extent to which that disability leads to the frustration of basic psychological needs—structure, self-esteem, and self-expression. Even the organicity-related behaviors, such as hyperactivity, short attention span, and emotional volatility, which are by no means omnipresent in cerebral palsy, are affected by the child's experience. The environment can moderate or exacerbate these difficulties. Structure, acceptance, consistency, controlled stimulation, support for success, and medication where needed all can help the child with these behaviors to function more adaptively.

For the most part, it is the need stresses to which persons with cerebral palsy are exposed that shape their adaptation. Let's now consider the impact of the disorder on their biological and psychological needs.

Survival

The concern here is not with health per se, although health problems such as epilepsy are clearly not trivial, but rather with treatment procedures that themselves can be a source of discomfort or pain. Repeated orthopedic surgical procedures in childhood or adolescence can make these children "old before their time" (Jewell, with Weiner, 1984). Even physical therapy can be stressful if the child is required to engage in prolonged exercises that are uncomfortable. The conflict this can produce in a child who is still too young to appreciate the benefits of muscle exercise is illustrated in this extraordinary statement by a nonambulatory youth: "I cannot remember any need to walk or talk, I was getting everything I wanted without it" (Cruickshank, Hallahan, and Bice, 1976).

Self-Esteem

Intimacy. As in autism (see Chap. 4), the disability itself can interfere with the development of normal parental attachment. Movement difficulties (e.g., rigidity or floppiness) can block normal "cuddling" behavior, and chewing and swallowing problems can make feeding situations labored and tedious (Neuer and Strom, 1983). Moreover, spastic infants and toddlers are often quite irritable, and like some autistic children, may cry for long periods during the day or night. Combining these difficult behaviors with the whole range of stresses thrust on parents of seriously ill or disabled children—physical, financial, and psychological—it is hardly surprising that one author (Boles, 1959) characterized mothers of cerebral palsied children as anxious and guilty in their parental role and conflicted in their marital one. There is also the possibility of friction with siblings, who see their disabled brother or sister getting a disproportionate amount of parental attention (Breslau, 1983). Indeed, one worker (Hall, 1963) saw the families of cerebral palsied children as being at high risk for breakdown, a condition more likely in low-income families (Breslau, 1983). As we'll see in the family of Geri Jewell (Jewell with Weiner, 1984), however, her parents were extremely loving and supportive, though the father's mother was not. She was much ashamed of her granddaughter. Happily, she lived in another city!

Another threat to self-esteem is the attitude of the developing child and adolescent with cerebral palsy toward his or her own body. By the early elementary school grades, the child becomes aware of the nature of his or her disability and its likely persistence (e.g., Minde et al., 1972); and with the probable loss of friendships with children with whom there were relationships in the preschool years, the difference between the affected child and his or her nondisabled peers becomes increasingly evident. In adolescence especially, the difference is likely to be very painful, perhaps even more so for girls (Magill and Hurlburt, 1986). Geri Jewell tells us how embarrassed she was to show her "sticklike" body in the girl's locker room in high school (Jewell, with Weiner, 1984). In a culture where beauty and fitness are much prized, the person who is deformed must look elsewhere for sources of self-esteem. Geri Jewell has actually capitalized on her disability by using it as the source of humor in her career as a comedienne.

Success. As is apparent at this point, the disabilities of cerebral palsy have an impact on virtually every area of endeavor. There are obstacles to performing tasks that the rest of us take for granted. We do not have to think about moving our hands and feet, maintaining our balance, or feeding, dressing, or toileting ourselves. We do not have to think about how we want to express ourselves so as to be understood. The frustration connected with performing even the simplest activities can be very damaging to a person's sense of worth. "I can't walk or even eat without some help. I get discouraged because I'm so helpless. You're stuck and you hate yourself for being stuck" (Cruickshank, Hallahan, and Bice, 1976).

One of the ironies of such a severe disability is that the need to rely so heavily on others for assistance can sap motivation for increasing self-sufficiency. The youth mentioned earlier who asserted his need to do nothing for himself was communicating a sense of acceptance of total dependence on others. Although assuredly a minority view, it reveals how the will to accomplish even the most basic functions can be subverted.

Autonomy. Diminished autonomy and excessive dependency are a common pattern. Parents or care givers tend to respond to the child's genuine physical needs in an overly protective manner and can produce the kind of total psychological and physical dependence just described. The reality of a cerebral palsied child's vulnerability, however, should not be minimized. Poor motor control and balance, susceptibility to seizures, and possible visual or hearing difficulties all have the effect of diminishing a child's natural self-protective abilities. The wheelchair-bound spastic quadriplegic child is truly limited in the capacity to avoid physically dangerous situations and must depend on others for basic protection. The consequence of highly protective care givers is a dependency pattern dubbed the "apron strings" syndrome. The child is seen as fearful, seeking of assistance, demanding of attention, overreacting to separation, submissive, and lacking in initiative (Cruickshank, 1976; Shere, 1954; Shere and Kastenbaum, 1966). In the extreme, there is a sense of perceived helplessness, a lack of independence in thought and action and reduced motivation for greater self-sufficiency. Happily, this attitude is not universal. In Chapter 1, a group of cerebral palsied young adults was described who insightfully noted that because of their inherently greater dependence they needed more, not fewer, experiences that would foster greater self-sufficiency (Mowatt, 1970). These young people were asking for less protection, for greater freedom to grow, and for a reduced state of dependency. Two of the pioneers in cerebral palsy, Crothers and Paine (1959), encouraged their fellow-physicians to avoiding fostering docility in their patients with cerebral palsy.

AGE-RELATED ADAPTIVE BEHAVIOR PROBLEMS

INFANCY AND EARLY CHILDHOOD (BIRTH TO AGE 6)

During the early developmental years, the normal child acquires relative mastery of his or her body and native tongue. The body can be moved easily and securely, and there is steady growth in the coordination of hands and eyes. But this process is going to be slowed, if not actually precluded, in the child with cerebral palsy. Self-help skills in feeding, dressing, and toileting are delayed, speech lacks clarity, and motor difficulties interfere with play. And these impairments, especially in speech and play, compound the child's difficulties because they tend to limit interactions with peers and nonfamily adults. More broadly, the physically imposed mobility restrictions reduce opportunities for general stimulation and result in a child who seems naive in comparison with agemates. Equally important are the potential personality problems and immaturity that can result when loving parents seem unduly protective of their cerebral palsied child's physical safety. How severe disabilities evoke such protective behavior and the pattern of dependency is illustrated in the following description of a young cerebral palsied child.

> Bobby is a 4-year-old with severe athetosis. Virtually helpless, he cannot move himself or speak clearly. He can briefly sit without support but then tends to slide backward. He has little use of his hands; they're typically clenched and show jerky, uncontrolled movements. Unable to stand by himself, he continues to be carried about by his parents. Early feeding problems around chewing and swallowing have eased, and he does have good bladder control.
>
> In spite of his motor limitations, there has been steady growth in his cognitive abilities. He recognizes things about him and knows their names. But access to new experiences is extremely limited. Accustomed to having others do for him, there is little opportunity for growth of personal coping skills. The severity of his disability fosters dependency, and this is intensified by parents who, overwhelmed by his impairment, see him as a helpless baby who needs the protection that they alone can offer.
>
> Nevertheless, they derive pleasure from Bobby, as do other parents of seriously disabled children. The disability feeds into parental and, particularly, maternal nurturing needs. Beyond that, his parents are pleased with his mental development as his general understanding is approximately at age level. (Adapted from Taylor, 1959)

SCHOOL AGE

General access to public school is a relatively recent phenomenon for the cerebral palsied child (Zadig, 1983). In the past, such children often were placed in private schools for physically disabled children, in day care programs primarily for preschool-age retarded children, or in institutions for mentally retarded individuals. Only the brightest and least impaired physically could enter the public schools. The main resistance to such admission centered around their limitations in mobility and in self-care.

Under the pressure of federal legislation, the school doors were opened, and pupils with cerebral palsy are now found in regular classes as well as in special classes for those with physical disabilities and/or mental retardation. And now, federal legislation has extended school opportunities down into the 3- to 5-year range (Public Law 99-457, 1986).

The learning problems of cerebral palsied students reflect their specific disabilities. With the majority of such students functioning at subaverage intellectual levels, basic progress in academic skills will be delayed (Dillon, 1966). When this delay is combined with eye-muscle focus problems that interfere with reading itself (Jones and Collins, 1966), visual-motor difficulties, problems in paying attention, indistinct speech, seizures, possible hearing and visual loss, emotional immaturity, and weak motivation, the educational challenge is not inconsiderable. Attention has been particularly called to the role of the guidance counselor with elementary school age cerebral palsied children (Parette and Hourcade, 1984b), but it is clear that assistance may be needed at all age levels.

During adolescence, likely academic difficulties will be complicated by the normal problems associated with that period—problems of social relationships, sexuality, vocational aspirations, and independence. The need for independence may be relatively muted in comparison with nondisabled peers. In the domain of sexuality, while cerebral palsy does not rob one of sexual feelings, its expression can be affected by the motor problems (Chipouras et al., 1979; Mooney, Cole, and Chilgren, 1975).

> Paul is 12 and has a left spastic hemiplegia. He is small and undeveloped for his age. His gait shows a marked limp, and his left arm and hand are stiff. His development was slower than that of an older brother. Speech was not present until 2½, but by 4 he was reasonably fluent and had good intelligibility. As a child he was hyperactive and had a short attention span. His parents enjoyed him, but he didn't play well with other children; they tended to overexcite him. By 7 his hyperactivity had lessened, but his attention span was still short. In school, he had special difficulty in understanding visual forms and spatial relationships, an area of expected impairment in light of

motor problems indicating right hemisphere damage. He has been in a special class for three years, enjoys school and his teacher, but peer problems persist. They tease him and he becomes angry and strikes out. At 12 he cannot read, though he's learned some street and bus signs. In spite of his many problems his parents take pride in Paul. His father does carpentry, and Paul has learned a little about tools and tries to be helpful. The parents' main concern is with his emotionality. They believe that he could get along better if he had more control of his feelings. Apart from emotional outbursts, his mother sees him as a gentle and sensitive youngster who is easily handled if one avoids direct confrontation. (Adapted from Taylor, 1959)

Geri Jewell, mentioned earlier, offers a fascinating picture of the effects of her disability on her life. Affected with athetosis and a mild hearing loss, she tells her story in an autobiography that covers the years of infancy to young adulthood. It is much recommended (Jewell with Weiner, 1984) as a means of understanding cerebral palsy from the "inside" from one who lives with its effects every day. The focus here is limited to the years of middle childhood and early adolescence.

Geri's early school years were marked by interminably long bus rides with other physically disabled children and family moves to find better special programs in the public schools. Following one such move, Geri experienced her first serious teasing and rejection. Ridiculed as "gimp," "freak," "cripple," and "retard," she emerged from that trauma with a new and diminished sense of self.

> Until that day I had never really felt at all different. [A difference that we see but that the disabled person does not.] I knew that I was different, but oddly enough, I didn't see my handicap the way other people did. Even now [at age 25], the only time I see it is when I'm walking toward a glass door or see my reflection in a mirror, because in my own mind I don't look like that. For years my parents' friends kept saying how desirable I was. . . . I'd even been a poster child.
>
> And now all my accomplishments suddenly amounted to zero [instantaneous fall in self-esteem]. I realized for the first time that I was just what these kids said I was: a cripple, someone to take advantage of, someone to hate and be afraid of. Nobody would ever know what I was really like on the inside because on the outside I was scary, ugly and different [a desirable human being imprisoned in a handicapped body]. (Jewell, with Weiner, 1984, p. 93)

Precisely the same difference between our own view of ourselves and that of others is reflected in a retrospective view of himself by another cerebral palsied person, Raymond Goldman, who describes a childhood visit to an orthopedist for the fitting of leg braces (Goldman, 1947; Wright, 1983). Raymond writes, "I preferred looking at folding doors to looking at the children. I couldn't stand the sight of them; they were ugly and sickening. I almost hated them. Their legs were thin and misshapen. Their faces, somehow, were too old and wise. I felt that way not realizing that I was there as one of them. If someone had reminded me that my legs were thin and deformed, ... I would have been shocked. (Goldman, 1947)

The issue here, in both cases, is one of *body image*. A person's body image appears to relate more to his or her attitude toward it than to its objective nature. And that attitude reflects our self-esteem, itself a product of how "significant others" have accepted us. Raymond, like Geri, experienced a sudden and catastrophic fall in self-esteem when he was teased and ridiculed by other children on his first day in public school. Both he and Geri had to learn to regard their bodies as only one aspect of themselves and to value their persons for that which was positive about them. It's a universal problem, since we are all a blend of wanted and unwanted qualities. If significant others accept us, then we can learn to accept ourselves, the good with the bad. This serves to underline the tremendous importance of society's attitude toward disabled persons. We must all recognize the power that we possess as individuals to affect how other people come to see and feel about themselves.

Let's now return to Geri, as she describes a school experience that gives us some sense of how enforced separation, another condition that affects self-esteem, is perceived by those who are separated (segregated). The school had a special-education facility that was physically set off from the regular class building by a playground. Children were not permitted to cross an imaginary playground line and play with each other. The involuntary separation and exclusion from contact with non-disabled peers created in Geri the sense of being a reject. She had always accepted the possible rejection by an individual child as the price of being different, but it was the official stamp given to it by the school that appears to have been particularly offensive to her. Both these experiences, of course, touch fundamentally on every person's need for intimacy, the need to be liked and approved of by those whose approval we seek.

In sixth grade Geri was mainstreamed, and her description of the effect of attending regular classes rather than special ones deepens our understanding of the benefits of normalization—of integration rather than separation of children, and adults, with disabilities.

> Got all Ds but at least I was seeing regular kids up close, watching what they did, how they acted, learning all the time, trying to blend in.

This is a superb statement of the importance of modeling as a teaching and learning method. Geri's wish to "blend in" also points up another difficult psychological situation: one of trying to fit simultaneously into two different worlds. Since Geri was relatively less impaired than her disabled peers, she could aspire to accomplishments appropriate to able-bodied youngsters, such as balancing on a skateboard, but she was always aware that she was not really "able-bodied." Indeed, as a preschooler, Geri seems to have tried to reduce the ambiguity in her self-image by deliberately choosing the handicapped role in her doll play. Needless to say, this horrified her mother. This same dilemma was expressed by a graduate student with cerebral palsy who is primarily impaired in her gait but whose speech and dexterity are grossly normal. In new social contacts, this woman is always "on guard" for the question that must ultimately come: "Why do you have difficulty in walking?" Until it is asked, she is simultaneously operating in two different roles—normal and disabled. This is painful to her, but once "the question" is asked, the ambiguity is removed and she can step into her "real" role, like that of Geri, a disabled person but only mildly so. This kind of role ambiguity would appear to stress one's need for structure.

In high school Geri was cautious in her emotional relationships. She distrusted the motives of an English teacher who seemed to be giving her special attention. Geri wondered whether the teacher was doing it "because she feels sorry for me." This evokes the question of how one should treat a handicapped person. This is Geri's comment on it:

> People don't know how to approach us. So they don't. And if they do, they wonder if its OK to bring up the subject of our affliction. My advice is "yes."

The graduate student mentioned earlier would agree. She and Geri assert that people have to feel that they can ask questions without feelings being hurt. Geri says,

> Ask any questions you want. First, because we're generally so hungry for any kind of interaction, we'll jump at a chance to talk about anything and, secondly, like everybody else, we enjoy talking about ourselves whenever possible. (Jewell with Weiner, 1984, p. 160)

Adolescence brings with it an increased sensitivity to one's own body and, of course, sexuality itself. Geri's observations here are also instructive:

> When you watch telethons, you probably hear handicapped people say that their handicaps don't get in the way of their sex lives. Whenever I hear that I start to laugh. The truth is, one of the reasons that . . . regular class kids were so afraid to get close to me was that they were afraid things might get sexual eventually . . . [and] nobody was identifying me with the idea of sex at all.

Geri was ashamed of her body:

> Others had fully formed figures, . . . I was a stick. I couldn't stand to take my clothes off and take showers with these girls. I felt so inadequate, so ugly, so handicapped.

In retrospect, Geri could recognize that her normal peers were not free of the same anxieties. A resident of the Los Angeles area, Geri notes:

> Everyone was California body-conscious, obsessive; everyone felt inadequate to the TV commercial ideal. You don't have to have CP to feel inadequate about your body in Southern California!

A description of Geri's only date in high school, with another cerebral palsied youth, conveys the degree of her social isolation and how the disability itself interferes with normal kinds of romantic activity:

> He had gotten his driver's license, and we decided to go to the drive-in movie. We were both expecting that we'd make out and neck like everybody else, but nothing seemed to happen. Just the act of holding hands created problems for us. He was on the left side of me and his right arm was spastic.

The rest of the episode offers some comic relief and shows us a side of Geri with which we can all identify:

> About ten minutes before the dumb movie ended, as we both sat there in frustration, . . . I told Steve to start the car. I wanted to leave before everyone else did so we wouldn't end up in a collision [Steve was agreeable] . . . In a panic, however, he put the car into forward instead of reverse, and the car lurched up onto the cement bumper and stalled there blocking the view of the other cars behind us. Since he'd forgotten to take the speaker out of the window as he drove away, he ripped it right off the pole. It cracked the window and hung there.

In his confusion Steve turns his headlights on, as Geri dryly observes, "a very big mistake at a drive-in," and horns begin blaring from all directions. "Headlights were flashing off and on and people were screaming. I did the only honorable thing I could do, I hid on the floor."

They decide to go for a Big Mac but Steve, still shaken, locks his keys in the car. After getting the food, he sets it on the hood while using a hanger to get the window opened (another accident waiting to happen). He's successful, they get into the car, forgetting the food on the hood, and Steve says, "Come on, Geri, let's go home." He drives off and "Big Macs, french fries, and vanilla milk shakes land on the windshield. . . I laughed so hard I soaked the seats of his mother's car (she also had occasional bladder control problems). Yup, I had a great social life in high school, no doubt about it." (Jewell with Weiner, 1984, pp. 183–184)

Little has been said about her school experience, as such. It was clearly very different from that of nondisabled students. Much time was spent in therapies—PT, OT, and speech, especially in elementary school. In retrospect, she felt that too little time was devoted to academics. Teachers were seen as having such a low expectation of what they could do with their lives that the days were filled with time-wasting projects that had little to do with schooling. She blames the school for allowing her to reach 21 thinking that Canada was one of our states! Yet two teachers had a major positive impact on her. One helped her and her disabled classmates to begin to explore and express their individual creativities ("self-expression") while the other did not ridicule her wish to be an actress.

ADULTHOOD

For the dependent individual with cerebral palsy and his or her family, adulthood presents its own special problems. For the family, the change from student to a more uncertain role can be stressful (Brotherson et al., 1986; Suelzle and Keenan, 1981). With many lacking job skills and, at least initially, having limited access to work settings, new demands fall on families, at a time, ironically, when fewer support services are available. The disabled adult finds less acceptance than the disabled child.

Employment

The cerebral palsied high school graduate has an uncertain future. Only about 25 to 50 percent have been readily employable. (Cohen, 1976; Kiernan and Morrison, 1983; Moed and Litwin, 1963; O'Grady, et al., 1985; O'Reilly, 1975), with those actually employed reflecting the lower end of that range (O'Reilly, 1975; McCavitt, 1966). The current national thrust in supported employment should significantly increase the number finding work. Commenting on her own experience, Geri says,

> You can't believe how hard it is to find a job when you have cerebral palsy. I couldn't type or be a waitress [due to motor problems], and a lot of companies wouldn't hire me because they don't know how the public would react to someone like me.

There are numerous obstacles to employment—motor, cognitive, communicative, and social-emotional. For those with cognitive impairments, vocational options are narrowed to relatively unskilled tasks, the kind found in sheltered workshops, but even this opportunity is limited by motor difficulties, although I saw one young man who stuffs envelopes with a head pointer. The pointer has a rubber tip that enables the young man to raise the flap of an envelope. Parenthetically, this young man was spending his days in an adult enrichment center, a day program providing vocational, recreational, and social experiences.

Along with physical problems, there are psychological ones. Excessive dependency on parents, lack of realism in job choices, limited awareness of the effects of one's own disability, fearfulness, immaturity, and weak motivation all constrain vocational potential.

Within this gloomy environment, however, numerous persons with cerebral palsy find employment. Such people tend to be mildly disabled, to have higher IQs, and to have been educated in integrated schools. The capacity for self-care and travel also seems to be important (O'Grady et al., 1985). Some years ago I had a colleague with athetosis who functioned as a teacher in a higher-education setting. I also remember a spastic individual who was a distinguished geneticist at a major university. While some individuals with cerebral palsy may seem to passively accept their lot, others, like the young adults in the British documentary film *Like Other People* (British Mental Health Film Council, 1972), demand for themselves greater self-determination and a chance to function in more normal adult roles.

Residential Status

Although the family home continues to be the primary residence for the young adult with cerebral palsy, group homes and other alternative living situations are becoming increasingly available. Movement into a nonfamily setting can be a step toward greater independence, and it also offers socialization possibilities likely reduced with departure from school (Knishkowy et al., 1986; Niestadt and Marques, 1984). In the family home, social isolation is a threat during evening and weekend hours when the wheelchair-bound person lacks access to day programs. And because it is simply easier to do things for severely disabled persons than to take the time and effort to teach them to do for themselves, they typically enter nonfamily settings with higher degrees of dependency than is necessary.

> George, age 37, has spastic diplegia, is mildly retarded, has a personality disorder, and is now in a group home for cerebral palsied adults. Another group home resident says it's hard to do for oneself at home because parents want to help us so much. Pat, now 25, urges parents to let their child do as much as possible, giving help only when necessary. "I wasn't independent at home like I am here. I was depending on my parents to do everything—mostly my mother."
>
> "If a child falls, let him get back up again. That's how they learn—fall down and get back up until you do it right." (Adapted from Knishkowy et al., 1986)

In recent years, so-called independent living centers, programs not facilities, have been created to provide services that enhance independence (Niestadt, 1987). Of special importance to the wheelchair-bound individual who needs assistance in basic self-care, the service can provide a personal attendant who lives with and cares for the person. If this has always been the family's role, residence in another environment requires the availability of equivalent support. With a personal attendant, the individual can live independently, in his or her own apartment, for example. Other independence-promoting services offered are barrier-free housing, transportation (always a problem where there are mobility limitations), counseling on rights and benefits, and counseling by peers who can serve as role models (Jones and Ulicny, 1986). Aspirations for greater independence may conflict, however, with established family roles; this is illustrated in the following vignette:

> Ben is a moderately retarded 26-year-old with mild cerebral palsy. He'd like to move to a group home and live with friends, but his mother is sure that he wouldn't be adequately cared for there [overprotective], and in any case, Ben is needed to assist a disabled grandmother who lives with them. [Ben in the role of "personal attendant".] Perhaps most important of all, the family depends on the financial assistance Ben receives as a permanently disabled adult. [They are more dependent on him than he is on them!] The family concerns are real; it is only that the disabled member has less freedom than his nondisabled counterpart to move into more age-appropriate roles, roles that would cause the family to find other ways of meeting needs that Ben now fulfills. (Adapted from Brotherson et al., 1986)

Apart from those who live independently or in family or group homes, persons with more severe cognitive and/or physical limitations are frequently found in public residential mental retardation settings and nursing homes.

Recreation

Given the nature of the disorder, recreational opportunities are necessarily reduced. With adaptations of recreational equipment, however, persons with cerebral palsy can participate in some of the same activities enjoyed by nondisabled ones. So-called adaptive bowling equipment is shown in Fig. 5-5.

Special adult day programs include recreational activities that have an educational as well as a play goal. Frisbie baseball teaches team play (cooperation) and the need to follow a particular sequence. Bake-offs also offer team competition and provide an activity that may be of greater interest to women. Even scavenger hunts provide a mix of fun and learning. The treasure seeker has to read directions in the quest for treasure. In larger communities, local parks and recreational departments may offer special programs in swimming, bowling, and fishing.

Socialization

Day programs are also intended to meet some of the social (intimacy) needs of clients. The wheelchair-bound adult who also lacks intelligible speech is very limited in access to social relationships. And even where

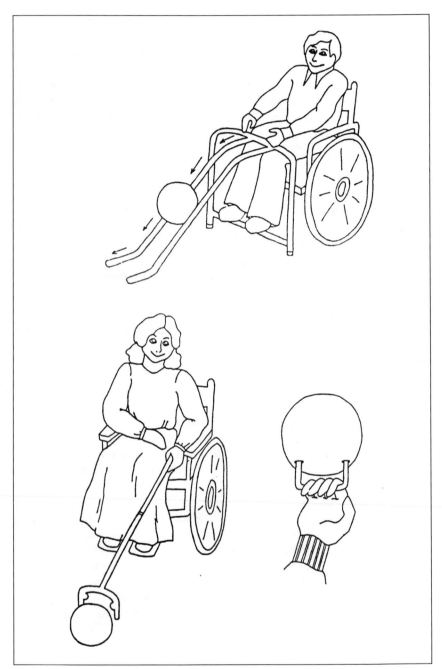

FIGURE 5-5. "Adaptive" equipment for bowling.
(*From Wehman et al., 1980.*)

such access is provided, the aesthetic aspects of the disorder hinder contact. I remember very clearly the autobiography of a cerebral palsied woman who felt herself to be an "alien," not like the rest of us. She saw herself as trapped in a deformed shell, different from the normal population that walked by her wheelchair without acknowledging her. Only in reading the autobiography of a similarly disabled person did she discover a kindred soul, one who had emotions like her own, and found a bridge to the rest of humanity.

But social isolation can even occur in settings housing other disabled individuals. The speech problem makes communication frustrating for both speaker and listener. In this regard, one of the great boons to communication has been the development of nonspeech devices. Using a communication board or a word processor, even the most immobilized person, with a head pointer, can engage in "verbal" discourse.

A Married Couple with Cerebral Palsy

Martin and Barbara are a cerebral palsied couple. He is 36, and she is 30. They reside in a special nursing home, a facility for physically disabled persons. Both are severely affected physically and move with the aid of walkers. Their speech is indistinct. Martin says,

> I was born in '44 when they didn't know too much about CP. I proved the doctors wrong; I walk and I talk. We don't think we are handicapped. Maybe we don't walk or talk so good but that doesn't stop us. We can walk, we can see, we can hear, and that means a lot to us. . . . We dress our own selves and we do everything but cook. [Here we see pride and a focus on abilities rather than disabilities; evidence of good self-esteem.]

Barbara says, "A lot of people think that because we're handicapped, we are retarded" (there seems to be nothing more feared than to be seen as retarded). Geri Jewell (Jewell, with Weiner, 1984) reveals the lengths to which she would go to avoid being thought retarded. At age nine during a visit to her speech therapist she burst into tears and told her that she wanted a pair of canes, those metal crutches with arm braces. When her teacher asked why she said that if she had canes people would know her problems were physical and that she wasn't mentally retarded. "I wanted to look like I had cerebral palsy so people would understand." (This may have been a factor in her mentioning her preschool doll playing when she treated her doll as if were handicapped.)

Barbara continues,

> In the special education schools they thought we couldn't learn. I didn't graduate; I finished ninth grade. . . . If we got a good teacher, we could learn a whole lot. . . . [Geri Jewell also stressed the importance of a good teacher,

one who had some expectations that, in spite of their disabilities, they could learn.] People don't understand CP. Especially little kids. They look at us because their folks don't teach them. What makes me so mad is that . . . people just stare. [Not only children can be cruel. Discomfiture at being stared at is a commonplace experience of people with visible physical differences.]

Martin says, "Our families couldn't believe it when they heard we were getting married. They were afraid. Her mom called the director . . . and said 'What can we do about Martin and Barbara?' The director said, 'Martin is fickle . . . don't worry it won't ever last.' And this coming August, it will be five years [continual parental fears about their disabled children as sexual beings].

"We have a good marriage. If we didn't . . . we couldn't stay in one room.

"That first year was hard for Barbara, being away from her folks [the dependency referred to earlier in the chapter]. Every time she got sick, she wanted her mom and I would call. But the last time she got sick in that first year . . . I said, "Barbara, no, I won't call your mom. Because some day, you won't have your mom and you will have to rely on me." And we fought about this. I put the phone on the bed and walked out. I was gone for about an hour. Then I came back and said I didn't realize that Barbara would miss her mom so much.

"I do feel that everyone should be married, because then he has a mate someplace in the world. I was very lucky to find Barbara, although sometimes I would like to give her back to her mom. She probably would feel the same way about me." (Orlansky and Heward, 1981, pp. 61–63)

SPECIAL SERVICE NEEDS

Medical needs are of particular concern and remain prominent into adulthood. The associated motor and speech problems give special significance to physical therapy, occupational therapy, and speech therapy. During the elementary school years, decisions are likely to be reached regarding further efforts to increase mobility in nonambulatory children. The child and family may have to accept the reality of a permanent wheelchair. Indeed, for some children, progressive orthopedic deformities may result in a loss of existing ambulatory skills and lead to a wheelchair (Taft and Matthews, 1983). Chronic muscle abnormalities also can require surgery in childhood and on into adulthood (Bleck, 1984). Spastic diplegic cerebral palsy, in which the legs are more involved than arms, is the form most amenable to surgical correction (Gage, 1983).

Technology has made major contributions to reducing or circumventing motor disabilities—notably in the speech area through augmentative communication devices and in general mobility (e.g., through the motorized wheelchair). The minicomputer also has been a boon. A problem with all these, however, resides in ensuring access to the existing technology.

Programs and services that support opportunities for more independent living, employment, recreation, and social integration mushroomed in the 1980s. Independent living services can provide a personal attendant and enable the physically disabled individual to receive the kind of basic care that earlier was available only from the family. Independent living is also facilitated by the reduction of architectural barriers, such as ramping buildings to make them wheelchair-accessible.

In the employment sphere, programs of supported employment and rehabilitation engineering in the workplace ensure greater job opportunities than have been heretofore available. Rehabilitation engineering involves making whatever physical changes are necessary (e.g., removal of architectural barriers) so that there can be access to employment.

Physical barriers to the use of community recreational resources persist and force the kind of social isolation that was described earlier. Moreover, apart from the concrete barriers, there are those in our hearts and minds. In our societal drive for excellence we have great difficulty in accepting our own imperfections as well as those of others. In a success-driven culture, those of us who do not fully measure up to the cultural ideals of beauty, intelligence, and other valued attributes are necessarily devalued. And we devalue ourselves as well as them. Cannot our perspective on human worth be broadened?

REFERENCES

Abercrombie, M. L. J. (1964). *Perceptual and visuomotor disorders in cerebral palsy.* London: Spastics Society.

Alexander, M. A., and Bauer, R. E. (1988). Cerebral palsy. In V. B. Van Hasvelt, P. S. Strain, and M. Hersen (Eds.), *Handbook of developmental and physical disabilities.* Elmsford, NY: Pergamon.

Asher, P., and Schonell, F. E. (1950). A survey of 400 cases of cerebral palsy. *Archives of Diseases of Children, 25,* 360–379.

Banker, B. Q., and Bruce-Gregoris, J. (1983). Neuropathology. In G. H. Thompson, I. L. Rubin, and R. M. Bilenker (Eds.), *Comprehensive management of cerebral palsy.* New York: Grune & Stratton.

Bice, H. V., and Cruickshank, W. M. (1966). Evaluation of intelligence. In W. M. Cruickshank (Ed.), *Cerebral palsy: Its individual and community problems,* 2d Ed. Syracuse, NY: Syracuse University Press.

Bleck, E. E. (1984). Where have all the CP children gone? The needs of adults. *Developmental Medicine and Child Neurology, 26,* 674–676.

Boles, G. (1959). Personality factors in mothers of cerebral palsied children. *Genetic Psychology Monographs, 59,* 159–218.

Brent, R. L., and Harris, M. I. (1976). *Prevention of embryonic, fetal, and perinatal disease* (DHEW Pub. No. NIH 76-853). Bethesda, MD.: National Institutes of Health.

Breslau, N. (1983). Family care: Effects on siblings and mothers. In G. H. Thompson, I. L. Rubin, and R. M. Bilenker (Eds.), *Comprehensive management of cerebral palsy.* New York: Grune & Stratton.

British Mental Health Film Council in Association with the Spastics Society. (1972). *Like other people.* London.

Brotherson, M. J., Backus, L. H., Summers, J. A., and Turnbull, A. (1986). Transition to adulthood. In J. A. Summers (Ed.), *The right to grow up.* Baltimore: Brookes.

Burks, H. (1960). The hyperkinetic child. *Exceptional Children, 27,* 18–26.

Byrne, M. (1959). Speech and language development of athetoid and spastic children. *Journal of Speech and Hearing Research, 24,* 231–240.

Capute, A. J. (1975). Cerebral palsy and associated dysfunctions. In R. H. Haslam and P. J. Valletutti (Eds.), *Medical problems in the classroom.* Austin, TX: PRO-ED.

Chipouras, S., Cornelius, D. A., and Daniels, S. M. (1979). *Education and counseling services for disabled people.* Washington, DC: George Washington University.

Cohen, J. C. (1976). Vocational guidance and employment. In W. M. Cruickshank (Ed.), *Cerebral palsy: A developmental disability.* Syracuse, NY: Syracuse University Press.

Cohen, S., and Warren, R. D. (1987). Preliminary survey of family abuse of children served by United Cerebral Palsy centers. *Developmental Medicine and Child Neurology, 29,* 12–18.

Crothers, B., and Paine, R. S. (1959). *The natural history of cerebral palsy.* Cambridge, MA: Harvard University Press.

Cruickshank, W. M. (Ed.). (1976). *Cerebral palsy: A developmental disability,* 3d ed. Syracuse, NY: Syracuse University Press.

Cruickshank, W. M., Bice, H. V., and Wallen, N. E. (1957). *Perception and cerebral palsy,* 2d ed. Syracuse, NY: Syracuse University Press.

Cruickshank, W. M., and Hallahan, D. P., with Bice, H. V. (1976). Personality and behavioral characteristics. In W. M. Cruickshank (Ed.), *Cerebral Palsy: A developmental disability,* 3d Ed. Syracuse, NY: Syracuse University Press.

Cruickshank, W. M., and Paul, J. L. (1971). The psychological characteristics of brain-injured children. In W. M. Cruickshank (Ed.), *Psychology of exceptional children and youth.* Englewood Cliffs, NJ: Prentice-Hall.

Denhoff, E. (1976). Medical aspects. In W. M. Cruickshank (Ed.), *Cerebral palsy: A developmental disability,* 3rd Ed. Syracuse, NY: Syracuse University Press.

Denhoff, E., and Holden, R. H. (1954). Family influence on successful school adjustment of cerebral palsied children. *Exceptional Children, 21,* 5–7.

Dillon, E. J. (1966). An investigation of basic psycholinguistic and reading abilities among the cerebral palsied. *Dissertation Abstracts, 27*(4A), 949.

Dolphin, J., and Cruickshank, W. M. (1951). The figure-background relationship. *Journal of Clinical Psychology, 7,* 228–231.

Donlon, E. T. (1976). Visual disorders. In W. M. Cruickshank (Ed.), *Cerebral palsy: A developmental disability,* 3d ed. Syracuse, NY: Syracuse University Press.

Drillien, C. M. (1974). Prenatal and perinatal factors in etiology and outcome of low birthweight. *Clinics in Perinatology, 1,* 197–211.

Eiben, R. M., and Crocker, A. C. (1983). Cerebral palsy within the spectrum of developmental disabilities. In G. H. Thompson, I. L. Rubin, and R. M.

Bilenker (Eds.). *Comprehensive management of cerebral palsy.* New York: Grune & Stratton.

Fassler, J. (1970). Performance of cerebral palsied children under reduced auditory input. *Exceptional Children, 37,* 201–209.

Finnie, N. R. (1975). *Handling the young cerebral palsied child,* 2d ed. New York: Dutton.

Gage, J. R. (1983). Surgical complications. In G. H. Thompson, I. L. Rubin, and R. M. Bilenker (Eds.), *Comprehensive management of cerebral palsy.* New York: Grune & Stratton.

Golden, N. L., and Rubin, I. L. (1983). Intrauterine factors and the risk for the development of cerebral palsy. In G. H. Thompson, I. L. Rubin, and R. M. Bilenker (Eds.), *Comprehensive management of cerebral palsy.* New York: Grune & Stratton.

Goldman, R. L. (1947). *Even the night.* New York: Macmillan.

Grossman, H. I. (Ed.). (1983). *Classification in mental retardation.* Washington, DC: American Association on Mental Deficiency.

Hall, W. J. (1963). Physical handicap and family stress. *Cerebral Palsy Review, 24*(4), 8–11.

Heinonen, O. P., Slone, D., and Shapiro, S. (1977). *Birth defects and drugs in pregnancy.* Acton, MS: Publishing Sciences Group.

Henderson, J. L. (1961). *Cerebral palsy in childhood and adolescence.* Edinburgh: Livingstone.

Hohman, L. B., and Freedheim, D. K. (1958). Further studies on intelligence levels in cerebral palsied children. *American Journal of Physical Medicine, 37,* 90–97.

Hopkins, T., Bice, H. V., and Colton, K. C. (1954). *Evaluation and education of the cerebral palsied child: New Jersey study.* Washington, DC: International Council for Exceptional Children.

Ingram, T. T. S. (1964). *Pediatric aspects of cerebral palsy.* Edinburgh: Edinburgh Press.

Irwin, O. (1972). *Communication variables of cerebral palsied and mentally retarded children.* Springfield, IL: Thomas.

Jewell, G., with Weiner, S. (1984). *Geri.* New York: William Morrow.

Jones, J. W., and Collins, A. P. (1966). *Educational programs for visually handicapped children.* Washington, DC: U.N. Office of Education.

Jones, M. L., and Ulicny, G. R. (1986). The independent living perspective: Applications to services for adults with developmental disabilities. In J. A. Summers (Ed.), *The right to grow up.* Baltimore: Brookes.

Katz, E. (1955). Intelligence test performance of "athetoid" and "spastic" children with cerebral palsy. *Cerebral Palsy Review, 16,* 17–18.

Kiernan, W. E., and Morrison, P. (1983). Rehabilitation and habilitation of the adult. In G. H. Thompson, I. L. Rubin, and R. M. Bilenker (Eds.), *Comprehensive management of cerebral palsy.* New York: Grune & Stratton.

Kirk, S. A., and Gallagher, J. J. (1976). *Educating exceptional children,* 3d ed. Boston: Houghton-Mifflin.

Klapper, M., and Birch, H. G. (1967). A fourteen year follow-up study of cerebral palsy: Intellectual change and stability. *American Journal of Orthopsychiatry, 37,* 540–547.

Klapper, Z. A., and Werner, H. (1950). Developmental deviations in brain-injured (cerebral palsied) members of pairs of identical twins. *The Quarterly Journal of Child Behavior, 2,* 288–313.

Knishkowy, B. N., Gross, M., Sundee, L. M., Reeb, K. G., and Stewart, D. L.

(1986). Independent Living: Caring for the adult with cerebral palsy. *The Journal of Family Practice, 23,* 21–27.

Koheil, R., Sochaniwskyj, A. E., Bablich, K., Kenny, D. J., and Milner, M. (1987). Biofeedback techniques and behavior modification in the conservative remediation of drooling children with cerebral palsy. *Developmental Medicine and Child Neurology, 29,* 19–26.

Laraway, L. A. (1985). Auditory selective attention in cerebral-palsied individuals. *Language, Speech, and Hearing Services in Schools, 16,* 260–266.

Largo, R. H., Molinari, L., Comenale Pinto, L., Weber, M., and Duc, G. (1986). Language development of term and preterm children during the first five years of life. *Developmental Medicine and Child Neurology, 28,* 333–350.

Lencione, R. M. (1976). The development of communication skills. In W. M. Cruickshank (Ed.), *Cerebral palsy: A developmental disability,* 3d ed. Syracuse, NY: Syracuse University Press.

Levitt, S. (1982). *Treatment of cerebral palsy and motor delay,* 2d ed. Oxford, England: Blackwell.

Magill, J., and Hurlburt, N. (1986). The self-esteem of adolescents with cerebral palsy. *The American Journal of Occupational Therapy, 40,* 402–407.

Malofayev, N. N. (1985). Characteristics of lexical vocabulary in cerebral palsy schoolchildren. *Defektologiya, 1,* 29–33.

Mastikova, Y. (1982). Clinical characterization of developmental backwardness in cerebral palsied children. *Defektologiya, 4,* 7–11.

Makley, J. T., and Kim, W. C. (1983). Spastic equinus deformities. In G. H. Thompson, I. L. Rubin, and R. M. Bilenker (Eds.), *Comprehensive management of cerebral palsy.* New York: Grune & Stratton.

McCarty, S., St. James, P., Berninger, V. W., and Gans, B. M. (1986). Assessment of intellectual functioning across the life span in cerebral palsy. *Developmental Medicine and Child Neurology, 28,* 369–372.

McCavitt, M. E. (1966). The cerebral palsied. *Rehabilitation Record, 7,* 2.

Miller, E., and Rosenfeld, G. (1952). The psychological evaluation of children with cerebral palsy and its implications in treatment. *Journal of Pediatrics, 41,* 613–621.

Minde, K. K., Hackett, J. D., Kollou, D., and Silver, S. (1972). How they grow up: 41 physically handicapped children and their families. *American Journal of Psychiatry, 128,* 1554–1559.

Mitchell, P. R. (1983). Ophthalmologic problems. In G. H. Thomson, I. L. Rubin, and R. M. Bilenker (Eds.), *Comprehensive management of cerebral palsy.* New York: Grune & Stratton.

Moed, J., and Litwin, D. (1963). The employability of the cerebral palsied: A summary of two related studies. *Rehabilitation Literature, 24,* 266–271, 276.

Mooney, T., Cole, R., and Chilgren, R. (1975). *Sexual options for paraplegics and quadriplegics.* Boston: Little, Brown.

Morris, T. (1973). Hearing impaired children and their education. *Public Health, 88,* 27–33.

Mowatt, M. H. (1970). Group therapy approach to emotional conflicts of the mentally retarded and their parents. In F. J. Menolascino (Ed.), *Psychiatric approaches to mental retardation.* New York: Basic Books.

Neistadt, M. E. (1987). An occupational therapy program for adults with developmental disabilities. *The American Journal of Occupational Therapy, 41,* 433–438.

Neistadt, M. E., and Marques, K. (1984). An independent living skills training program. *The American Journal of Occupational Therapy, 38,* 671–676.

Nelson, K. B., and Ellenburg, J. H. (1986). Antecedents of cerebral palsy: Multivariate analysis of risk. *New England Journal of Medicine, 315,* 81–86.

Neuer, N., and Strom, G. A. (1983). Guidance and support for parents. In G. H. Thompson, I. L. Rubin, and R. M. Bilenker (Eds.), *Comprehensive management of cerebral palsy.* New York: Grune & Stratton.

Neuman, S. S. (1983). Intellectual disabilities. In G. H. Thompson, I. L. Rubin, and R. M. Bilenker (Eds.), *Comprehensive management of cerebral palsy.* New York: Grune & Stratton.

Nussbaum, J. (1962). An investigation of the relationship between the self-concept, mother concept and reality orientation of adolescents with cerebral palsy. *Dissertation Abstracts, 22,* 4410–4411.

Nober, E. H. (1976). Auditory processing. In W. M. Cruickshank (Ed.), *Cerebral palsy: A developmental disability,* 3d ed. Syracuse, NY: Syracuse University Press.

O'Grady, R. S., Nishimura, D. M., Kohn, J. G., and Bruvold, W. H. (1985). Vocational predictions compared with present vocational status of 60 young adults with cerebral palsy. *Developmental Medicine and Child Neurology, 27,* 775–784.

O'Reilly, D. E. (1975). Care of the cerebral palsied: Outcome of the past and needs for the future. *Developmental Medicine and Child Neurology, 17,* 141–149.

Orlansky, M. D., and Heward, W. L. (1981). *Voices.* Columbus, OH: Merrill.

Paneth, N., Kiely, J., Stein, Z., and Susser, M. (1981). The incidence of cerebral palsy: Which way are we going? Paper presented at the Annual Meeting of the American Academy of Cerebral Palsy and Developmental Medicine.

Parette, H. P., and Hourcade, J. J. (1984a). An analysis of effective therapeutic intervention programs with young mentally retarded children who have cerebral palsy. *Journal of Human Behavior and Learning, 1*(2), 27–35.

Parette, H. P., and Hourcade, J. J. (1984b). The student with cerebral palsy and the public schools: Implications for the counselor. *Elementary School Guidance Counseling, 19,* 141–146.

Perlstein, M. A. (1949). Medical aspects of cerebral palsy. *Nervous Child, 8,* 125–151.

Phelps, W. M. (1948). Let's define cerebral palsy. *Crippled Children, 26,* 3–5.

Powell, T. G., Pharoah, P. O. D., Coke, R. W. I., and Rosenbloom, L. (1988). Cerebral palsy in low-birth-weight infants: I. Spastic hemiplegia: Association with intrapartum stress. *Developmental Medicine and Child Neurology, 30,* 11–18.

Powell, T. G., Pharoah, P. O. D., Coke, R. W. I., and Rosenbloom, L. (1986). Cerebral palsy in low-birth-weight infants: II. Spastic diplegia associations with fetal immaturity. *Developmental Medicine and Child Neurology, 30,* 19–25.

Rothman, J. G. (1978). Effects of respiratory exercises on vital capacity and forced expiratory volume in children with cerebral palsy. *Physical Therapy, 58,* 421–425.

Rutter, M., Graham, P., and Yule, W. (1970). *A neuropsychiatric study in childhood.* London: Heinemann.

Sacks, O. (1984). *The man who mistook his wife for a hat and other clinical tales.* New York: Summit.

Schleichkorn, J. (1983). *Coping with cerebral palsy: Answers to questions parents often ask.* Austin, TX: PRO-ED.

Schonell, F. (1956). *Educating spastic children.* Edinburgh: Oliver and Boyd.

Shapiro, B. K., Palmer, F. B., Wachtel, R. C., and Capute, A. J. (1983). Associated dysfunctions. In G. H. Thompson, I. L. Rubin, and R. M. Bilenker

(Eds.), *Comprehensive management of cerebral palsy.* New York: Grune & Stratton.

Shere, M. D. (1954). An evaluation of the social and emotional development of the cerebral palsied twin. Unpublished doctoral dissertation, University of Illinois.

Shere, M. D., and Kastenbaum, R. (1966). Mother-child interaction in cerebral palsy: Environmental and psychosocial obstacles to cognitive development. *Genetic Psychology Monographs, 73,* 255–335.

Simonova, N. V. (1981). Formation of notions of space and time in children with cerebral palsy. *Defectologiya, 4,* 82–87.

Stanley, F. J., and English, D. R. (1986). Prevalence of and risk factors for cerebral palsy in a total population cohort of low-birthweight (<2000 gm) infants. *Developmental Medicine and Child Neurology, 28,* 559–568.

Strom, G. A., and Oppenheimer, C. (1983). Maturation and sexual awareness. In G. H. Thompson, I. L. Rubin, and R. M. Bilenker (Eds.), *Comprehensive management of cerebral palsy.* New York: Grune & Stratton.

Suelzle, M., and Keenan, V. (1981). Changes in family support networks over the life cycle of mentally retarded persons. *American Journal of Mental Deficiency, 86,* 267–274.

Taft, L. T. (1984). Cerebral palsy. *Pediatrics in Review, 6,* 35–45.

Taft, L. T., and Matthews, W. S. (1983). Cerebral Palsy. In M. D. Levine, W. B. Carey, A. C. Crocker, and R. T. Gross, *Developmental-behavioral pediatrics.* Philadelphia: Saunders.

Tarnowski, K. J., and Drabman, R. S. (1986). Increasing the communicator usage skills of a cerebral palsied adolescent. *Journal of Pediatric Psychology, 21,* 573–581.

Taylor, E. M. (1959). *Psychological appraisal of children with cerebral defects.* Cambridge, MA: Harvard University Press.

Thompson, G. H. (1983). Hip and knee deformities. In G. H. Thompson, I. L. Rubin, and R. M. Bilenker (Eds.), *Comprehensive management of cerebral palsy.* New York: Grune & Stratton.

Thompson, G. H., Rubin, I. L., and Bilenker, R. M. (Eds.). (1983). *Comprehensive management of cerebral palsy.* New York: Grune & Stratton.

Thompson, R. J., and O'Quinn, A. N. (1979). *Developmental disabilities.* New York: Oxford University Press.

Towbin, A. (1970). Central nervous system damage in the human fetus and newborn infant. *American Journal of Diseases of Children, 119,* 529–542.

Wedell, K. (1961). Follow-up study of perceptual ability in children with hemiplegia. In *Hemiplegic cerebral palsy in children and adults* (pp. 76–85). London: Spastics Society/Heinemann.

Wehman, P., Schleien, S., and Kiernan, J. (1980). Age appropriate recreation programs for severely handicapped youth and adults. *Journal of the Association for the Severely Handicapped, 5,* 395–407.

Wolfe, W. (1950). A comprehensive evaluation of fifty cases of cerebral palsy. *Journal of Speech and Hearing Disorders, 15,* 234–251.

Wright, B. A. (1983). *Physical disability: A psychosocial approach,* 2d ed. New York: Harper & Row.

Yost, J., and McMillan, P. (1983). Communication disorders. In G. H. Thompson, I. L. Rubin, and R. M. Bilenker (Eds.), *Comprehensive management of cerebral palsy.* New York: Grune & Stratton.

Zadig, J. (1983). The education of the child with cerebral palsy. In G. H. Thompson, I. L. Rubin, and R. M. Bilenker (Eds.), *Comprehensive management of cerebral palsy.* New York: Grune & Stratton.

CHAPTER 6

Epilepsy

OVERVIEW

This chapter describes a condition that is generally better known for its medical than its developmental consequences. Although epilepsy is commonly associated with each of the developmental disabilities presented in the preceding chapters, in its own right it can create extraordinary adaptive difficulties. As in earlier chapters, this chapter examines (1) the nature of epilepsy, (2) its prevalence, (3) causation, (4) associated disorders, (5) adaptive consequences, and (6) special service needs.

NATURE OF EPILEPSY

Epilepsy, or *seizure disorder*, refers to an abnormality in the electrical activity of the brain that causes recurrent seizures (convulsions, fits). It is the *recurrent* character of the seizures rather than their occurrence per se that warrants the designation of epilepsy. (Keranen, Sillanpaa, and Riekkinen, 1988). Generally not regarded as epilepsy even though they may recur are seizures in infancy and early childhood associated with fever, the so-called febrile convulsions. Typically first appearing between 9 and 18 months of age, these seizures usually disappear by age 6 (Livingston, 1972).

In addition to their tendency to recur, *epileptic seizures* have several other common features: (1) a sudden onset, (2) an altered state of consciousness, (3) a similar length of time per type of seizure, (4) abnormal movement or posture change, (5) spontaneous cessation, and (6) a lapse of time before returning to the pre-seizure state.

HISTORICAL ASPECTS

Few human maladies have evoked the mystique of epilepsy (e.g. Temkin, 1971). The "falling sickness" or "sacred disease" was first described by the Greek physician Hippocrates in 350 B.C. He sought to dispel the then popular view that the disorder was really demonic possession with these words: "It is thus with regard to the disease called Sacred; it appears to me to be nowise more divine nor more sacred than other diseases, but has a natural cause from which it originates like other affections . . . [from] things which enter and quit the body . . . [and] the brain is the cause of this affection" (Adams, 1939). However, it would be 2000 years before the first effective treatment was found, when an English physician, Lacock, in 1857, introduced bromide therapy (Livingston, 1972). In the meantime, and continuing to this very day, epilepsy carries with it psychological baggage evoking associations of crime and violence and, in the affected person, fears of mental illness, mental retardation, and social stigmatization.

While epilepsy refers to a variety of types of seizures, it is the generalized tonic-clonic (grand mal) seizure that is most clearly associated with the disorder and is its most dramatic representative. A mother describes the first such episode in her son:

> It was Christmas and the children were about to open their presents. Suddenly one of them said, "Something's wrong with Jonathan." He was sitting quite still and with a fixed stare. Slowly his head turned to the left and his eyes moved laterally. His body stiffened and he began to slide off the bed on which he was sitting. For seconds he got tighter and tighter, his face paled and then it became a horrible blue. Small jerking movements began in his arms and legs. They weren't violent but they were forceful and not to be restrained. He grunted with each jerk as if it was a major physical effort. This seemed to go on forever, but it could not have been more than 30 seconds with his color steadily worsening.
>
> Then it stopped, fairly quickly, and he lay there with his eyes turned up, motionless, not even seeming to breathe. I felt for his pulse, it was still there, and as I held his wrist he took a few deep, gasping breaths. His color began to return and the blueness disappeared. He coughed, spit, and I wiped his lips because of the accumulation of saliva.
>
> When his breathing had returned to normal, he was carried to his bed where he slept for about 15 minutes. When he got up, he was a bit tired and quiet, but he was soon back to normal and returned for more opening of presents. The whole episode lasted less than half an hour, but those 30 minutes changed our family life. (Adapted from Linnett, 1982)

FORMS OF EPILEPSY

Systems of classification of the different types of seizures have been based on their symptoms and severity. Within these systems, the three most common seizures are *grand mal, petit mal,* and *psychomotor* or *temporal lobe seizures.* Less frequent are *local motor* and *minor motor seizures.* The International Classification of Epileptic Seizures, the current major classification system (Epilepsy Foundation of America, 1981; Gastaut, 1970), continues the symptomatic description but divides seizures according to their place of origin in the brain. Two broad groups are recognized, *partial seizures,* those originating at a site (locus) in either hemisphere of the brain, and *generalized seizures,* those originating simultaneously in both hemispheres.

Partial Seizures

Partial seizures are themselves divided into three types: (1) those with elementary symptoms (*focal motor or sensory*), (2) those associated with some impairment of consciousness (*complex partial*), and (3) those with both impairment of consciousness and bilateral movements; convulsive movements beginning on one side of the body and spreading to the other; so-called *partial seizures secondarily generalized*. The list of partial seizures and their traditional designations are shown in Table 6-1.

The manifestations of each type of partial seizure depend on the particular brain area affected. These involve (1) the motor cortex in the frontal lobes and convulsive movements of the body parts innervated by the discharging motor nerve cells (e.g. hands and fingers and legs), (2) parietal cortex and sensory phenomena (e.g. numbness and tingling in a limb), (3) occipital cortex and bright, flashing lights, and (4) temporal cortex and speech disturbance and/or complex motor and psychological phenomena. Following a partial seizure, there may be a brief weakness in the affected limb, so-called postictal (postseizure) posture or Todd's paralysis (Dreifuss, 1975).

Simple Partial (Focal). These seizures commonly involve convulsive movements on one side of the body, face, and/or limbs. The muscles first become rigid (*tonic* phase), and then jerking usually follows (*clonic* phase). Commonly, these seizures last for about 30 seconds without loss of consciousness.

Also included here are seizures manifested in tingling and numbness on one side of the body (partial sensory seizures), or the perception of flashes of light or strange smells and tastes (partial seizures with special sensory symptoms).

Complex Partial (Temporal Lobe or Psychomotor). In this type of seizure there is some impairment of consciousness. Although *appearing* to be conscious, the person has at least some unawareness of his or her environment and there is no memory of the episode. The seizure is often preceded by an *aura*, a somatic or sensory experience that alerts one to its imminence (e.g., a strange sensation in the stomach that moves up to the chest and throat or such sensory experiences as an unpleasant odor or a ringing bell). One also may feel a dreamy sense of unreality, déjà vu (strange objects or people seem familiar), or emotions (e.g., fear,

Table 6-1. Partial seizures

Partial seizures	*Traditional designation*
Simple (with elementary symptoms)	Focal
Complex (altered consciousness)	Psychomotor or temporal lobe
Partial seizures secondarily generalized	Focal and/or grand mal*

*A grand mal seizure, although typically generalized in origin, can result from the spread of an originally focal seizure to the whole brain.

anxiety, rage, or even bliss). Distinct from the aura, there can be a sense of increased irritability and unease for hours or even days. The unique feature of this type of seizure is the seemingly purposeful inappropriate actions that are carried on without awareness, *automatisms* (e.g., chewing, smacking of the lips, fumbling with buttons, moving about). Whether simple or complex, these acts are actually manifestations of the seizure.

Partial Seizures Secondarily Generalized. These are *partial* seizures caused by abnormal electrical activity originating in a specific area of the brain that become *generalized* as the activity spreads throughout the brain.

Generalized Seizures

Generalized seizures result from abnormal electrical activity in both hemispheres of the brain. The initial symptom is loss of consciousness. The types of generalized seizures are shown in Table 6-2.

Tonic-Clonic (Grand Mal). These are the most common of the generalized seizures and the prototype of epilepsy. This type of seizure was depicted in the earlier description of Jonathan. The seizure begins with unconsciousness. If standing, the person falls stiffly to the ground. The body muscles are rigid (tonic phase). There is a fixed contraction of the diaphragm and chest muscles causing an expulsion of air and the so-called epileptic cry. Muscle rigidity also interferes with breathing, and the temporary loss of oxygen produces the bluish or cyanotic appearance of the face. The rigidity is quickly replaced by jerking (clonic) movements of the head, face, and limbs. There may be loss of bladder control. Breathing returns in the clonic phase but is "snoring" in quality. The eyes may roll up or turn to the side. The jerking movements gradually subside with the convulsive phase usually not exceeding 5 min-

Table 6-2. Generalized seizures

Generalized seizures	Traditional designation
Tonic-clonic	Grand mal
Tonic (only)	Limited grand mal
Clonic (only)	Limited grand mal
Absence	Petit mal
Atonic	Drop attack, minor motor
Myoclonic	Bilateral massive epileptic
Infantile spasms	Jackknife, salaam, hypsarrhythmia

utes; 1 to 3 minutes is typical. The seizure is often followed by confusion. The person may be difficult to arouse and may sleep for several hours, or the person may awaken with a headache or muscle soreness. While most tonic-clonic seizures require no medical intervention, where they are continuous, a condition called *status epilepticus*, immediate medical attention is necessary. If seizures continue for more than one hour there may be permanent brain damage (Hermann, Desai, and Whitman, 1988).

Tonic (Only) and Clonic (Only). Following loss of consciousness, there is either rigidity (tonic) or jerking (clonic).

Absence (petit mal). There is brief loss of consciousness manifested in vacant staring, usually for only a few seconds. There also may be some rhythmic blinking as well as brief automatisms (e.g., lip smacking, chewing and swallowing movements, and mumbling speech). The seizure ends as rapidly as it began, with immediate resumption of normal activity. If the seizure occurs while the person is standing, there may be some swaying but usually no falling. These seizures can vary in frequency from an occasional episode to more than 100 per day. They occur in about 6 to 12 percent of all children with epilepsy, about half of whom also have tonic-clonic seizures. A mix of more than one type of seizure is common in epilepsy. Sometimes these seizures are confused with complex partial seizures because of the automatisms. Absence seizures are much briefer, lasting seconds rather than minutes, and they end with an instant return to clear consciousness.

Atonic (Drop Attack, Minor Motor). Usually these seizures start between the ages of 2 and 5. The legs simply give way and the child falls. There is no tonic or clonic phase; the muscles are limp. This type of seizure lasts for less than a minute, and there is quick recovery of alertness and use of the legs. Affected children wear protective head gear to prevent injury during falls.

Myoclonic (Bilateral Massive Epileptic). These seizures consist of sudden shocklike contractions that can affect the entire body or be limited to the head (head bobbing), trunk, or limbs. Jerking may be rapidly repetitive or relatively isolated (the person may spill beverages or actually be propelled out of a chair).

Infantile Spasms (Hypsarrhythmia, jackknife, salaam). Onset in these types of seizures occurs between 3 months and 2 years of age. The seizure lasts for seconds, during which the head, neck, and trunk flex forward and the knees draw up. They can occur repeatedly. If a seizure occurs while the child is standing, it can result in a violent fall against which the child cannot protect him- or herself. Protective headgear is worn. The great majority of children so affected eventually show mental retardation of a moderate to profound degree.

PREVALENCE

Although epilepsy is the most common neurologic disorder, estimates of its prevalence vary tremendously. International surveys (e.g., in the United States, Poland, Japan, and Norway) have found rates of 1 to 5 per 1000 persons, or 0.1 to 0.5 percent (Zielinski, 1986), while practitioners and advocacy groups report much higher rates, that is, 1 to 2 per 100, or 1 to 2 percent, (e.g., Livingston, 1972; Epilepsy Foundation of America, 1983). The most accurate data pertain to people under active treatment, a population in the United States of about 5 per 1000 or 0.5 percent (Goodridge and Shorvon, 1983; Hauser, 1978). With significant numbers of persons either never diagnosed (e.g., Zielinski, 1974) or seizure-free and no longer under treatment, it is likely that the number of individuals who have *ever* had seizures is, indeed, between 1 and 2 percent.

AGE OF ONSET

Epilepsy is chiefly a disorder of the developmental years, with 75 percent of first seizures occurring by age 18 (Commission for the Control of Epilepsy . . . , 1977).[1] During this period, initial seizures occur most often between (1) birth to 2 years, (2) the beginning school years, ages 5 to 7, and (3) early adolescence, ages 11 to 13 (Ziegler, 1982).

SEIZURE TYPES

As noted earlier, the three most common seizures are tonic-clonic, complex partial, and absence. Estimates of their prevalence are compounded by the frequent occurrence of multiple seizure types in the same person. In a major American study, one-third of seizures were generalized (34 percent) and two-thirds were partial (Hauser & Kurland, 1975). With regard to age, the frequency of generalized seizures is higher in children than in adults, and when originating in adulthood, these seizures decline in frequency with age. In populations 15 years of age and older, partial seizures are likely to predominate (e.g., Keranen, Sillanpaa, and Riekkinen, 1988), complex partial seizures being the most common type found in adults (Hermann, Desai, and Whitman, 1988).

---

[1]In future references simply noted as the Epilepsy Commission, 1977.

SEIZURE TYPES AND AGE

Some forms of epilepsy are relatively age-specific. Infantile spasms and myoclonic seizures occur most often between 5 months and 4 years of age; absence seizures between 5 and 15 years, rarely first appearing in adulthood; and complex partial seizures usually not before age 10 or early adolescence.

SEIZURE FREQUENCY IN AFFECTED PERSONS

The Epilepsy Commission (1977) indicates that about a third of persons under treatment have an average of less than one seizure per year, one-third have between 1 and 12 seizures per year, and the final third have more than 1 seizure per month. Of those with at least monthly seizures, the majority have them at least weekly. It is the last group whose seizures would be regarded as largely uncontrolled by antiepileptic medication.

For many persons epilepsy is truly a *chronic* condition. While the great majority, about 80 percent, can anticipate reduction in seizure frequency with anticonvulsants, even those who have been seizure-free for as long as 2 years are at some risk of recurrence (Annegers et al., 1979). The prognosis differs for children and adults as well as between sexes (Masland, 1982). Children with absence and/or tonic-clonic seizures who have been fully controlled for at least 4 years by adolescence can, with an 80 percent probability, anticipate complete weaning from antiepileptic treatment and a seizure-free future. With complex partial seizures, however, only about a third (35 percent) can be expected to remain seizure-free for 5 years without medication. Adults, in particular, are likely to require lifelong maintenance on anticonvulsants. As for the sexual differences, recurrence is more likely among young females, typically around puberty (Arts et al., 1988).

CAUSES OF DEATH

A common fear among persons with epilepsy is that a seizure may cause death (Mittan, Wasterlain, and Glocke, 1982)—a fear shared by their parents. That this is not entirely unfounded is evident from studies of causes of death, direct and indirect, attributable to the disorder (Aird, Masland, and Woodbury, 1984; Woodbury, 1978a, 1978b). *Direct* causes constituted 27 percent of the total, of which 22 percent were associated with seizures and 5 percent with status epilepticus. Among the *indirect* causes, suicide and drowning occur with some frequency, 9 and 6 percent, respectively. The apparently increased suicide rate (Aird, Masland, and Woodbury, 1984) is related to the greater risk of depression and other mental health problems, a topic addressed later in the section "Associated Disorders."

GENDER

Males are at greater risk for epilepsy, at least in part due to their being twice as likely as females to sustain a head injury (Hermann, Desai, and Whitman, 1988).

CAUSES OF EPILEPSY

Epileptologists have commonly distinguished between two types of causation: (1) *symptomatic epilepsies,* which are those associated with either a structural brain abnormality (e.g., cerebral palsy or brain tumor) or an accompanying systemic disease (e.g., kidney failure), and (2) *idiopathic epilepsy,* which is epilepsy without structural brain disorder or other disease. The latter is thought to have a genetic component and carries a small but increased risk in offspring (6 percent where one parent is affected and 9 percent where both parents are affected (Masland, 1982).

The various causes of epilepsy are shown in Table 6-3. The table is organized according to time of origin, from conception to postnatal life (Aird, Masland, and Woodbury, 1984; Dreifuss, 1975; Marsden and Reynolds, 1982). Of all the causes, brain infections are the most common (Epilepsy Commission, 1977).

ASSOCIATED DISORDERS

The effects of epilepsy are not limited to the relatively brief periods during which seizures occur. While those who are seizure-free and no longer dependent on anticonvulsants can aspire to essentially normal lives, where seizures persist, antiepileptic drugs are a permanent fact of life. While these medications are often effective against seizures, they can produce unwanted side effects—physical, cognitive, psychomotor, and personality (e.g., Aird, Masland, and Woodbury, 1984). Major side effects are presented in the subsequent section "Adaptive Behavior."

Table 6-3. Causes of epilepsy

Conception:
  Genetic: Genetic susceptibility to
    abnormal brain waves (electrical
    activity); to idiopathic
    (cryptogenic) seizures in
    childhood, primarily tonic-clonic
    and absence; and to inherited
    disorders in which epilepsy is a
    symptom (e.g., phenylketonuria)
  Chromosomal: Trisomy 13-15 (D)
    (Patau syndrome); fragile X
    (Musumeci et al., 1988)
Prenatal:
  Infections: Congenital rubella,
    syphilis, toxoplasmosis, and
    cytomegalovirus
Natal and perinatal:
  Birth trauma
  Anoxia
  Bleeding into the brain
  Low blood sugar
  Maternal-fetal blood incompatibility
  Prematurity

Postnatal:
  Brain infections: Encephalitis and
    meningitis; abscess; fever
  Head injury: Closed or open
  Toxins: Lead and mercury,
    alcohol, drugs (e.g.,
    amphetamines), allergic
    factors, toxemia of pregnancy
  Metabolic and nutritional disorders:
    Imbalances of sodium,
    potassium, calcium,
    magnesium, and water;
    carbohydrate metabolism
    (e.g., hypoglycemia and
    diabetes); protein metabolism
    (e.g., phenylketonuria,
    porphyria); fat metabolism
    (e.g., lipid storage diseases);
    vitamin B_6 deficiency;
    endocrine disorders (e.g.,
    adrenal, thyroid, estrogens);
    kidney and liver failure
  Circulatory disease: Brain
    hemorrhage; stroke;
    arteriosclerosis; hypertensive
    encephalopathy; syncope
  Neoplasms: Brain tumor; blood
    vessel tumor; vascular
    malformations; familial and
    degenerative brain diseases

EPILEPSY AND INTELLIGENCE

General Intelligence (IQ)

Numerous studies indicate a reduction in average IQ of from 5 to 10
points in populations with epilepsy (Bagley, 1971; Dodrill, 1982a, 1982b;
Tarter, 1972; Vislie and Henrikson, 1958), especially in individuals with
chronic seizures (e.g., Bourgeois et al., 1983; Giordani et al., 1985). This
difference also includes a somewhat higher rate of retardation (e.g., Bagley, 1971), particularly in the generalized seizures of infancy and early
childhood-infantile spasms and myoclonic epilepsy of infancy, seizures
associated with brain damage (Livingston, 1972; Ounsted, Lindsay, and
Norman, 1966).

Apart from epilepsy itself, other factors that can affect intelligence are epilepsy's age of onset, causation, seizure type, seizure frequency, and anticonvulsant medication.

Age of Onset

Chronic seizures arising in childhood carry greater risks to intellectual development than those originating in adolescence or adulthood (DeHaas and Magnus, 1958; Dodrill, 1982a; Taylor and Falconer, 1968). In one study there was an average difference of 10 IQ points between those with onset before age 5 and those with onset between age 10 and age 25 (Dikmen, Matthews, and Harley, 1977). The respective IQs in the two groups were 81 and 91. Several explanations for this suggest themselves—the just-noted likelihood of organic brain damage in early-onset epilepsy, the side effects of long-term exposure to antiepileptic drugs (e.g., Bourgeois et al., 1983; Stores, 1978), and the number of seizures experienced (Dodrill, 1988).

Causation

The effect of causation of the epilepsy on intelligence is clearly seen in a study of epileptic children with major cognitive impairment (Bagley, 1971). Of these, the great majority (73 percent) had symptomatic or organic epilepsy, while of those with the idiopathic form, only 22 percent suffered from cognitive impairment. And in an adult population (Matthews and Klove, 1967), a slight difference in average IQ (100 versus 96) was found in favor of those whose epilepsy was of unknown origin in comparison with those whose epilepsy was associated with brain injury.

It is important to add, however, that *all* levels of intellectual development are found in the organic epilepsies, including IQs of 120 and above. Organicity does not ensure intellectual impairment.

Type of Seizure

Except for the epilepsies of infancy and early childhood, those associated with clear organic brain abnormality (infantile spasms and myoclonic seizures), there appears to be no particular relationship between intelligence and seizure type (Giordani et al., 1985).

Frequency of Seizures

There seems to be at least a modest relationship between the frequency of seizures and intellectual functioning (Chaundry and Pond, 1961; Dodrill, 1988; Dikmen and Matthews, 1977; Ounsted, Lindsay, and Norman, 1966; Trimble, 1988). The effect has been observed in both complex partial and generalized tonic-clonic epilepsy. With reference to the former, the hippocampus, the memory-related structure in the temporal lobes, is said to be particularly vulnerable to damage from seizures (Aird, Masland and Woodbury, 1984). As regards tonic-clonic epilepsy, Dodrill (1988) has found that individuals who over the course of their lifetime had experienced 100 or more seizures were functioning about 10 IQ points below their counterparts with fewer than 100 seizures (94 versus 103).

Effects of Anticonvulsant Medications

It has been noted that while antiepileptic drugs can either eliminate or significantly reduce seizures, their side effects can affect cognition (Dam, 1982; Masland, 1982; Reynolds, 1983; Trimble, 1988; Trimble and Reynolds, 1984). Impairments in attention and concentration are common and are sometimes associated with drug-induced hyperactivity, a phenobarbital side effect. Teachers will note that sometimes the children seem "out of it." Moreover, some antiepileptic drugs, notably phenytoin (Dilantin) and phenobarbital, have been found to produce a progressive decline in intelligence in persons with epilepsy and mental retardation (Trimble, Thompson, and Huppert, 1980), while other drugs are less likely to have this effect (Schaon, Ward, and Guthrie, 1977). The drug carbamazepine (Tegretol) seems to produce less cognitive impairment (Andres et al., 1985; Schaon, Ward, and Guthrie, 1977).

OTHER COGNITIVE EFFECTS

As just indicated with regard to seizure type, epileptic foci in the temporal lobes (complex partial seizures) can affect memory as well as language. A lesion in the left temporal lobe, the side dominant for language in most individuals, may impair word-finding and verbal memory, while a comparable lesion in the right temporal lobe could interfere with the memory for complex visual stimuli (Engel, Crandall, and Rausch, 1983; Hermann et al., 1987; Milner, 1975; Russell, 1975).

SCHOOL LEARNING PROBLEMS

Given the potentially adverse effects of epilepsy on intellectual functioning, it is not surprising that frequency of school learning problems is increased (Holdsworth and Whitmore, 1974; Myklebust, 1977; Pazzaglia and Frank-Pazzaglia, 1976; Rodin, Shapiro, and Lennox, 1977; Seidenberg et al., 1986; Svoboda, 1979; Ziegler, 1985). Reading and arithmetic difficulties are commonplace (Bagley, 1971; Rutter, Graham, and Yule, 1970).

An electroencephalographic (EEG) study indicated that the children at greatest risk for learning problems had abnormalities in the temporal and frontal lobes (Baird et al., 1980). Attention deficits were particularly prominent. Temporal lobe abnormalities also can affect language, math, or visuospatial functions depending on the lobe(s) involved (Svoboda, 1979). Parenthetically, the EEG test is very important in the diagnosis of epilepsy because the seizure-causing electrical activity is reflected in characteristic abnormalities in brain waves.

With attention deficits and problems of language, memory, and visuospatial functioning, it would be expected that *learning disabilities per se* would be common (e.g., Ziegler, 1985), and Seidenberg and colleagues (1986) found underachievement relative to IQ in spelling, reading comprehension, and word recognition.

EPILEPSY AND MOTOR FUNCTIONS

Apart from motor impairments caused by epileptogenic lesions in the parts of the brain that control movement, the motor cortex in the frontal lobes, antiepileptic medications also can produce motor side effects, notably hyperactivity on the one hand and slowing on the other (Ounsted, 1955; Reynolds, 1981). In one study (Bagley, 1971), about 10 percent of the children showed hyperactivity.

Anticonvulsants also can affect the structure in the brain that controls balance, the cerebellum. A toxic level of the drug in the blood may also impair gait (Dam, 1982).

EPILEPSY AND PERSONALITY

This is one of the more fascinating aspects of epilepsy, since numerous studies show a heightened frequency of personality and behavior problems in children and young people with epilepsy and psychiatric disorders in the adult. Surveys of school populations show that a little more than a quarter of the children are so characterized (27 percent, Mellor, Lowitt, and Hall, 1974; 29 percent, Rutter, Graham, and Yule, 1970). And in adults in particular, a range of aberrant behaviors is found, both as manifestations of seizures themselves and during seizure-free periods. From 2 to 4 percent of epileptic adults are subject to psychoses, with the frequency increasing to 11 to 14 percent in the complex partial form (Aird, Masland, and Woodbury, 1984).

As in the case of cognitive problems, children with seizures originating in early childhood are at greater risk for mental health problems than those with a later onset (Betts, 1982; Bagley, 1971; Pond and Bidwell, 1959; Stores, 1978), although if seizures come to be well-controlled by adolescence, adult adjustment is grossly normal. Boys are at a greater risk for both cognitive and behavioral problems (Stores, 1978).

Nature of Personality Disorders

In the epilepsy literature there is reference to the "epileptic personality" (e.g., Betts, 1982). Self-centered, irritable, and clinging are all qualities identified with the behavioral picture (e.g., Blumer, 1982), although there appears to be no uniformity of personality among affected individuals. Some traits are more frequently seen—anxiety, fearfulness, and insecurity, all of which contribute to a common pattern of *dependency* (Bridge, 1949; Bagley, 1971; Hughes and Jabbour, 1958; Livingston, 1972). Personality and behavior problems are more probable in children whose seizures are not fully controlled, the remainder being largely free of significant behavior disorders.

In adults with epilepsy, Dodrill (1982b) calls attention to the frequent presence of psychological difficulties—anxiety, guilt, and depression—poor interpersonal relationships, vocational problems, and financial concerns. As with children, these problems are more typical of the adults whose seizures are not adequately controlled.

Personality effects are most evident in complex partial seizures (psychomotor/temporal lobe). In at least some individuals there are tendencies to humorlessness, excessive circumstantiality in speech or writing (e.g. Hoeppner et al., 1987), a deep concern with religious or philosophical topics, and a relative disinterest in sex. It also would appear that the intensity of emotional experiences is heightened (see the Leonard Wolf case history in the later section on social concerns of the adult) and that in social interactions there is difficulty in "separating" or terminating them (Bear, Freeman, and Greenberg, 1984; Bear and Fedio, 1977).

In seeking to explain increased personality disorders in epilepsy, Hermann and Whitman (1986) call attention to three factors: the psychosocial environment to which the person with epilepsy is exposed, the disorder itself, and the medications used to treat it. The psychosocial environment is thought to be of greatest significance.

Personality and Psychosocial Factors

The most characteristic feature of the environment of the individual with epilepsy is the real or presumed threat of social rejection if the disorder is known to others (Dell, 1986; Vinson, 1975; West, 1986). The person with epilepsy perceives him- or herself as stigmatized by it, a presumption based on discrimination in important aspects of life. Only in recent years has the general public acknowledged that epilepsy is not to be equated with insanity and have state laws that had prohibited marriage and parenthood been repealed. The laws derive from the eugenics concerns of the 1920s and 1930s; that is, epilepsy was seen as inherited, and also as contributing to criminal behavior, a 19th century residual (Hermann, Desai, and Whitman, 1988). It was feared that without such restrictions, its frequency would be increased. In fact, as earlier noted, it is only the idiopathic form of epilepsy that carries a genetic risk, and even this is very slight. Even with the repeal of stigmatizing legislation and a softening of the public attitude, however, young people and adults with epilepsy continue to face restrictions unknown to their non-epileptic peers. The vocational area seems to be a particularly discriminating domain. Driving restrictions, a rational limitation tied to seizure control, still have the effect of adding to a person's sense of "different-ness." Such restrictions also mean a lesser degree of mobility and, possibly, greater dependence on others.

The widespread fear of social rejection resides in the fear of being "found out." Epilepsy is an "invisible" disability. Except for the period of seizures and their aftermath, the person with epilepsy, by hiding the condition, can try to pass as normal. Evasion and outright denial are commonly employed in job-seeking because of employer resistance to hiring persons with the disorder, but these behaviors are also much used in the social sphere. Knowledge of one's epilepsy may be a "family secret" or may be entrusted only to the closet friends. The later section on adaptive behavior will present numerous examples of how individuals see themselves as stigmatized by epilepsy. Stigma, of course, is not unique to this condition. The same fear of being "found out" is seen in mental retardation, but since retardation is a potentially broader adaptive problem, there is less opportunity to avoid at least some recognition.

The very nature of seizures presents the threat of embarrassment and humiliation. A seizure can occur anywhere and at any time. Indeed, the unpredictability of seizures is one of their most stressful aspects. Falling unconscious in the local mall, grotesquely convulsing, involuntarily urinating, and foaming at the mouth all evoke horror and repulsion in the naive observer. In this respect, I would remind the reader again that *knowledge* of ordinarily frightening disorders can genuinely reduce fear. If we understand the physiology of a tonic-clonic (grand mal) seizure, its occurrence is less frightening. Knowledge of what we are looking at "distances" us psychologically from it; we respond with our minds as well as with our emotions.

Given the ever-present threat of public exposure and humiliation, however, protecting self-esteem by avoiding being recognized as epileptic becomes a central driving force and the price paid for such evasion is anxiety, fear, and social isolation. Another major consequence of this psychosocial environment, especially as it relates to the family, is the degree to which parents seek to protect and shelter their epileptic child. It is out of excessive parental caution and experiential restriction that children come to learn that they cannot trust their own judgment and then become unduly dependent on others. The inevitable tie to daily medication represents one kind of permanent umbilical cord, but the parent who can think developmentally as well as protectively can try to maximize rather than minimize the child's exposure to normal experiences and opportunities to make decisions. Attitudes of learned helplessness, not uncommon in individuals with epilepsy, are inculcated by undue protection and are not inherent in the disorder. In the adaptive behavior section we'll read of individuals who are proud of their independence (autonomy) and are grateful to their parents for helping them become self-confident adults.

Effects on Personality of the Disorder Itself

As noted earlier, the effect of seizures on personality seems most evident in complex partial epilepsy, seizures usually originating in the temporal lobes (Aird, Masland, and Woodbury, 1984; Dam and Dam, 1986; Bear, Freeman, and Greenberg, 1984; Betts, 1982; Blumer 1982; Sands, 1982). Within the temporal lobes are structures that affect emotions and sexuality as well as language and memory. Impairment in these functions can result from either seizure-causing lesions in these structures or repeated generalized tonic-clonic episodes.

Emotions. The characteristic effect is rapid mood change—from calm, warm, and friendly at one moment to extreme irritability or even explosive rage at another. Some forms of complex partial epilepsy, those involving the inner or medial portion of the temporal lobes, can be treated by surgical excision of the diseased area (anterior temporal lobectomy), and apart from seizure reduction, a common behavior change is diminished irritability (Engel, Crandall, and Rausch, 1983; Walker and Blumer, 1984).

Another emotional feature is the earlier-mentioned deepening of feelings. This can lead to the investing of interest in things with a degree of emotional significance that seems exaggerated. Seemingly related to emotional deepening is a general seriousness and preoccupation with religion or philosophy.

Sexuality. A reduced sexual drive is frequently found particularly with the onset of temporal lobe seizures in childhood or adolescence. Sexual activity may either originate or revive following seizure control, whether achieved through anticonvulsants or surgery.

Memory. Memory loss for recent events is a common postseizure (postictal) phenomenon. A severe complex partial seizure involving the temporal lobes may even cause *amnesia*, a memory loss extending back for weeks or months. Some complex partial seizures also can be manifested in *fugue states*, in which there is wandering or even seemingly purposeful travel for which there is no recall.

"Viscosity" (Clingingness). This is a tendency to circumstantial thought and "adhesive" behavior (Blumer, 1982; Walker and Blumer, 1984). In the cognitive realm it is expressed in extreme, methodical, and tedious elaboration either in speech or writing, and in the social sphere in undue prolongation of social interactions.

Psychosis. Found in about 12 percent of persons with complex partial seizures as opposed to only 3 percent of the general population, a flurry of seizures can produce a state of confusion or delirium. Prominent in the past, it is now rare because of more effective anticonvulsant drugs. More frequently seen is a schizophrenic-like psychosis that, paradoxically, occurs *during* periods of being seizure-free. Consciousness is clear and symptoms may be manic-depressive or paranoid in nature. Tending to occur after many years of epilepsy (e.g., 14 years), unlike classical schizophrenia, emotions are well preserved. Particularly striking is the sometimes inverse relationship between psychosis and seizure control. The onset of psychosis may coincide with the cessation of complex partial seizures or even appear to be precipitated by their control. The reader may be aware that the deliberate induction of a tonic-clonic seizure by electric shock has long been used in the treatment of schizophrenia and depression. Seizures and psychosis appear to be truly related.

Auras. In describing the characteristics of complex partial epilepsy, reference was made to the *aura,* an experience that precedes the seizure and which may be experienced as strange or unusual (e.g., déjà vu). Parenthetically, auras may also precede secondarily generalized partial seizures. Curiously, antiepileptic drugs can result in the inhibition of seizures but also can accentuate the aura, resulting in so-called continuous aura, as the following illustrates.

> An adult female with both complex partial and occasional tonic-clonic seizures experienced a sense of dread and terror as her aura. The seizure that followed consisted of staring and of the common automatisms of lip smacking and repetitive hand movements. When her seizures were reduced by a combination of antiepileptic medications she began to experience an almost continuous state of dread and anxiety, a feeling that something terrible was about to happen. After as many as 10 days of such severe anxiety, either deliberately or unconsciously, she fails to take her medicine and a seizure occurs. She is much relieved by the seizure, claiming that "her tension lifts off like a weight." (Adapted from Aird, Masland, and Woodbury, 1984.) Once again, an inverse relationship between seizures and psychological distress is apparent.

The continuous aura also can have the classically psychotic character of hallucinations, both auditory and visual:

> I start to hear my own thoughts, they get louder and louder. I become more interested in what I'm thinking than what I'm doing. I begin to hear voices, [a common auditory hallucination], usually just one; it tells me stories. After a week or two it breaks down and then I hear two or three voices. They come from different parts of my head and usually sound different. They can sound evil, or good, or just neutral and sometimes they all talk at once. I get confused, upset, and then begin to visually hallucinate. I see colors or ghosts, the dead or people from outer space. I begin to believe that my hallucinations are real and I talk to the figures I see. By this time I feel physically ill and seek medical help. (Adapted from Aird, Masland, and Woodbury, 1984.)

Treatment may involve modification of the anticonvulsant medication and/or the use of antipsychotic (psychotropic) drugs.

Depression. Another apparent emotional consequence of complex partial seizures is depression (Robertson, 1986). The risk of depression increases with age and as overt expressions of anger lessen. A psychodynamic relationship between anger suppression (repression) and depression has long been assumed. With depression there is threat of suicide, paradoxically, at a time when seizures themselves may be fully controlled. Again, there is a seemingly inverse relationship between seizure frequency and psychiatric disorder in temporal lobe epilepsy.

Effects of Antiepileptic Drugs on Personality

Anticonvulsant drugs also can have personality side effects. These range from heightened aggressiveness and restlessness, especially in young children, to psychotic states (Livingston, 1972). At least one anticonvulsant, carbamazepine (Tegretol), seems also to improve mood and lessen depression (Aird, Masland, and Woodbury, 1984).

ADAPTIVE BEHAVIOR

The preceding material makes clear that adaptive problems are frequent in epilepsy. This will certainly characterize the developmentally disabled segment of the epileptic population, those in whom either other developmental disorders are present (e.g., mental retardation or cerebral palsy) or seizure type or frequency seriously interferes with the capacity to function. Age considerations aside, impairment in everyday functioning is likely in the approximately one-third of persons with epilepsy who have seizures at least monthly, and often weekly. With regard to type of seizure, poorly controlled tonic-clonic or complex partial seizures particularly affect adaptation.

As an introduction to common adaptive patterns in children, young people, and adults, it is important to first review the *stresses* that epilepsy imposes on the family and the affected person and the coping mechanisms typically adopted. It is out of these experiences that emerge such behavior patterns as avoiding stigmatization and excessive dependency.

STRESSES ON THE FAMILY

Seizures as Dangerous

The onset of seizures is an extraordinarily stressful event for the family as well as for the child. At whatever the child's age, seizures evoke fears of a life-threatening illness, especially those of the generalized tonic-clonic type. Even when parents are assured that the seizure itself poses little danger, its manifestations are viewed with alarm. There are fears of swallowing the tongue, injury during the clonic (jerking) phase of the tonic-clinic seizure, and injury by falling either during the tonic phase (stiffness) of the tonic-clonic seizure or because of atonic epilepsy.

Unpredictability and Chronicity

Apart from fear of the consequences of seizures, there is the awareness that, to varying degrees, seizures are unpredictable in their occurrence. Moreover, the underlying brain disorder is generally not curable, as in the case of an acute illness, and treatment may last for years, even a lifetime. The final irony is that the medications used to treat epilepsy can themselves create problems. There is also the financial burden of chronic illness.

Causation

With the characterization of epilepsy as a chronic brain disorder, there are going to be fears about its possible effect on the child's thinking and behavior. School progress is threatened, no small consequence for the family that values education and achievement. When causation is clearly linked to a structural brain abnormality, as in symptomatic epilepsy, such fears will be intensified, and when the cause is unknown, as in idiopathic epilepsy, the knowledge vaccuum is certain to cause frustration and a search for "answers" that fit one's own predelictions. Self-blame or the blaming of others (scapegoating) are likely outcomes, especially where emotional stress itself can trigger seizures.

Stigma

Family members, as well as the affected individual, are sensitive to the stigmatic character of the illness. Epilepsy is a condition about which family members may feel shame, and they may seek to hide or disguise the disorder.

Summary

Given this forbidding array of stresses, it is to be expected that families or individuals with epilepsy show more than their share of anxiety, fear, and frustration, along with feelings of sadness and guilt (Ford, Gibson, and Dreifuss, 1983; Voeller and Rothenberg, 1973).

FAMILY RESPONSES TO STRESS

Overprotection

Given the pervasiveness of fears for the welfare of the epileptic child, it is not surprising that parents tend to be overprotective. They impose greater restrictions on activities in which the child can engage, an area of potential conflict when the epileptic child is an adolescent, and they try to guard their child from ridicule and stigmatization. Parents are also likely to set fewer behavioral limits, a parenting style intended to minimize the child's discomfort, especially where stress can trigger seizures, or as a way of compensating the child for the burden he or she must bear. The literature on epilepsy abounds with professional concern about overprotection and its role in producing children who are insecure and dependent (Aird, Masland and Woodbury, 1984; Ford, Gibson, and Driefuss, 1983; Ritchie, 1981; West, 1986).

Minimizing Stigma: "To Conceal or Not to Conceal"

As noted earlier, except for the seizures themselves, epilepsy carries no visible mark of its presence. Parents can choose how "public" they wish their child's disorder to be, and a mother or father who is ashamed of the child's illness frequently will severely limit outside contact, as the following illustrates.

> Eight-year-old Jenny is forbidden to play with other children. Viewing her child as "an epileptic," she [the mother] even avoids using public transportation when they make clinic visits for her medication. Even vacations are avoided so as to "hide" the child. Questioned about the effect of such restrictiveness on Jenny's development, the mother merely replied, "she hasn't had to go out to look for anything." (West, 1986, p. 259)

As much as we may deplore behavior that appears intended to protect the parent from exposure at least as much as the child, the children can be treated very cruelly by their peers, as indicated in the following.

> Recalling a classmate in her childhood, a woman describes her as a "pure outcast." Nobody used to say very much to her. "You dare not talk to her; she's not right in the head" (West, 1986, p. 254). Commenting on a child who had just had a tonic-clonic seizure, a classmate exclaims, "The way she foams at the mouth . . . like a mad dog . . . they ought to shoot her!" (West, 1986, p. 258)

And the stigma from which Jenny's mother seeks protection, although partly a projection of her own attitude, can be extended from child to family: "People shy away, and they immediately think there's something wrong with the whole family. . . ." (West, 1986, p. 255)

In contrast to efforts to hide and conceal, other parents, less defensive about the disorder, insist on their child's access to normal experiences. They recognize the child's vulnerability to teasing and ridicule but regard peers as educable.

A college senior whose seizures began at 13 credits his parents with not putting any restrictions on him. They never said that he couldn't do anything because he might have a seizure. His seizures were eventually controlled and he was able to get a driver's license. Getting the license did make his mother apprehensive but all she ever said was "Did you take your medicine?"

Amidst family coping patterns varying from concealment to openness, the most common seems to be selective disclosure, most often to the child's teachers or to those in activities that are potentially hazardous to the child, for example, swimming or climbing (West, 1986).

STRESSES ON THE CHILD, YOUNG PERSON, OR ADULT

The Threat of Recurrence

As defined earlier, epilepsy refers to *recurrent* seizures. Whatever their frequency, from less than yearly, to monthly, to weekly, or even daily (as in absence), the *threat* of recurrence cannot be entirely eliminated. Adherence to a regimen of daily medication for years or even a lifetime is an ever-present reminder of that threat. And even when medication is finally discontinued after a seizure-free period of several years, the possibility of a future seizure still remains.

Unpredictability

One can never know when a seizure may occur, and since its occurrence can be devastating, either psychologically or physically, a certain level of anxiety and caution is to be expected. The unpredictability can be extraordinarily stressful. This refers to the basic psychological need for structure, the need for events to make sense. While the normal person may bemoan the hand that life has dealt, at least he or she knows what it is and can try to deal with it as best as possible. The "enemy" in epilepsy, however, is silent and invisible and may give no clue to its readiness to strike. Admittedly, for some, the time of a seizure or its precipitant is fairly predictable (e.g., while the person is asleep in the early morning or when the person is under emotional stress), but since the actual occurrence of seizures is still irregular, one cannot know from one day to the next what to expect. While life inevitably has a certain degree of uncertainty, it is clearly heightened in epilepsy.

Seizures Themselves

This chapter has described the various kinds of seizures along with the associated disorders found with epilepsy. Although the prototype of epilepsy, the tonic-clonic seizure, generally requires no medical attention—indeed it is usually over before such assistance could arrive—such a seizure is not without physical risk. There is the possibility of injury connected with unprotected falling (Trimble, 1988) or subsequent thrashing; hence it is recommended that something soft be placed under the convulsing person's head. One study found an average decline of 21 points in IQ connected with falling-related head injuries in 15 percent of a large group of epileptic children (Trimble, 1988). And if seizures are prolonged or continue without interruption, as in status epilepticus, a genuine medical emergency exists.

Apart from potential physical hazards, activities may go on out of consciousness that are psychologically devastating, for example, public undressing or overt sexual behavior such as occasionally seen in complex partial seizures or involuntary urination such as seen in tonic-clonic seizures. For the school-age child, persistent absence seizures will interfere with attention to what is going on in the classroom. And seizures themselves appear capable of injuring the brain, especially the memory-related structure, the hippocampus, in seizures originating in the temporal lobes. Some intellectual deterioration is also thought to result from the chronic seizures associated with the genetic mental retardation disorder tuberous sclerosis (Gomez, 1979).

Anticonvulsant Side Effects

The common adverse side effects of antiepileptic medications were mentioned earlier. The drugs are powerful, exerting cognitive, motor, behavioral, and physical effects. Among the physical effects, enlargement of the gums and heightened and unwanted hair distribution associated with use of phenytoin (Dilantin) are particularly troubling to the adolescent female (Arts et al., 1984; Livingston, 1972). In a survey of epilepsy centers (Collaborative Group for Epidemiology of Epilepsy, 1986), the most common physical effects were sleepiness (32 percent), gum enlargement (22 percent), rhythmic oscillation of the eyeballs, i.e., hystagmus (15 percent), and ataxia (10 percent).

Activity Restrictions

Caution must be exercised with respect to activities that could either trigger seizures or would be dangerous if a seizure occurred during them, thus the concerns about swimming and climbing. Persons with epilepsy are encouraged to have adequate rest, keep regular habits, avoid excessive stimulants, and beware of alcohol (Aird, Masland, and Woodbury, 1984). Alcohol is a common precipitant of seizures, and care must be taken regarding its consumption, to say nothing of the use of "recreational" drugs. Society also expresses its concern, notably in limiting access to driving contingent upon achieving full seizure control.

Stigma and Discrimination

The following paragraphs describe a college girl who experienced the stigma of the disorder through her physician father (rejection of the word "epilepsy").

Her epilepsy was diagnosed when she was a freshman. She was afraid that she had a brain tumor and was overjoyed when the neurologist said it was epilepsy. She didn't know what it meant, but she knew she wasn't dying. *The doctor warned her never to tell anyone she had epilepsy for fear of being ostracized.* He told her to call it a "seizure disorder" because fewer people would be frightened by that label. He also told her to choose a field that would be relatively free of stress ["stress" as a precipitant of seizures]. For a long time she followed his advice and told no one because she was afraid she'd lose her friends.

The term *epilepsy* was also rejected by her father, himself a pediatrician. He said she had a "seizure disorder" not epilepsy and when she said they meant the same thing, he turned away. She realized that her father, himself a doctor, didn't accept her illness.

But she's gradually come to terms with it. Her roommates at college have won her trust. They don't treat her with pity; she still has seizures but they get along together just like other friends. Her seizures usually occur at night, and they treat them with "attentive disregard."

Along with the fears of rejection by peers are the realities of facing discrimination in employment when school is over. A later section will describe the frustrations created by the negative attitudes of prospective employers as well as difficulties in obtaining health and life insurance.

RESPONSES TO STRESSES

Effects on Self-Esteem: Intimacy, Success, and Autonomy

A disorder that has such widespread ramifications for the person, his or her family, friends, and the community at large is bound to affect self-esteem. This is particularly true where seizures are not fully controlled. Needs for intimacy are threatened by fears of rejection. The afflicted person's tie to the people from whom only love and support should be expected, his or her parents, also may be jeopardized.

The need for success is also likely to be threatened by feelings that the epileptic person cannot cope with daily challenges in the same way as his or her peers. The classroom is particularly likely to evoke such feelings, because the seizures themselves, anticonvulsant medications, and/or the brain abnormalities that underlie the disorder can create impediments to learning.

Certainly, one dimension of self-esteem likely to be adversely affected by epilepsy is the need for autonomy. The person's life is to a great degree controlled by others—parents, doctors, the condition itself. Surrounded by restrictions, there is less opportunity to develop the kind of growing self-determination that is the hallmark of the journey from childhood to adulthood. Instead, there is likely to be insecurity and dependency—in short, diminished autonomy.

While these threats to self-esteem are amply documented in the epilepsy literature, it is clear that ultimately many achieve an essentially normal adaptation, largely as a result of gaining freedom from seizures. Even in the school-age population, where about a quarter were seen as having significant behavior difficulties, the large majority were functioning in ways not different from their peers. Certainly the presence of epilepsy per se has not been an insurmountable barrier to extraordinary achievement; witness some of history's greatest figures—Caesar, Napolean, and Dostoyevsky. And in a more contemporary mode, tonic-clonic seizures did not interfere with the basketball skills of Bobby Jones, an All-American in college and an All-Star as a defensive specialist in the National Basketball Association.

ADAPTATION IN INFANCY AND EARLY CHILDHOOD

Non-fever-related seizures in infancy and early childhood do pose some serious risks. Indeed, those occurring in the first months of life are sometimes associated with life-threatening neurologic conditions. The developmental hazards connected with the two generalized epilepsies of the early years, infantile spasms and myoclonic seizures, have already been noted. Presumptively tied to organic brain abnormality, they commonly result in delayed motor development and mental retardation (Livingston, 1972).

For parents, the onset of epilepsy can be expected to produce the whole range of painful emotional responses found in other developmental disorders. Ziegler (1982) has noted reactions of shock, denial, a sense of loss of the baby-not-to-be, shame and guilt, anger and blaming others, and depression. A mother conveys her feelings:

> It's hard not be angry at the world. . . . Doctors say that if my baby had been treated earlier he might not be so badly retarded. We tried but couldn't find a doctor who understood it was epilepsy until too late.
> Billy's seizures began when he was 2½. He has mixed generalized seizures—absence, tonic-clonic, and atonic. The following year was a difficult one. His seizures were hard to control, and our reactions ranged from extremes of denial to overconcern, with occasional moments of calm acceptance. [Initial reactions to severe stress will be highly emotional.] By 4½,

behavior problems of an "organic" nature were present—a short attention span, hyperactivity, poor control of anger, and general developmental delay. Speech was poorly articulated, and there was impairment in visual-motor skills and general coordination. Bobby is now in a preschool program where his seizures and behavior present some problems, as does his learning difficulty. (Adapted from Ziegler, 1985)

ADAPTATION IN THE SCHOOL YEARS: LATER CHILDHOOD AND ADOLESCENCE

Epilepsy can have an impact on all developmental spheres—academic, behavioral, social, and vocational. These were enumerated in the earlier section entitled "Associated Disorders."

Academic

Mark, age 11, has poor visual-motor abilities, apparently related to an epilepsy-causing lesion in his right hemisphere. He has difficulty in drawing and in understanding how pieces, as in a puzzle, fit together.

Chrissy, age 13, began having absence seizures 2 years ago, and in the past year she's begun to have tonic-clonic ones as well. This is a common developmental pattern of absence seizures preceding tonic clonic ones. She has several absence seizures per day and, over the past year, five tonic-clonic ones as well. Her school achievement has significantly declined.

As indicated in the earlier review of the cognitive impairments associated with epilepsy, school learning problems are common, reading and math difficulties being noted in the elementary grades (Bagley, 1971).

Behavioral

Children with epilepsy are prone to a variety of behavioral problems—some connected to the disorder itself, some to medications, and some to the developmental experiences of the children. Such children may be viewed by their parents as immature and dependent and by their teachers as moody, irritable, restless, and aggressive. And for those in whom the seizures occur during school hours, the postseizure confusional states can cause classmates to regard them as crazy or weird (Ziegler, 1982). Again, it should be pointed out that this picture, along with attention deficit and a general slowing of reactions, is more characteristic of children whose seizures are not fully controlled.

Social

It is the interpersonal consequences of epilepsy that appear to create the greatest concern as young people (and adults) describe the impact of epilepsy on their lives. The particular focus is on its stigmatic aspect.

Chrissy, the 13-year-old mentioned earlier, complains of her class-mates teasing. "Everybody picks on me about it. I'm not very popular. They're like, 'Get out the way—if you look at her she'll have a seizure.' They say I have AIDS and pick on me about being gay."

Her first tonic-clonic seizure occurred in school. "All I know, I was there at my locker and then I was in the faculty lounge." She has come to know about her tonic-clonic seizures; she falls, starts shaking, and when its over she's confused about who and where she is for 30 minutes to an hour. Regarding teasing, she says that others just don't know how badly it affects one. "I mean it really hurts deep inside when people pick on you about being epileptic." Her two suggestions for youth who have contact with a person with epilepsy are to learn how to help someone during a seizure and to avoid teasing them about it ["helping" again means largely putting something soft beneath the head, turning the person sideways to allow saliva to drain from the mouth, and just getting out of the way and waiting for it to end. Only if the seizure lasts longer than 10 minutes or a second one immediately follows is there need for medical attention (Epilepsy Foundation of America, 1981)].

Steve, age 20, dropped out of college because of memory lapses. He says that potential employers treat you like a mental patient or a "re-tard."

Apart from stigmatic concerns, the school years are likely to evoke conflicts over activity restrictions. These are more likely to occur during adolescence when the very need for increasing self-determination (au-tonomy) is so strong.

Mark is 17 and has complex partial seizures that have been increasing in frequency. His mother says that he is sleeping less, smoking more, and had recently watched a late night TV program about a race car driver. He'd gotten very excited about it. His seizures have prevented him from getting a driver's license.

Interviewed when his parents were not present, Mark bitterly com-plained that they would use the threat of more seizures as a way of preventing him from doing things they didn't like.

Beth, a college senior, began having tonic-clonic seizures at 4, but they occurred rarely. All told she's had five, all tonic-clonic. Although she's had none for six years, she still is uneasy. She says that it's difficult not knowing whether she'll have one again. She also knows that epilepsy could reduce her chances for marriage and motherhood. She would like to have a baby but she knows that her anticonvulsant medication can damage the fetus. But since pregnancy increases the risk of seizures she would not want to discontinue her medication. She's in a real "Catch 22" situation.

Vocational

The degree of seizure control is an important vocational consideration. For high school students who have been seizure-free for at least 4 years by their freshman or sophomore years, Livingston (1972) suggests that they plan for the future as if they have never had epilepsy. On the other hand, as indicated earlier, young people whose epilepsy first appears in adolescence are less likely to achieve permanent freedom from seizures.

Apart from seizure control, the student's school experience will have provided a basis for post–high school consideration. Is postsecondary education appropriate, academic or vocational, or should the youth seek immediate employment? High school students with epilepsy can particularly benefit from vocational counseling because of a likely more narrow view of what is possible.

> Stephen, age 18, was seen by his high school counselor as capable of college work. He'd had tonic-clonic seizures since 9, and they were well-controlled, although he was still on medication. His parents "took epilepsy calmly" and saw that he had good medical care. With his seizures under good control, his epilepsy had no significant effect on his school adjustment. He enjoyed dating and dances, and because he'd never had a "public" seizure, few knew of his condition.
>
> With "above average" intelligence, an IQ of 114, he aspired to college and wanted to study business administration. During his freshman year he took a part-time job as a bookkeeper, and when, at the end of the session, he was offered it full-time, he accepted it and left school.
>
> But his job was not without stress. He later told a vocational rehabilitation counselor who had been assisting him that he was working under severe pressure because he had never told his employer about his epilepsy. He lived in daily fear of a seizure on the job. Encouraged to inform his employer that his epilepsy was well controlled, he was reluctant. He admitted that he was quite sensitive about being epileptic, although he'd never experienced any social rejection about it, and that "the stigma attached to epilepsy by non-understanding persons tormented him at all times." He feared being fired if he told the truth. [Concealing epilepsy from employers is common.] Counseling did not appear to result in a "confession" but reduced his fears about another seizure, in effect, removing the need for confession. (Adapted from Wright, 1975.)

ADAPTATION IN ADULTHOOD

In adulthood, as before, the degree of seizure control affects adjustment, although the psychological consequences of epilepsy may create the most difficult challenges. The focus here is on the vocational and social effects of epilepsy in the postschool years.

Vocational

The vocational domain has long been a special "sore point" for persons with epilepsy because of the pervasiveness of negative employer attitudes. Safety and related financial concerns appear to weigh heavily. Employers fear increased health insurance costs because of possible seizure-related injury on the job and loss of work time because of seizures (e.g., Sinick, 1975). With reference to safety, the record of individuals with epilepsy appears to compare quite favorably with that of the nonepileptic population (e.g., Udel, 1960). A New York State study found that the frequency of industrial accidents from seizures was less than half of that resulting from sneezing and coughing (U.S. Department of Health, Education and Welfare, 1969). There are, however, legitimate concerns about working conditions that could precipitate seizures. Some individuals are particularly sensitive to emotional upset, others to irregular work hours, others to physical conditions in the work environment. With regard to work environment conditions, noise at high levels can precipitate seizures.

Steve, age 29, complains about employer attitudes. He has seizures at about three-week intervals, and when they learn that he has epilepsy, takes medications, and can't drive, they refuse to hire him. With bitterness he exclaims, "They treat you like a mental patient or a retard."

Another young man, Mitchell, age 27, has nothing but praise for his employer. "My boss doesn't look at epilepsy like most people do. It's hard to get jobs for people like me. A lot of employers won't give people a chance. . . . That's my big beef."

In the face of such employer attitudes, it is to be expected that there will be resistance to divulging the illness. Indeed, if seizures never occur during working hours, some justification for nondisclosure might be found (Fraser and Smith, 1982). On the other hand, even when seizures occur only in nonworking hours, their aftereffects can interfere with the ability to work that day. In any case, most applicants feel uncomfortable about evasion and prefer to be open with an employer, even at the risk of rejection (Perlman, 1977).

Despite these difficulties, the great majority of persons with epilepsy are employed, about 75 percent, though disproportionately, at low-wage jobs. Nor does one need to be completely seizure-free to work. Among young adults in whom the majority had at least monthly seizures, most had some work history (Frazier, Erikson, and Thompson, 1978). Still 40 percent, at an average age of 28, had never worked. Their histories of dependency and social isolation were serious barriers; this is a population much in need of vocational assistance (Muthard, 1975).

While professional sports is an unlikely career choice, the former professional basketball player, Bobby Jones, proved that epilepsy was no hindrance to an extraordinary career. Now married and a parent, he had his first seizure, a tonic-clonic one at age 20, while he was a sophomore in college; a second at age 24; and then a third at age 26. In retrospect, he views his illness as having had at least one positive effect; he became more careful about his health.

Social Concerns

Apart from vocational problems, it is the social sphere that most troubles the person with epilepsy. The descriptions that follow present examples of extreme overprotection, of how people cope with stigma, and of how some put their lives back together after initial seizures in adulthood. First, some brief comments about marriage and sexuality.

Sexuality. Most persons with epilepsy lead normal sexual lives. Sexual problems tend to be associated with complex partial seizures and in those with poor seizure control. Generally the main sexual dysfunction is lack of interest rather than inability to perform (Lechtenberg, 1984). In the later self-descriptions of Leonard Wolf, his complex partial seizures appear to have not adversely affected his sexual activity.

Marriage. Males with epilepsy are somewhat less likely to marry. Whereas about 69 percent of men and 70 percent of women in the general population marry, in epilepsy, only 56 percent of men but virtually the same percentage of women (69%) ever marry. Factors reducing the marriage rate in males include seizure onset before age 20, degree of seizure control, and employment potential (Lechtenberg, 1984).

Mary, age 24, has had complex partial seizures since age 11. Usually lasting for about 2 minutes, objects appear to shrink in size and the familiar seems strange ("jamais vu"). They occur often, usually early in the morning and are unaffected by antiepileptic drugs.

Her parents' reaction was one of extreme overprotectiveness and control. They decided to have no more children, and her mother gave up her job in order to devote full time to her care. Mary was forbidden to go out by herself or to play with other children. When she did go out, she was always accompanied by her mother.

Following school, during which there was much absence, she sought employment, but anxiety about her seizures seemed to increase their frequency and she couldn't hold a job. Her life was one of staying at home and helping her mother with household chores. Her social life was not wholly absent, however, since she frequented a center serving young adults with epilepsy *but always accompanied by her mother*. Somehow she managed to marry a young man whom she met there, and they moved into a house, but only a few doors from her parents. Still her pattern of dependency was beginning to moderate. Both counseling and anticonvulsants began to reduce her seizures and increase her desire for greater independence. This was rejected by her mother who regarded it as "ingratitude." (Adapted from Betts, 1972)

Arlene, a young mother, tells of her long battle to overcome the stigma of epilepsy. Her first seizure occurred in adulthood and at a surprise party she was giving for her mother. Guests arrived to find her unconscious on the hotel dining room floor, her body strangely rigid. Her diagnosis presented her with an illness that "can be an invisible barrier between you and me, composed largely of ancient fears and prejudices that refuse to die. What dies, indeed, or seriously weakens, is one's self-confidence." Illustrating epilepsy's psychological impact is her observation, "My doctors were able to control my seizures before I could control my shaken self-esteem. Signing my name to this article is my first step in restoring my dignity." She had written an unsigned piece 12 years before. At that time she wrote, "I have never robbed a bank, committed murder, or served time, yet I cannot sign this article." She later observes that the concealment of her name typified the many falsehoods with which she has had to live.

She came to know that honesty about the disorder made it hard to find work, that driving privileges were lost, that for some there would be the embarrassment and humiliation of unpredictable public seizures and that others faced being labeled retarded, insane, or dangerous (unprovoked rage is sometimes seen in complex partial seizures involving the temporal lobes). Though initially relieved that her seizures were not due to a brain tumor, she was to learn that "public opinion was going to be more of a problem than my seizures."

"The early warnings came from my family. My mother was so pained by the word 'epilepsy' that she called it my "neurological" . . . Her mother-in-law persuaded her not to "burden her children with anything so—uh—difficult." Her friends encouraged the conspiracy of silence. Said one, "I'll never tell a soul and you shouldn't either."

So traumatized was Arlene that she couldn't even write the words "I have epilepsy" on a health identification card for her wallet. "Write the words? I couldn't even say them."

Gradually she's emerged from hiding. "Now I've placed the 'I have epilepsy' card in my wallet and I drive to the local pharmacy to buy my own antiepileptic medication." (Her husband used to do this for her.)

A teacher, prior to her illness, she began writing while waiting for her seizures to be controlled and has since devoted herself fulltime to writing and lecturing about epilepsy.

Leonard, an English professor, had his first seizure at 54. His story is told in some detail. We hear about his aura and seizures, what they were like, and how he eventually regained his psychological equilibrium and resumed his life and career.

His first attack occurred while in bed and reading. His wife recalls, "I saw your head fall sharply forward; your eyes were closed and you were very still, as if asleep . . . I called sharply but you didn't answer. After a minute, you came out of it, very slowly . . ."

Perplexed, Leonard and his wife, Debbie, concluded that he'd fainted because the room was too hot. Two days later while reading what he later described as a "melodrama," he found himself deeply touched by the character's violent death. "The room darkened and there welled up in me an unbelievable anguish for Pepe (the main character), his mama, his family, and for the entire human race. There was a final moment when I was stern with myself, thinking, it's sad, but it's not *that* sad! Then the darkness gathered me in. [He is describing the deepening of emotion associated with the onset of an aura.]

"I was not frightened. Rather I felt myself privileged to be enclosed by a soft silent grandeur, (like) a brooding river was flowing over me. I was glad to merge into that horizonless river, in which, for an instant, I could watch and sustain the world's grief. Then the river and I faded and there was nothing more to see (the kind of "mystical" experience also associated with drug use).

Returning to consciousness, he was disoriented and frightened. His cheek rested on his desk and out of a corner of his mouth saliva oozed. He staggered into the office of a colleague who exclaimed, "For God's sake, what's the matter with you?" I said, "I don't know but I'm scared." I was to be scared for a long time.

Eventually diagnosed as complex partial seizures, his epilepsy was attributed to an abnormality in the temporal lobes.

"Epilepsy! I heard it as in the old days I might have heard the warning of the leper's bell [an apt analogy]. I thought of armies of tremor-ridden Jukes and Kallikaks [pseudonyms for families connected with retardation] and of epileptic women burned at the stake for being witches . . . I recalled when an 8th grade classmate moaned and fell . . . into the aisle to thrash about while the rest of us, including the teacher, stood terrified and helpless." [My own first experience at seeing a tonic-clonic seizure was very frightening]

He began to learn about epilepsy and its possible side effects—skin rash, gum problems, sleepiness, depression, or even a feeling of depersonalization.

"Now I knew something . . . but I was still afraid. What was I afraid of? The usual things . . . my classes, my writing, my family. And that All-American question: What about my sex life?"

He speaks of his continual self-monitoring. "Each day, I watched my behavior for signs of a coming fit or the side effects of the Dilantin (a popular anticonvulsant). Whenever I stumbled I was sure that the worst was about to happen." He describes an episode on a bus when, after feeling his body tingling, a possible seizure indicator, he initiated conversation with a fellow passenger as a deliberate way of distracting himself from what he was feeling. This had been suggested to him by his doctor as a means of inhibiting a seizure. Though this was successful in that instant, the awareness of an ever-possible seizure did not lessen. . . . "The waiting for something to happen persisted."

His life was not eased by the loss of his driver's license and his being forbidden by his doctor to ride his horse. He did resume riding but with a "hard hat" that masqueraded as a hunting cap!

"I was getting used to being an epileptic. I'm afraid I was aggressive to my friends, asserting the word "epilepsy" as if it was a condition anyone would be a fool not to envy [overcompensating for his initial revulsion to the disorder] . . . An interesting by-product . . is the way people appeared out of nowhere . . . to whisper to me that they were epileptics [he learns that "whispers" are in order].

His daily job responsibilities helped him to begin to think about something else beside his illness. "My family and I simply have too much to do to play footsies very long with despair . . . Epilepsy . . . settled into its proper place. I would much rather not have it, but I have it. I see no reason to be ashamed of having it [rejects being stigmatized]. For the time being my job is secure, my friends steadfast. I do the work I care about and take my pills . . . life is neither more nor less tumultuous than before . . . as for my sex life, as far as I may be permitted to describe it, it ranges between spectacular and splendid." (Adapted from Wolf, 1977).

SPECIAL SERVICES NEEDS

Two kinds of services are needed by individuals with epilepsy—medical and habilitative. Medical services are directed toward maximizing seizure control, eliminating the seizures completely if possible, while habilitative services are focused on its psychosocial aspects.

CONTROLLING SEIZURES

Antiepileptic Drugs

It will be recalled that a medical treatment for epilepsy was not discovered until the 1850s. At that time, a bromide salt was introduced, and it continued to be the main anticonvulsant medication until the introduction of phenobarbital in 1912. Phenytoin (Dilantin), perhaps the best known anticonvulsant, has been widely used since the late 1930s (Livingston, 1972). The current armamentarium consists of 18 major anticonvulsants (Aird, Masland, and Woodbury, 1984), within which phenobarbital is still prominent.

With current drugs, a 75- to 100- percent reduction in seizures is achievable in half of affected persons. A lesser degree of control is obtained in another third, while about a fifth obtain no benefit at all (Aird, Masland, and Woodbury, 1984). Total elimination is a reasonable expectation with absence and generalized tonic-clonic seizures originating in childhood, but not for infantile spasms or atonic or myoclonic seizures. With respect to infantile spasms, greater control has recently been reported with the anticonvulsant Valproate, although lessening of seizures did not alter the cognitive impairment associated with this form of epilepsy (Siemes et al., 1988). For those with an adult onset, however, lifelong adherence to an anticonvulsant regime is likely. In those with seizure onset in adolescence or adulthood, the response to treatment during the first 2 years is a good predictor of future seizure control (Reynolds, 1987).

In the use of anticonvulsants, the goal is to achieve the greatest degree of control with the fewest drugs, only one, if possible. For some individuals, combinations of drugs are necessary, but combinations increase the risk of side effects (Aird, Masland, and Woodbury, 1984; Thompson and Trimble, 1982). Fortunately, at least 80 percent of the more common types of seizures are controllable by a single drug (Elwes et al., 1986; Reynolds and Shorvon, 1981).

ACTH Hormone

ACTH, adrenocorticotropic hormone, is used to treat either infantile spasms or severe seizures not controllable with other drugs (Epilepsy Foundation of America, 1986; Jeavons and Bower, 1974).

Psychological Procedures

Seizure reduction also can be achieved through psychological means, ordinarily as adjuncts to anticonvulsants (Williams, 1982). Psychological methods include the use of biofeedback (to try to normalize brain waves); desensitization to experiences that trigger seizures; the use of relaxation, psychotherapy, or counseling; and the interrupting of a behavior chain leading to a seizure, as in the case of Leonard (Fraser and Smith, 1982). With regard to stress, anxiety and frustration are commonly reported precipitants of seizures (Aird, Masland, and Woodbury, 1984).

Psychotherapy itself has been particularly employed in the treatment of "psychogenic" seizures, those presumed to be primarily psychological rather than organic in origin, or where emotional states, such an anxiety and frustration, trigger organically based ones (e.g., Bouchard et al., 1975).

Dietary Treatment

In preschool-age children for whom anticonvulsants have been ineffective, there may be resort to a special ketogenic diet, a diet high in fat and low in carbohydrates. Because the diet can involve fasting as well as narrowed food intake, children resist it, and implementation is difficult (Livingston, 1972; Epilepsy Foundation of America, 1986).

Surgery

Where seizures are unresponsive to other procedures and are due to a brain lesion that is operable, surgery may be employed. Most commonly done for complex partial seizures that originate in the temporal lobes, surgery is said to be effective in either eliminating or reducing seizures in about 75 percent of cases (Aird, Masland, and Woodbury, 1984; Engel, Crandall, and Rausch, 1983). One of the hazards, however, is that surgical intervention in brain areas involving memory, language, and emotions can leave lasting deficits.

HABILITATIVE SERVICES

Much of this chapter has been devoted to the psychological and social problems created by epilepsy, but the importance of the psychological side has not always been appreciated.

> We cannot overemphasize the importance of discussing with the parents and the patient . . . the nature of the disorder . . . at the initial interview or very early in . . . treatment. The treatment of epileptic patients in most clinics, including our own [Johns Hopkins Hospital Epilepsy Clinic], many years ago consisted almost exclusively of giving medication and telling him to return later if his seizures were not helped. As time went on, we realized that medical attention should be directed not only to the seizures per se, but to the "whole individual" since the epileptic patient is frequently confronted with many problems . . . over and above the seizures. We soon learned that when we took time to sit down . . . and discuss what epilepsy is . . . and is not, what the patient can do and . . . should not do and explained . . . the complications, hazards, restrictions and unwarranted stigma . . . our overall results . . . became progressively better. We *now believe that the consideration of such problems as how to cope with epilepsy, and what the future holds is just as important as the administration of antiepileptic medication.* (Livingston, 1972, p. 475; italics added)

In coping with epilepsy, for parents and the child (youth or adult) there is the problem of finding a healthy balance between restriction and freedom. The price of too much restriction or external control is a diminished sense of personal autonomy and competence and a dependent lifestyle. Yet the encouragement of full participation in age-appropriate activities, in a commendable effort to reduce the sense of difference, is not without risks. The dilemma of parents who want their child to be as normal as possible is illustrated in the following episode:

Richie, 8½, was brought to a hospital emergency room after a seizure while bike riding. He had a large black eye and needed stitches in his forehead. When doctors learned of his epilepsy as the cause of his accident and injuries, his mother was criticized for allowing him to ride his bike. She complains, "The doctors tell you to try and treat him normally. Let him be an active boy, but when they saw him bleeding they stitched him up and rushed him to the hospital (with a special seizure clinic). *They act like I did something wrong.* (Adapted from Ziegler, 1981, p. 343; italics added)

When families are encouraged to accept risks, professionals have to be prepared to provide the emotional support those risks entail. After all, it is the parent and the affected individual who must live with the consequences of our advice.

While some unhappiness from restrictions can produce difficulties in the preadolescent child, in adolescence the need for autonomy and "to be like others" is likely to create even greater stress in parent-child relationships. Open access to a professional who understands the inherent conflict between restriction and freedom and the stress that difference can impose on self-esteem is crucial to earning the adolescent's trust and willingness to comply. Other adolescent psychological concerns will be peer acceptance, academic progress and assessment of one's abilities, and a beginning attention to the future. However, psychological concerns are clearly of no less relevance to the individual whose epilepsy originates in adulthood, as the following illustrates.

Eve, 31, wife and mother, felt that in her job she always had to prove to others that she was as good as them. She began to see a counselor who was knowledgeable about epilepsy and "she helped me to understand that just because I was an epileptic, I wasn't any different than anybody else . . . I don't know what makes it so difficult for an epileptic to understand that but it's the hardest thing to ever accept. It really is."

Apart from the sense of difference, the adult with epilepsy is often troubled by fears of death, mental deterioration or mental illness, unemployment, and social isolation. One of the extraordinary consequences of the development of support groups is that many individuals for the first time meet other people with the same disorder. Inevitably, this reduces the sense of personal isolation, allows for a sharing of common experiences, and permits learning about how others are coping with similar problems.

Independent Living Skills

Adults whose seizures have interfered with employment are likely to have continued to reside in the family home and to have never acquired the skills necessary for a more independent adjustment. Areas of particular educational attention in habilitative programs include public transportation (a major problem for those not permitted to drive), budgeting, housekeeping, shopping, nutrition, grooming, and health care (Fraser and Smith, 1982).

Residential Alternatives

In the past, nonfamily residential services were largely limited to individuals with combinations of seizures and mental retardation or mental illness. In 1976, about 30 percent of the institutionalized retarded population had seizures, while about 10 percent of the institutionalized mentally ill group were so affected (Levinson, 1982). More recently, local and state epilepsy societies have begun to establish group homes, principally for young adults who are either employed or in vocational training.

REFERENCES

Adams, F. (1939). *The genuine works of Hippocrates.* Baltimore: William & Wilkins.

Aird, R. B., Masland, R. L., and Woodbury, D. M. (1984). *The epilepsies: A critical review.* New York: Raven Press.

Andres, D. G., Bullen, J. G., Tomlinson, L., Elwes, R. D. C., and Reynolds, E. H. (1985). A comparative study of the cognitive effects of phenytoin and carbamazepine in new referrals with epilepsy. *Epilepsia, 26,* 268–278.

Annegers, J. F., Hauser, W. A., Elveback, L. R., and Kurland, L. T. (1979). Remission of seizures and relapses in patients with epilepsy. *Epilepsia, 20,* 729–737.

Arts, W. F. M., Visser, L. H., Loonen, M. C. B., Tsiam, A. T., Straink, M., Stuurman, P. M., and Poortvliet, D. C. J. (1988). Follow-up of 146 children with epilepsy after withdrawal of anti-epileptic therapy. *Epilepsia, 29,* 244–250.

Bagley, C. (1971). *The social psychology of the epileptic child.* Coral Gables, FL: University of Miami Press.

Baird, H. W., John, E. R., Ahn, H., and Maisel, E. (1980). Neurometric evaluation of epileptic children who do well and poorly in school. *Electroencephalography and Clinical Neurophysiology, 48,* 683–693.

Bear, D., Freeman, R., and Greenberg, M. (1984). Behavioral alterations in patients with temporal lobe epilepsy. In D. Blumer (Ed.), *Psychiatric aspects of epilepsy.* Washington, DC: American Psychiatric Press.

Bear, D. M., and Fedio, P. (1977). Quantitative analysis of interictal behavior in temporal lobe epilepsy. *Archives of Neurology, 34,* 454–486.

Betts, T. A. (1982). Psychiatry and epilepsy. In J. Laidlaw and A. Richens (Eds.), *A textbook of epilepsy,* 2d ed. Edinburgh: Churchill-Livingstone.

Blumer, D. (1982). Specific psychiatric complications in certain forms of epilepsy and their treatment. In H. Sands (Ed.), *Epilepsy: A handbook for the mental health professional.* New York: Brunner/Mazel.

Bouchard, R., Lorilloux, J., Guedeney, C., and Kipman, D. S. (1977). *Childhood epilepsy: A pediatric-psychiatric approach.* New York: International University Press.

Bourgeois, B. F., Prensky, A. L., Palkes, H. S., Talent, B. K., and Busch, S. G. (1983). Intelligence in epilepsy: A prospective study in children. *Annals of Neurology, 14,* 438–444.

Bridge, E. (1949). *Epilepsy and convulsive disorders in children.* New York: McGraw-Hill.

Brown, J. K. (1982). Fits in children. In J. Laidlaw and A. Richens (Eds.), *A textbook of epilepsy,* 2d ed. Edinburgh: Churchill-Livingstone.

Chaundry, M., and Pond, D. (1961). Mental deterioration in epileptic children. *Journal of Neurology, Neurosurgery and Psychiatry, 24,* 213–219.

Collaborative Group for Epidemiology of Epilepsy (1986). *Epilepsia, 27,* 323–330.

Commission for the Control of Epilepsy and its Consequences (1977). *Plan for nationwide action on epilepsy.* (DHEW Publication No. NIH 78276). Washington, DC: National Institutes of Health.

Dahl, J. A., Melin, L., and Leissner, P. (1988). Effects of a behavioral intervention on epileptic seizure behavior and paroxysmal activity: A systematic replication of three cases of children with intractable epilepsy. *Epilepsia, 29,* 172–183.

Dam, M. (1982). Adverse reactions to antiepileptic drugs. In J. Laidlaw and A. Richens (Eds.), *A textbook of epilepsy.* Edinburgh: Churchill-Livingstone.

Dam, M., and Dam, A. M. (1986). Is there an epileptic personality? In M. R. Trimble and T. G. Bolwig (Eds.), *Aspects of epilepsy and psychiatry.* New York: Wiley.

DeHaas, A., and Magnus, D. (1958). In A. DeHaas (Ed.), *Lectures on epilepsy.* New York: Elsevier.

Dell, J. L. (1986). Social dimensions of epilepsy: Stigma and response. In S. Whitman and B. P. Hermann (Eds.), *Psychopathology in epilepsy: Social dimension.* New York: Oxford University Press.

Dikmen, S., and Matthews, C. G. (1977). Effect of major motor seizure frequency upon cognitive-intellectual functions in adults. *Epilepsia, 18,* 21–28.

Dikmen, S., Matthews, C. G., and Harley, J. P. (1977). Effect of early versus late onset of major motor epilepsy on cognitive-intellectual performance: Further considerations. *Epilepsia, 18,* 31–43.

Dodrill, C. B. (1982a). Neuropsychology. In J. Laidlaw and A. Richens (Eds.), *A textbook of epilepsy,* 2d ed. Edinburgh: Churchill-Livingstone.

Dodrill, C. B. (1982b), Psychological assessment in epilepsy. In H. Sands (Ed.), *Epilepsy: A handbook for the mental health professional.* New York: Brunner/Mazel.

Dodrill, C. B. (1988). Correlates of generalized tonic-clonic seizures with intelligence, neuropsychological, emotional, and social functioning in patients with epilepsy. *Epilepsia, 27,* 399–411.

Dreifuss, F. E. (1975). The nature of epilepsy. In G. N. Wright (Ed.), *Epilepsy rehabilitation.* Boston: Little, Brown.

Elwes, R. D. C., Johnson, A. L., Shorvon, S. D., and Reynolds, E. H. (1984). The prognosis for seizure control in newly diagnosed epilepsy patients. *New England Journal of Medicine, 311,* 944–947.

Engel, J., Jr., Crandall, P. H., and Rausch, R. (1983). The partial epilepsies. In R. N. Rosenberg, R. G. Grossman, A. Schochet, and E. R. Heinz (Eds.), *The clinical neurosciences,* Vol. 2. New York: Churchill-Livingston.

Epilepsy Foundation of America (1981). *How to recognize and classify seizures.* Landover, MD: Epilepsy Foundation of America.

Epilepsy Foundation of America (1986). *A patient's guide to medical treatment of childhood and adult seizure disorders.* Landover, MD: Epilepsy Foundation of America.

Ford, C. A., Gibson, P., and Dreifuss, F. E. (1983). Psychosocial considerations in childhood epilepsy. In F. E. Dreifuss (Ed.), *Pediatric epileptology.* Boston: John Wright, PSG Inc.

Frazier, R., Erikson, K., and Thompson, J. (1978). The role of specialized vocational services in comprehensive treatment of the individual with epilepsy. Paper presented at the Epilepsy International Symposium, Vancouver, B.C., Canada. September.

Fraser, R. T., and Smith, W. R. (1982). Adjustment to daily living. In H. Sands (Ed.), *Epilepsy: A handbook for the mental health professional.* New York: Brunner/ Mazel.

Gastaut, H. (1970). Clinical and electroencephalographical classification of epileptic seizures. *Epilepsia, 11,* 102–113.

Giordani, B., Berent, S., Sackellares, J. C., Rourke, D., Seidenberg, M., Dreifuss, F. E., and Boll, T. J. (1985). Intelligence test performance of patients with partial and generalized seizures. *Epilepsia, 26,* 37–42.

Gomez, M. (1979). Clinical experience at Mayo Clinic. In M. Gomez (Ed.), *Tuberous sclerosis.* New York: Raven Press.

Goodridge, D. M. G., and Shorvon, S. D. (1983). Epilepsy in a population of 6,000: I. Demography diagnosis and classification and the role of hospital services. *British Medical Journal, 287,* 641–647.

Hauser, W. A. (1978). Epidemiology of epilepsy. In B. S. Schoenberg (Ed.), *Advances in Neurology,* Vol. 19. New York: Raven Press.

Hauser, W. A., and Kurland, L. T. (1975). Epidemiology of epilepsy in Rochester, Minnesota, 1935 through 1967. *Epilepsia, 16,* 1–66.

Hermann, B. P., Desai, B. T., and Whitman, S. (1988). Epilepsy. In V. B. Van Hasselt, P. S. Strain, and M. Hersen (Eds.), *Handbook of developmental and physical disabilities.* Elmsford, NY: Pergamon.

Hermann, B. P., and Whitman, S. (1986). *Psychopathology in epilepsy: Social dimension.* New York: Oxford University Press.

Hermann, B. P., Wyler, A. R., Richey, E. T., and Rea, J. M. (1987). Memory function and verbal learning ability in patients with complex partial seizures of temporal lobe origin. *Epilepsia, 28,* 547–554.

Hoeppner, J. B., Garron, D. C., Wilson, R. S., and Koch-Weser, M. P. (1987). Epilepsy and verbosity. *Epilepsia, 28,* 35–40.

Holdsworth, L., and Whitmore, K. (1974). A study of children with epilepsy attending ordinary schools: I. Their seizure patterns, progress and behavior in school. *Developmental Medicine and Child Neurology, 16,* 746–758.

Hughes, J. G., and Jabbour, J. T. (1958). The treatment of the epileptic child. *Journal of Pediatrics, 53,* 66–68.

Jeavons, P. M., and Bower, B. D. (1974). Infantile spasms. In P. J. Vinken and G. W. Bruyn (Eds.), *Handbook of clinical neurology,* Vol. 15. New York: Elsevier.

Keranen, T., Sillanpaa, M., and Riekkinen, P. J. (1988). Distribution of seizure types in an epileptic population. *Epilepsia, 29,* 1–7.

Lechtenberg, R. (1984). *Epilepsy and the family.* Cambridge, MA: Harvard University Press.

Levinson, R. W. (1982). Resources for epilepsy: Access and advocacy. In H. Sands (Ed.), *Epilepsy: A handbook for the mental health professional.* New York: Brunner/Mazel.

Linnett, M. J. (1982). People with epilepsy—the burden of epilepsy. In J. Laidlaw and A. Richens (Eds.), *A textbook of epilepsy*, 2d Ed. Edinburgh: Churchill-Livingstone.

Livingston, S. (1972). *Comprehensive management of epilepsy in infancy, childhood and adolescence.* Springfield, IL: Thomas.

Marsden, C. D., and Reynolds, E. H. (1982). Neurology, Part 1. In J. Laidlaw and A. Richens (Eds.), *A textbook of epilepsy.* Edinburgh: Churchill-Livingstone.

Masland, R. L. (1982). The nature of epilepsy. In H. Sands (Ed.), *Epilepsy: A handbook for the mental health professional.* New York: Brunner/Mazel.

Matthews, C., and Klove, N. (1967). Differential psychological performances in major motor, psychomotor and mixed seizure classifications of known and unknown etiology. *Epilepsia, 8,* 117–128.

Mellor, D. M., Lowit, I., and Hall, D. J. (1974). Are epileptic children behaviorally different from other children? In Marris, Mawdsley, Epilepsy Proc. Hans Berger Cent. Symp. pp. 313–316. Edinburgh: Churchill-Livingstone.

Milner, B. (1975). Psychological aspects of focal epilepsy and its neurosurgical management. In D. P. Purpura, J. K. Penry, and R. D. Walter (Eds.), *Advances in neurology,* Vol. B. New York: Raven Press.

Mittan, R. C., Wasterlain, C., and Locke, G. (1982). Fear of seizures. In H. Akimoto, H. Kazamatsuri, and M. Seino (Eds.), *Advance in epilepsy—1981.* New York: Raven Press.

Musumeci, S. A., Colognola, R. M., Ferri, R., Gigli, M. A., Petrella, M. A., Sanfilippo, S., Bergonzi, P., and Tassinari, C. A. (1988). Fragile-X syndrome: A particular epileptogenic EEG pattern. *Epilepsia, 29,* 41–47.

Muthard, J. E. (1975). Vocational counseling of the epileptic client. In G. N. Waight (Ed.), *Epilepsy rehabilitation.* Boston: Little, Brown.

Myklebust, H. (1977). Educational problems of the child with epilepsy. In Plan for nationwide action on epilepsy. Report of the Commission for the Control of Epilepsy and its Consequences, Vol. 2, Part 1 (pp. 474–490). Washington, DC: (DHEW Publication No. 78276).

Ounsted, C. (1955). The hyperkinetic syndrome in epileptic children. *Lancet, 2,* 303.

Ounsted, C., Lindsay, J., and Norman, R. (1966). *Biological factors in temporal lobe epilepsy.* London: William Heinemann Medical Books.

Pazzaglia, P., and Frank-Pazzaglia, L. F. (1976). Record in grade school of pupils with epilepsy: An epidemiological study. *Epilepsia, 17,* 301–366.

Perlman, L. G. (1977). *The person with epilepsy: Lifestyle, needs, expectations.* Chicago: National Epilepsy League.

Pond, D., and Bidwell, B. H. (1960). A survey of epilepsy in fourteen general practices, II: Social and psychological aspects. *Epilepsia, 1,* 285–299.

Reynolds, E. H. (1981). Biological factors in psychological disorders associated with epilepsy. In E. H. Reynolds and M. R. Trimble (Eds.), *Psychiatry and epilepsy.* Edinburgh: Churchill-Livingstone.

Reynolds, E. H. (1983). Mental effects of antiepileptic medication: A review. *Epilepsia,* 24(Suppl. 2), S85–S95.

Reynolds, E. H. (1987). Early treatment and prognosis of epilepsy. *Epilepsia, 28,* 97–106.

Reynolds, E. H., and Shorvon, S. D. (1981). Monotherapy or polytherapy for epilepsy? *Epilepsia, 22,* 1–10.

Ritchie, K. (1981). Research note: Interaction in the families of epileptic children. *Journal of Child Psychology and Psychiatry, 22,* 65–71.

Robertson, M. M. (1986). Ictal and interictal depression in patients with epilepsy. In M. R. Trimble and T. G. Bolwig (Eds.), *Aspects of epilepsy and psychiatry*. New York: Wiley.

Rodin, E. A., Shapiro, H. L., and Lennox, K. (1977). Epilepsy and life performances. *Rehabilitation Literature, 38,* 34–39.

Russell, E. W. (1975). A multiple scoring method for the assessment of complex memory functions. *Journal of Consulting and Clinical Psychology, 43,* 800.

Rutter, M., Graham, P., and Yule, W. (1970). A neuropsychiatric study in childhood. In *Clinics in Developmental Medicine*, No. 35/36. Philadelphia: Lippincott.

Sands, H. (1982). Psychodynamic management of epilepsy. In H. Sands (Ed.), *Epilepsy: A handbook for the mental health professional.* New York: Brunner/Mazel.

Schaon, R. J., Ward, J. W., and Guthrie, D. (1977). Carbamazepine as an anticonvulsant in children. *Neurology, 27,* 476–480.

Seidenberg, M., Beck, N., Geiser, M., Giordani, B., Sackellares, J. C., Berent, S., Dreifuss, F. E., and Boll, T. J. (1986). Academic achievement of children with epilepsy. *Epilepsia, 27,* 753–759.

Siemes, H., Spohr, H. L., Michael, T., and Nan, H. (1988). Therapy of infantile spasms with valproate: Results of a prospective study. *Epilepsia, 29,* 553–560.

Sinick, D. (1975). Job placement and postplacement services for the epileptic client. In G. N. Wright (Ed.), *Epilepsy rehabilitation.* Boston: Little, Brown.

Stores, G. (1978). School children with epilepsy at risk for learning and behavior problems. *Developmental Medicine and Child Neurology, 20,* 502.

Svoboda, W. B. (1979). *Learning about epilepsy.* Baltimore: University Park Press.

Tarter, R. E. (1972). Intellectual and adaptive functioning in epilepsy: A review of fifty years of research. *Diseases of the Nervous System, 33,* 763.

Taylor, D. C., and Falconer, M. A. (1968). Clinical socio-economic and psychological changes after temporal lobectomy. *British Journal of Psychiatry, 114,* 1247.

Temkin, O. (1971). *The falling sickness.* Baltimore: Johns Hopkins University Press.

Thompson, P. J., and Trimble, M. R. (1982). Anticonvulsant drugs and cognitive functions. *Epilepsia, 23,* 531–544.

Towne, A. E. (1975). Appendix B: Case Histories. In G. N. Wright (Ed.), *Epilepsy Rehabilitation.* Boston: Little, Brown.

Trimble, M. R. (1988). Cognitive hazards of seizure disorders. *Epilepsia,* 29(Suppl. 1), S19–S24.

Trimble, M. R., and Reynolds, E. H. (1984). Neuropsychiatric toxicity and anticonvulsant drugs. In W. B. Matthews and G. H. Glaser (Eds.), *Recent advances in clinical neurology.* Edinburgh: Churchill-Livingstone.

Trimble, M. R., Thompson, P. J., and Huppert F. (1980). Anticonvulsant drugs and cognitive abilities. In R. Cnager, F. Angelari, and J. K. Penry (Eds.), *Advances in epileptology.* New York: Raven Press.

Udel, M. M. (1960). The work performance of epileptics in industry. *Archives of Environmental Health, 1,* 257–264.

U.S. Department of Health, Education and Welfare (1969). *Epilepsy: Hope through research.* Washington, DC: U.S. Government Printing Office.

Vinson, T. (1975). Towards demythologizing epilepsy: An appraisal of public attitudes. *Medical Journal of Australia, 26,* 663–666.

Vislie, H., and Henrikson, G. (1958). Psychic disturbances in epileptics. In A. M. De Haas (Ed.), *Lectures on epilepsy.* Amsterdam: Elsevier.

Voeller, K. K., and Rothenberg, M. B. (1973). Psychosocial aspects of the management of seizures in children. *Pediatrics, 51,* 1072–1082.

Walker, A. E., and Blumer, D. (1984). Behavioral effects of temporal lobectomy for temporal lobe epilepsy. In D. Blumer (Ed.), *Psychiatric aspects of epilepsy.* Washington, DC: American Psychiatric Press.

West, P. (1986). The social meaning of epilepsy stigma as a potential explanation for psychopathology in children. In S. Whitman and B. P. Herman (Eds.), *Psychopathology in epilepsy: Social dimensions.* New York: Oxford University Press.

Williams, D. T. (1982). The treatment of seizures: Special psychotherapeutic and psychobiological techniques. In H. Sands (Ed.), *Epilepsy: A handbook for the mental health professional.* New York: Brunner/Mazel.

Wolf, L. (1977). Congratulations, you're an epileptic. *Psychology Today,* December, 94–99, 144.

Woodbury, L. A. (1978a). A brief consideration of the prognosis of epilepsy. In *Report of the Commission for the Control of Epilepsy and Its Consequences: Plan for nationwide action on epilepsy,* Vol. 4. Washington, DC: National Technical Information Service, Dept. of Commerce.

Woodbury, L. (1978b). Shortening of the life span and mortality of patients with epilepsy. In *Plan for nationwide action on epilepsy. Report of the Commission for the Control of Epilepsy and its Consequences,* 4, 107–114. Washington, DC: U.S. Dept. of Health, Education and Welfare.

Wright, G. N. (1975). Rehabilitation and the problem of epilepsy. In G. N. Wright (Ed.), *Epilepsy rehabilitation.* Boston: Little, Brown.

Ziegler, R. G. (1981). Impairments of control and competence in epileptic children and their families. *Epilepsia, 22,* 339–346.

Ziegler, R. G. (1982). The child with epilepsy: Psychotherapy and counseling. In H. Sands (Ed.), *Epilepsy: A handbook for the mental health professional.* New York: Brunner/Mazel.

Ziegler, R. G. (1985). Risk factors in childhood epilepsy. *Psychotherapy and Psychosomatics, 44,* 185–190.

Zielinski, J. J. (1974). *Epidemiology and medical and social problems of epilepsy in Warsaw.* Washington, DC: U.S. Government Printing Office.

Zielinski, J. J. (1986). Selected psychiatric and psychosocial aspects of epilepsy as seen by an epidemiologist. In S. Whitman and B. P. Hermann (Eds.), *Psychopathology in epilepsy.* New York: Oxford University Press.

A Brief Summary: What Have We Learned?

PURPOSE AND ORGANIZATION OF THE BOOK

PURPOSE

The intent of this book has been to convey the impact of a developmental disability on individuals—as children, young people, and adults. This was to be accomplished, in part, by describing each of the major developmental disabilities—mental retardation, autism, cerebral palsy, and epilepsy—in such a manner as to reveal their specific effects on basic human resources—cognitive; language; sensory, motor, and health; and personality. Thus each of the disorders was characterized in terms of its *psychological* effects. But our *attitudes* toward persons with disabilities shape our behavior toward them, and these attitudes, commonly negative in nature, add to the burden already imposed on disabled persons by their diminished adaptive capacities (resources, skills). It is the attudinal response to disability—by parents, family, peers, and the general society—that gives to the disability its social aspect, having its greatest impact on personality, particularly on how the disabled person comes to see himself or herself in terms of self-esteem. It is the latter aspect of disability that gives to it its *social* dimension and which, together with the *psychological* one, warrants our treatment of disabilities in terms of their *psychosocial* consequences.

It was also the intent of this book to portray the psychosocial effects of disability through autobiography as well as through external description, since only those who have to live with these disorders can truly know their impact. In seeking to give an "inside" view of what it feels like to be retarded, autistic, cerebral palsied, or epileptic, I was responding to my perception that our traditional views of these disorders are necessarily narrow and incomplete because their nature is typically conveyed by those who do not suffer them. Our knowledge cannot help but be secondhand. Most of us cannot truly walk in the shoes of others. Yes, we have some empathy, we can have some sensitivity to other's feelings, but without having actually undergone the same experience, our depth of understanding is necessarily constrained. This is why self-help groups consisting of individuals who share a common problem are so beneficial. The professional cannot know what the condition that is being treated really feels like unless he or she has experienced it.

ORGANIZATION

The nature of these developmental disorders has been made explicit by describing them through the filtering mechanism of a personality model that gives special visibility to human capacities or abilities (resources) and to human biological and psychological needs. The personality model described in Chapter 1 speaks in some measure to what it means to be human and serves as a bridge to the understanding of both ourselves and others. We sometimes regard those with a chronic and highly devalued disability as "different," "not like us" in some very fundamental way. It is as if they are not really human. But our study of these individuals reveals that they share the same hopes and fears as the rest of us, hopes and fears that spring from the same set of needs—survival, structure, self-esteem, and self-expression. My goal has been to show how developmental disabilities affect gratification of these basic needs and thus lead to lives of varying degrees of contentment and satisfaction. This has been carried out by showing how the resource deficits created by the disabilities affect adjustment at major life stages—infancy and early childhood, school age, and adulthood.

But adaptation is not only a function of the nature and degree of disability; it is also determined by the kinds of assistance that we offer. Chapter 2 described the general range of services required by people with the traditional developmental disabilities—disorders that typically interfere with learning and which pose serious obstacles to achieving age-appropriate developmental progress. The thrust of that chapter was that the potential for adjustment is tied to services as well as to disability, and that through services the effects of disability can be reduced to varying degrees. The reader who wears eyeglasses has a visual impairment, a "disability" if you will, but through the corrective function of glasses, that disability is essentially removed. While this kind of total correction is generally not possible with the disorders described in this book, their effects can be moderated through access to a range of habilitative services. Therefore, each chapter and its respective disability has been organized into a description of both adaptation and services. With regard to services, each of the disability chapters dealt with only the special service needs of that disability, the general or common service needs having been presented in Chapter 2.

THE PSYCHOLOGICAL IMPACT OF DEVELOPMENTAL DISABILITIES

Each of the disability chapters has characterized the disorder in terms of resources—its effects on our human capacities to think, to communicate, to use our bodies, and to express our personalities. The severity of the disabilities is a function of *both* the intensity or degree of impairment of any given resource (e.g., the degree of motor impairment in cerebral palsy) *and* the number of resources affected (e.g., speech as well as mobility impairment in cerebral palsy). Of the four disorders described, all except epilepsy are typically associated with multiple resource limitations. Thus cognitive, communicative, and personality difficulties are all commonly found in mental retardation, autism, and cerebral palsy. Their inclusion in the original group of disorders labeled *developmental disabilities* reflected their similarities in general effects and their corresponding need for similar services. Within the developmental disabilities framework, epilepsy was best known as a concomitant of these three conditions, an important aspect of their multidisabling nature, one of their common associated disorders. However, where epilepsy exists alone, is limited to childhood, or either disappears or comes under complete medical control, its effects may be quite limited. The afflicted person may function in the world in a manner not distinguishably different from individuals without the disorder. Thus many individuals with epilepsy may be free of the multiple substantial functional limitations tied to the diagnostic criteria for developmental disabilities and so not labeled as developmentally disabled. But this is certainly not true of the other three disorders. Their psychological or resource difficulties can only be eased, not erased, and they constitute lifelong obstacles to adjustment—hence the need for services at each major life stage.

THE SOCIAL IMPACT OF DEVELOPMENTAL DISABILITIES

While the resource or psychological deficits are the direct expression of the disorders, typically a consequence of their clear or presumed association with some kind of organic brain abnormality, their social effects derive largely from the impact of the disorders on other people. As a culture, we are not neutral about these conditions. While we are not really indifferent to any disability, all being conditions that we would prefer *not* to have, there are differences in our degrees of acceptance of them. We value intelligence, beauty, physical grace, and a good personality, and we devalue people who deviate in whatever degree from these standards. While the standards are generally implicit rather than explicit, they are no less real and pervasive. It is the cruel irony of persons with such disorders as mental retardation, autism, cerebral palsy, and epilepsy that they not only have to try to meet developmental expectations with diminished psychological resources, but that their very deficits evoke additional social burdens. Not only is it more difficult for them to get up on the horse that they wish to ride, but it is as if the horse itself does not want to be ridden.

Throughout this book we read of disabled persons lamenting how they are perceived by others. The retarded person who knows that he or she is retarded is not comfortable with that designation. The desire is to shed it and to be seen as "like everybody else." The cerebral palsied individual, sometimes literally imprisoned in a body that does not work and is deformed by its muscle abnormalities, may feel like an alien, not really human, rejected by others and sentenced to a life of loneliness. Recall the cerebral palsied woman who only discovered her humanity from reading the autobiography of a similarly affected person. In the discovery that her feelings were shared by another, this woman found a bridge to the recognition of herself as a person, at one with and not different from those who moved past her deformed body as though she did not exist.

Nowhere is the lament more painful than in the stories that persons with epilepsy tell us. Often free of major cognitive impairments and thus fully sensitive to the effect of their condition on other people, they report a sense of being pariahs—of carrying some terrible curse. Should their condition be known, they anticipate rejection and exclusion in virtually every aspect of life. We cannot be surprised that persons with epilepsy or other commonly "invisible" disabilities seek to protect their sense of worth by denying that the disorder exists whenever that is possible. They carry a permanent burden of fear that their terrible secret will be found out and that the price they will pay will be social rejection.

The normalization movement, with its goal of greater integration of disabled individuals into the general society, offers one potential antidote to our traditional patterns of avoidance and rejection of those we see as different. Xenophobia is not just an ethnic response to the stranger, it is also our individual one to persons who have characteristics we would not wish for ourselves, and about whom our lack of contact ensures the perpetuation of cultural stereotypes, fears, and propensities for avoidance. It is only through contact, and in settings that enable us to move beyond the apparent differences and to see and experience their abilities as well as their disabilities, that our fears can be eased and we can find ourselves reaching out, befriending, admiring, and loving our disabled peers. We are *all* disabled in the sense that none of us is perfect, a point made earlier. We can all look around and see others who surpass us in resources—who are brighter, more eloquent, better athletes, and more caring. It is only that our deficiencies are not so great that they impair our ability to meet the expectations that our culture sets for us. Hence though not perfect and, like our disabled peers, often beset by feelings of diminished self-worth—we all have fragile egos—we are still not perceived as disabled. We all exist on a continuum of ability, often envying those who are at the desired extreme and feeling sorry for those who are at the other, glad that it is them and not us. I am reminded of a former student who expressed his pleasure at the presence of disabled students on our campus: As long as he could see them, he could feel good about himself.

It is only through allowing ourselves to get to know people who are different that it is possible to reduce social barriers and create conditions that can elevate the disabled's sense of worth. In so doing we inevitably broaden our perception of what it means to be human, what it means to be a person. If the reader turns the last page in this book with at least the thought that we are all part of a common humanity, I will feel that the effort has been worthwhile.

Author Index

Subject Index